FIRST EDITION

PROBLEMS IN US HISTORY

Edited by Jim Cook | *California State University — Stanislaus*

Bassim Hamadeh, CEO and Publisher
Michael Simpson, Vice President of Acquisitions and Sales
Jamie Giganti, Senior Managing Editor
Miguel Macias, Graphic Designer
Kristina Stolte, Senior Field Acquisitions Editor
Michelle Piehl, Project Editor
Alexa Lucido, Licensing Coordinator
Allie Kiekhofer, Interior Designer

Printed in the United States of America

ISBN: 978-1-5165-0644-6 (pbk)/ 978-1-5165-0645-3 (br)

www.cognella.com   800-200-3908

CONTENTS

CHAPTER ONE

The Columbian Exchange

FROM *Food in World History*

BY JEFFREY PILCHER

INTRODUCTION

BY JIM COOK

Go to the grocery store today and look at the ingredients for most food. What you'll find is that most food products are made of corn. There are a number of practical reasons for this, but the main reason is that corn is cheap to grow, and its annual yields are high. More corn is produced in the United States than any other crop.[1] Potatoes make up fewer of our grocery store products, but then we have McDonald's French fries to pick up the slack. In the United States McDonald's buys over 45 billion pounds of potatoes each year.[2] Yet, as Jeffrey Pilcher points out in his chapter on the Columbian Exchange (from the book *Food in World History*), corn and potatoes were considered more fitting for pigs in sixteenth-century Europe.[3] What happened to transform these crops into the modern foods they are today? That is partly what Pilcher explores.

One tragedy of history that brings the importance of these foods into perspective is the Irish Potato Famine of the early nineteenth century. The Irish peasantry, mostly Catholic, was under the subjugation of a Protestant ruling class that had started with Protestant England's invasion of Ireland in the seventeenth century. A primary staple of the Irish peasant diet was the potato. It may surprise some to know that a diet of potatoes and milk gives a person every nutrient they need to live well. So this wasn't exactly a starvation diet for these Irishmen. They were relatively *thriving* on it. But in the

---

1   United States Department of Agriculture (USDA), Economic Research Service. www.ers.usda.gov.
2   Eric Schlosser, *Fast Food Nation* (New York: Houghton Mifflin, 2001).
3   Jeffrey Pilcher, *Food in World History* (Chapter 2, The Columbian Exchange).

1840s disease infected the potato crop. A million Irishmen starved to death. Many fled to the United States as desperate immigrants, hoping for a new life in America. What killed the Irish potato crop? It was a fungus called *Phytophthora infestans*.[4] It ravaged Ireland's potato supplies, leading to this epic disaster. What is interesting is that the source of the Irish potato is the Inca in South America. But the Inca had over one hundred types of potato. Why so many? We do have different types of potatoes available to us today: russet potatoes, red potatoes, Yellow Finns, Yukon Golds, and so on. But we'd be hard pressed to find one hundred different kinds of potatoes in a grocery store today. The answer seems to be that different types of potatoes have different susceptibility to disease. If you have only one type of potato, like the Irish did in the 1840s, and that type gets wiped out by a fungus, you're in trouble. If you grow many different types of potatoes, as the Inca did, then perhaps one type being wiped out does not cause a famine. So the potato came to Europe via the Inca, and eventually became an important food source. But the technology of growing them was left behind with the Inca. There's a lesson for all of us. And that's another point Pilcher makes in this chapter: technologies that should have travelled from the New World to the Old World never made it across the Atlantic.

* * *

---

4   J. M. Duncan, "Phytophthora-an abiding threat to our crops," *Microbiology Today* 26 (1999):114–16.

Columbus's 1492 voyage in search of a western passage to the Spice Islands began a fundamental transformation in the eating habits of all humans. The immediate biological and environmental consequences of contact between Europe and the Americas were dramatic, as exposure to Old World diseases killed more than 80 percent of the New World population within a hundred years. Aided by this unintentional germ warfare, Spanish conquistadors quickly subdued the vast Aztec, Maya, and Inca empires. European plants and animals flourished in the fields left open by demographic decline, transforming the ecology of the Americas, but the Spaniards succeeded only partially in their goal of establishing colonial replicas of their homeland. Surviving natives intermarried with European colonists and with African slaves, creating new ethnic blends. Highly productive food crops domesticated in the New World not only persisted as essential staples for both natives and newcomers alike, they were also carried back across the Atlantic and launched a demographic revolution in the Old World, helping set the stage for modern population growth.

Yet these changes were far from uniform. Peasants in China, Africa, and the

Middle East began planting American staples as soon as they arrived in the sixteenth century, but in Europe and India these crops were largely ignored for hundreds of years. Fruits and vegetables likewise spread in an irregular fashion, and Europeans who had pioneered the new trade routes to America were the least likely to adopt the crops they had discovered. The circuitous routes by which new plants traveled also led to popular uncertainty about their origins.

Material and cultural factors combined to determine the acceptance of new foods. Ecology had a role, for plants grew best in environments similar to those in which they had been domesticated. Tropical crops could not resist freezing temperatures, but changes in altitude and microclimates allowed ecological flexibility. Productivity and compatibility with existing rotations also mattered to farmers considering new crops. Cooks likewise had their say, for an unfamiliar plant, however prolific, was unlikely to gain favor if it could not be prepared in a tasty and appealing fashion. Although a global process, the Columbian Exchange was nevertheless negotiated at the local level.

Mexico

The absence of domesticated animals, apart from turkeys and small dogs, distinguished the civilizations of Mesoamerica from other classical empires. Native Americans excelled at foraging for protein but still depended overwhelmingly on their staple grain, maize. Human labor provided the main source of energy, as women ground maize by hand while men carried heavy loads on their backs. The introduction of livestock by Spanish conquistadors therefore had the potential for improving livelihoods but also posed great environmental dangers for indigenous farmers unaccustomed to pastoral herds.

The Mesoamerican maize complex provided the foundation for a basically vegetarian diet. The grain supplied carbohydrates and up to 80 percent of total calories while beans added protein; complementary amino acids magnified the nutritional value of the pair by forming a complete protein when eaten together. Chiles, squash, tomatoes, and avocadoes offered vitamins, minerals, and interesting flavors. Native Americans supplemented this vegetarian cuisine by consuming virtually all available animal protein: deer, ducks, rabbits, seafood, and even rodents, insects, and lake algae.

Indigenous techniques for preparing maize tortillas were extremely labor-intensive. Mesoamerican women first simmered the kernels in a mineral solution, which loosened the indigestible husk and released niacin, a vitamin necessary to avoid the disease pellagra. The next step involved hand-grinding the wet dough, called *nixtamal*, while kneeling painfully over a grinding stone. Women then patted the smooth dough into thin, round tortillas and cooked them briefly on an earthenware griddle.

Because tortillas quickly went stale and *nixtamal* fermented overnight, women had to rise hours before dawn to cook for men going to work in the fields. Midwives warned newborn girls: "Thou wilt become fatigued, thou wilt become tired; thou art to provide water, to grind maize, to drudge." The subjugation of the grinding stone inspired a particularly oppressive version of patriarchy in Mesoamerica.

With limited supplies, social hierarchies governed food distribution. Well-fed nobles stood some ten centimeters taller than commoners in the classical Maya city of Tikal (fourth–eighth centuries CE). A terrible famine in the year One Rabbit (1454), in the early stages of Aztec imperial expansion, focused attention on food supplies for the island capital of Tenochtitlan. At the time, Moctezuma the Elder used canoes to distribute maize to starving people, and in later years, the Great Feast of the Lords recalled this imperial beneficence through ceremonial handouts of tamales (maize dumplings) from canoes. The Aztec Empire demanded tribute of food and other goods from subject peoples, especially in the productive raised fields of Lake Chalco-Xochimilco. Among the warrior elite, civic and religious banquets assumed a competitive nature, with each host attempting to serve the finest chile pepper stews, tamales, and hot chocolate. Spanish conquistadors spoke with awe about the hundreds of lavish dishes served daily to Moctezuma the Younger (ruled 1502–1520).

Nevertheless, mutual disgust marked the culinary encounter between Spaniards and Native Americans. Moctezuma's emissaries reported that European bread tasted "like dried maize stalks," while Bernal Díaz del Castillo complained of the "misery of maize cakes" that served as rations during the conquest. Natives ranked pork fat among the tortures brought by the Spaniards, who were equally disgusted by the indigenous consumption of rodents and insects, dubbed "*animalitos*." Catholic missionaries attempted to propagate wheat in order to replace maize gods with the Holy Eucharist, but peasants found the Europe grain unproductive, expensive to grow, and prone to disease, although some entrepreneurial natives cultivated it for sale to urban Hispanic markets. As a result, wheat bread and maize tortillas became status markers within the racial hierarchy called the system of castes.

Even more devastating was the invasion of European livestock, as cattle and sheep reproduced at exponential rates and overran the countryside. The simultaneous growth of herds and collapse of human population due to disease made it appear as if the livestock were eating the natives. For a few decades in the mid-sixteenth century, meat sold for a pittance in Mexico City, but with uncontrolled grazing, herbivores soon exceeded the carrying capacity of the land, exposing the soil to erosion and rendering it unfit for farming or herding. In just a few decades, sheep turned the fertile Mezquital Valley into a barren desert, and by the end of the century, meat was again scarce in colonial markets.

Devastation and disgust notwithstanding, culinary fusion had already begun in sixteenth-century Mesoamerica. Although retaining their staple maize, native cooks learned to whip pork fat into tamales, giving the cakes a lighter texture and richer flavor. Spanish settlers meanwhile acquired a taste for beans and chile peppers, even while paying high prices for familiar wheat bread. This process of cultural blending was repeated in South America as well.

Peru

The Andes Mountains rise like some Brobdingnagian terraced field, with separate ecological niches providing a wealth of different foodstuffs. Abundant supplies of fish and shellfish supported complex societies as early as 2500 BCE in the otherwise desert climate on the Pacific coast, where strong currents bring fog but no rain. Ascending the slopes into temperate highland valleys, the Mesoamerican maize complex coexisted with the Andean grain, quinoa. Farther up, in the cold, rainy zone above the treeline, human settlements depended on potatoes and other root crops such as *oca* and *ulloco*. At the highest elevations grazed llamas, domesticated camelids used to carry trade goods up and down the mountains, as well as smaller alpacas, which provided fine wool. Coca leaves,

cultivated along the eastern slopes, were chewed as a stimulant by people living in the highlands. The exchange of food and other goods between such diverse climates became a central aspect of the diets and lives of Andean peoples.

To transport food such great distances without spoiling, Andean cooking relied heavily on methods for preservation. Highland farmers exposed potatoes to frost and sun to make freeze-dried *chuño*. Shepherds dried llama meat into *charqui* (hence the English word "jerky") and cooked blood into gruel similar to European black puddings. Meanwhile, salted and sun-dried fish arrived from the coastal lowlands. Guinea pigs, another important source of animal protein, reproduced so quickly as to obviate the need for preservation; they were simply boiled or roasted. Andean women likewise boiled and toasted maize. Without the need for laborious daily maize grinding, women worked as shepherds and farmers, planting and harvesting potatoes while men turned the soil with footplows, and as a result, they had greater social equality than in Mexico.

The Inca Empire (1438–1532) built a highly productive economy on Andean traditions of reciprocity, whereby leaders organized labor and redistributed wealth for the benefit of the entire community. Having conquered a vast realm, stretching 3,000 kilometers from present-day Ecuador to Chile, the Inca restructured these societies for maximum efficiency, for example, by resettling entire highland villages at lower elevations in order to increase the production of maize. The Inca not only uprooted communities but also dispersed them up and down the Andes Mountains, creating social "archipelagos" known as *ayllu*, in which kinfolk lived at different elevations and harvested seafood, maize, potatoes, and coca for exchange within these geographically extended families. *Ayllus* also had a responsibility for supplying labor tribute to herd llamas and to produce food, clothing, and other goods for the imperial government. The Inca maintained enormous granaries, both as military depots and as distribution centers, and kept careful records of food supplies using *quipus*, indigenous balance sheets that recorded numbers using a system of knots tied on strings. Local lords, called *kurakas*, served as intermediaries between the state and the people by allocating tribute duties and distributing food. The ideal of equality notwithstanding, nobles ate far more meat than commoners. According to early chronicles, Topa Inca (ruled 1471–1493) even ordered runners to carry "fresh fish from the sea, and as it was seventy or eighty leagues from the coast to Cuzco ... they were brought alive and twitching."

Disease and brutality made the conquest of Peru as devastating as that of Mexico, but prior pastoral experience helped mitigate the environmental consequences of the Columbian Exchange. The rapacious Spaniards systematically looted Inca warehouses, seizing any treasure and selling off the foodstuffs. By the fall of 1539, less than a decade after their arrival, people were starving in Cuzco, despite the rapid population decline. Disease also decimated llamas, although from an indigenous source rather than a pathogen imported from Europe. Inca shepherds had carefully culled any animals infected with *caracha*, but after the breakdown of the native administration, this disease spread through the herds, killing two-thirds of the indigenous camelids. The conquistadors ordered Andean shepherds to tend cattle and sheep instead, a policy that at least helped protect indigenous farmers. Nevertheless, Spaniards often purposely turned livestock loose to damage indigenous fields and irrigation works in order to claim the land for their own uses, especially to grow wheat and sugar cane.

The development of food habits in post-conquest Mexico and Peru provides an interesting comparative study in cultural accommodation. Both colonies became productive centers for European agriculture, with diverse ecological niches supporting wheat, sugar cane, and livestock. Nevertheless, two other mainstays of the Mediterranean diet, olive oil and wine, flourished in Peru but not in Mexico. Favorable climates existed in both regions although unpredictable frosts frustrated early attempts at winemaking in Mexico. Nor does Spanish trade policy explain the differences because decrees establishing peninsular monopolies for these products came only after regional agriculture patterns had become fixed. Perhaps colonists in Mexico simply came to prefer the taste of substitutes – pork fat and hot chocolate–along with chiles and beans. Indigenous nobles in both colonies claimed status by adopting European foods, but commoners preferred their accustomed staples, maize and potatoes, and accepted imports at the margins of their diet; for example, *anticuchos* (grilled beef heart) became a street food of indigenous Peruvians in urban areas. Meanwhile, American crops had begun to transform the Old World.

Return passages

In America, Columbus encountered foods that ultimately yielded far more benefits than the Asian spices he had originally sought, but Europeans proved curiously slow in exploiting those new culinary treasures. Instead of taking root in Iberian fields, these crops passed by way of Spanish and Portuguese merchants to the Middle East, Africa, and Asia. They gained European acceptance hundreds of years later. A number of factors helped determine the spread of new crops, including their productivity and fit within agricultural regimes, their ease of preparation and adaptability to culinary systems, and the cultural associations that they evoked.

Maize, the most versatile and productive plant domesticated in the Americas, illustrates the ambivalent reception of new crops. Columbus carried it back to

Spain in 1493, but lacking the gluten to make leavened bread, it was prepared as porridge and considered to be a famine food at best. In 1597, John Gerard described it as "a more convenient food for swine than for men." By contrast, the American grain diffused rapidly in the Middle East, where porridges did not have such inferior status. Arriving in Lebanon and Syria by the 1520s, corn helped spur population growth under the Ottoman Emperor Süleyman the Magnificent (ruled 1520–1566). As a result, many Europeans referred to maize as the "Turkish" grain while in India it was known as "Mecca" corn. The Portuguese introduced it to West Africa, where it surpassed the productivity of millet and sorghum, although the latter was still more drought-resistant. From northern India, maize spread through inland Chinese provinces of Yunnan and Sichuan in the seventeenth century. The labor-intensive technique of making *nixtamal*, however, remained limited to Mesoamerica; Old World cooks prepared the new cultivar using familiar methods, either roasting it on the cob like a vegetable or else grinding it into flour for porridge or, in China, noodles.

Chile peppers likewise spread most rapidly in cuisines that already used spices liberally. Although colonists in New Spain quickly acquired a taste for chile sauces prepared by Native American cooks, western Europeans accustomed to powdered cinnamon, nutmeg, and pepper, hesitated to touch the hot plant, which burned the hands as well as the mouth. The principal staging point for the chile's invasion of the Old World was therefore India, where they were introduced by Portuguese traders and fit naturally into the complex spice blends, prepared as pastes and generically called "curry" by Europeans. Areas of Indian cultural influence such as Thailand quickly adopted the new condiments, and they were also carried overland on the Silk Road to Sichuan and Yunnan, Chinese regions now known for fiery dishes, as well as to Turkey and hence Hungary, where people became addicted to the chile powder, paprika. Chiles also spread widely through Africa as a complement to spices arriving from the Indian Ocean trade.

Social conditions influenced the diffusion of American crops, as can be seen by comparing the experience of China and India. Despite intensive agriculture, China's population had reached its ecological limits in the final years of the Ming dynasty (1368–1644). As famines struck, starving peasants eagerly adopted American foodstuffs, particularly the sweet potato, which provided multiple crops with a greater caloric yield even than rice, did not require laborious transplanting and paddy maintenance, and could be grown on otherwise marginal land. Whether baked, boiled, mashed, or ground into flour for noodles and porridge, sweet potatoes became a fixture of virtually every meal in South China. Maize and peanuts likewise complemented existing crop rotations, multiplying agricultural productivity.

In India, by contrast, the Mughals ruled a more mobile society with considerable available land and relatively slow population growth. Farmers thus had little incentive to intensify production and largely ignored the American staples maize and potatoes until the nineteenth century.

European reluctance to adopt American crops begins to make sense when viewed from a broader perspective. Recurring bouts of plague left room for population growth until famines drove northern Europeans to adopt the potato, starting with Ireland in the seventeenth century and moving east through France, Germany, and Russia in the eighteenth and nineteenth centuries. Maize likewise became a staple in southern Europe but without losing its initial association as an animal fodder. Even the tomato, which had arrived in Naples by the 1550s, did not appear in Italian cookbooks until the end of the seventeenth century, although peasants had no doubt eaten it sooner. Thus, the lethargy with which medieval Europeans adopted Muslim crops continued to characterize the early modern spread of American foodstuffs.

Conclusion

Religious imperatives drove both Aztec and Inca imperial expansion, but the common belief in reciprocity took different forms in Middle and South America. The Inca, like the Chinese, emphasized the distribution of food as essential to good government, while the

Aztec tribute system functioned primarily to supply food to the metropolis, as in imperial Rome, in addition to sacrificial victims for the maize gods. It is difficult to explain these differences considering material causes alone, but the labor-intensive production of maize tortillas does help account for the greater inequality of gender relations in Mesoamerica.

A broad view of material and cultural factors is likewise necessary to explain the uneven nature of the Columbian Exchange. Demographic pressure encouraged the adoption of new crops in Europe and Asia, while population declines helped spread livestock in the Americas. Landholding patterns and agricultural regimes also influenced the selection of new crops. Native Americans cultivated wheat only under Spanish compulsion because of the expense of heavy plows, grinding mills, and ovens. Disgust and fear also delayed the spread of both tomatoes and potatoes, which were considered potentially dangerous in Europe.

Although seeds often traveled independently of farmers, agricultural and culinary knowledge had an important role in the Columbian Exchange. Because Native American women, with their knowledge of *nixtamal*, did not travel to the Old World, populations that adopted maize as the staple grain were subject to the dietary deficiency disease pellagra. The limited inward migration to Europe during the early modern period may have slowed the

diffusion of crops; indeed, American crops took hundreds of years to achieve their full demographic effect. By that time, Europeans had developed new systems of production and trade with profound historical consequences.

Further reading

This chapter was inspired by Alfred W. Crosby, Jr., *The Columbian Exchange: Biological and Cultural Consequences of 1492* (Westport, CT: Greenwood Press, 1972). See also, Sophie Coe, *America's First Cuisines* (Austin, TX: University of Texas Press, 1994); John C. Super, *Food, Conquest, and Colonization in Sixteenth-Century Spanish America* (Albuquerque, NM: University of New Mexico Press, 1988); and Elinor G. K. Melville, *A Plague of Sheep: Environmental Consequences of the Conquest of Mexico* (Cambridge: Cambridge University Press, 1997). On the diffusion of American foods, William Langer, "American Foods and Europe's Population Growth, 1750–1850," *Journal of Social History* 8(2) (Winter 1975): 51–66; Nelson Foster and Linda Cordell (eds), *Chiles to Chocolate: Food the Americas Gave the World* (Tucson, AZ: University of Arizona Press, 1992); Sucheta Mazumdar, "The Impact of New World Food Crops on the Diet and Economy of China and India, 1600–1900," in Raymond Grew (ed.), *Food in Global History* (Boulder, CO: Westview Press, 1999); and Arturo Warman, *Corn and Capitalism: How a Botanical Bastard Grew to Global Dominance*, trans. Nancy L. Westrate (Chapel Hill, NC: University of North Carolina Press, 2003).

DISCUSSION QUESTIONS

1. Where did new crops from America immediately flourish? Where did it take some time for them to catch on?
2. What did grinding corn in Mexico have to do with the subjugation of women?
3. What was the effect of domesticated animals from Europe on America?
4. Why did olive oil and wine (two Mediterranean staples) become popular in Peru but not Mexico?

CHAPTER TWO

A Short History of the Puritans

FROM *Saints, Sinners, and the God of the World*

BY ANDREW MALLORY

INTRODUCTION

BY JIM COOK

John Calvin's doctrine of predestination weighed heavily on the Puritans. Essentially it said that because God is all-powerful, all-knowing, and not bound by time, it must be true that he knew from before the beginning of time who would be saved and who would be lost. By knowing this before it happened, God was determining that it would happen. It would be impossible to do other than what God has determined, because if you did, you would make God less than all-knowing and all-powerful.[1] What a tremendous concept to deal with on a personal level! How did one know whether he or she was saved or damned? This must have bothered many Puritan minds.

Ironically, many scientists and philosophers today would agree with Calvin. They argue that we simply don't have free will. In a universe ordered by cause and effect, it is impossible for us to have free will. We may go about our lives *as if* we have free will, but scientifically and philosophically it is impossible, or so the argument goes. Scientists have conducted experiments since the 1960s that seem to support this determinist view. By monitoring brain activity, they have shown that subjects who choose to lift their right arm, for instance, do so believing that they have made that choice. Yet their brain activity shows invariably that in regions of the brain that are part of the unconscious mind (i.e., the part of the brain we normally don't associate with decision making) neuron activity has already decided to raise the right arm *before* the person actually does it. The conscious

---

1   R.T. Kendall, *Calvin and English Calvinism to 1649* (Oxford: Oxford University Press, 1979).

FIGURE 2.1.

Fig. 21: Edward Oliver Skelton, "The Puritans," https://commons.wikimedia.org/wiki/File:The_story_of_New_England,_illustrated,_being_a_narrative_of_the_principal_events_from_the_arrival_of_the_Pilgrims_in_1620_and_of_the_Puritans_in_1624_to_the_present_time_(1910)_(14596575418).jpg. Copyright in the Public Domain.

part of the brain then tricks us into thinking we made the choice. Cognitive scientists call this the "readiness potential."[2] The subject did not choose to raise his right arm. Instead, his brain (the unconscious, supposedly non—decision making part of his brain) made the decision a second before he did. Our brain tricks us into thinking we have free will when the truth is we live in a deterministic universe of cause and effect.

Would knowing that scientists and philosophers would eventually agree with them have helped the Puritans? Probably not, for their world was not dominated like ours is by the material and empirical. Their world was dominated by a God who had chosen them to do His will. And no matter how many psychological tricks they may have had to play on themselves in order to reconcile their world to predestination, it was all worth it for the pleasure of being in God's grace. As much as the Puritans eschewed the pleasures of this world, they certainly longed for this pleasure with God.

In Andrew Mallory's book, *Saints, Sinners, and the God of the World,* he begins with an introduction to how we should approach the world of the Puritans. He brings many Puritan scholars into this discussion, including the incomparable Perry Miller. A common statement among Puritan scholars, as well as in graduate schools all over the world, is that you can't begin to deal with the Puritans until you've dealt with Perry Miller first. He is the gold standard of Puritan scholarship. Another idea that you often

---

2   Kornhuber and Deecke, "Readiness for movement –The Bereitschaftspotential-Story," *Current Contents Life Sciences* 33 (1990): 14.

hear from Puritan scholars is that we really need to understand the Puritans in order to understand ourselves as Americans today. That's not a completely self-serving idea, because it is true that many things about Americans today can still be explained in terms of those odd and stubbornly serious Englishmen who immigrated to America in the early seventeenth century. Their odd theology made them odd people. If we could ever be thought of as an American family, maybe the Puritans are that slightly grumpy uncle who everyone says is odd, and always makes family gatherings uncomfortable.

* * *

The Hartford Sermon Notebook is a product of the Reformation, and with the rise of humanism and the popularity of the cults of antiquity, Europeans since before the time of Luther and Calvin had been reaching back many centuries for answers to questions about their world. Donatism, with its pursuit of a perfect church on Earth, and St. Augustine's distinction between the visible and invisible churches, are only fragmentary examples of the impact of early Christianity on what would become Protestantism, and ultimately for this book, Puritanism.[3] In other words, Puritanism did not spontaneously erupt somewhere in England during the sixteenth century. The ideas that shaped it took centuries to grow,

and in terms of the Reformation as a movement, the story of the Puritans is but one of its chapters.

In The New England Mind: the Seventeenth Century, Perry Miller tells us, "The soul of Puritan theology is the hidden God, who is not fully revealed even in His own revelation. The Bible is His declared will; behind it always lies His secret will."[4] Miller notes that the Puritan religious ethos as determined by scripture was not restrained to Sunday devotions. Puritans used the Bible as a kind of blueprint for behavior, and not simply personal behavior, but in matters of theology, politics, economics and military exploits, the Bible was the instructive source.[5]

Similarly, the historian David Hall credits the uniqueness of the Bible over all other books by virtue of its status as the "Word." "All other texts were copies of this one original; all other forms of

---

3   Edmund S. Morgan, Visible Saints: the History of a Puritan Idea (Ithaca: Cornell University Press, 1963), 2–3. In addition, in an interesting article "Were There Any Puritans in New England?" The New England Quarterly 74, no. 1 (March 2001), 118–138, the historian Michael Winship argues that the very meaning of the term "Puritan" is problematic and in need of reassessment. This book uses the term "Puritan" throughout its pages. I believe "Puritan" is a recognizable historical term that, while objectionable to some, is an accepted point of reference for most historians and theologians.

4   Perry Miller, The New England Mind, Vol. 1: The Seventeenth Century (Cambridge Massachusetts: The Belknap Press of the Harvard University Press, 1982), 21.
5   Perry Miller and Thomas H. Johnson eds., The Puritans: A Sourcebook of their Writings, 43.

truth were incomplete or partial next to Scripture. It was the living speech of God, the "voice" of Christ, a text that people heard."[6] The important distinction made by Hall is that people "heard" the sermon, which enhances the uniqueness of the *Hartford Sermon Notebook*, since the sermons it contains were not edited or prepared for the printing press. Indeed, as Paul Lucas writes in *The Valley of Discord*, seventeenth century Connecticut had no printing press of its own, which clearly limited the publishing possibilities for its ministers.[7]

Puritans were English Protestants, and England's Reformation spanned the years 1527–1660. According to the historian and minister Charles Hambrick-Stowe, "Puritanism in England, whatever else it accomplished in the economic, ecclesiastical, political, and social turmoil of the period, was a devotional movement dedicated to the spiritual regeneration of individuals and society."[8] As mainland Europe struggled over the ideas of men like Luther and Calvin, England wrestled with its own Protestant Reformation.

England's Protestant movement was rooted in the fourteenth century dissenter tradition of John Wycliffe, the Oxford theologian. Wycliffe, like Luther, insisted that lay people improve themselves spiritually by reading the Bible.[9] In 1519, Luther discovered that his work was influencing England, and that an Augustinian friar named Robert Barnes, in Cambridge, at a place called the White Horse Inn, was leading discussions there. Known as "Little Germany," the island, like the mainland, was moving toward its divorce from Rome.[10]

In *Puritans in the New World*, David Hall briefly explores the origin of the name "Puritan," as an interesting historical aside. Hall's reference is from Bradford's *Of Plymouth Plantation*, where the term "Puritan" is traced to the fourth century C.E., and was apparently a kind of mockery that grew from a controversy within the Christian church. The name grew legs in the sixteenth century and became a caricature in popular theater: "the Puritan as a zealous busybody."[11] As Hall explains it, the Puritans of the seventeenth century embraced the term, and it became more generally associated with piety and commitment to God.[12]

6 David D. Hall, *Worlds of Wonder, Days of Judgment*, 24.

7 Paul R. Lucas, *Valley of Discord: Church and Society along the Connecticut River, 1636–1725* (Hanover New Hampshire: The University Press of New England, 1976), 212.

8 Charles E. Hambrick-Stowe, *The Practice of Piety: Puritan Devotional Disciplines in Seventeenth-Century New England* (Chapel Hill: The University of North Carolina Press, 1982), 23.

9 James D. Tracy, *Europe's Reformations, 1450–1650* (Lanham Maryland: Rowman & Littlefield, 1999), 185.

10 Ibid.

11 David D. Hall, *Puritans in the New World: A Critical Anthology* (Princeton: Princeton University Press, 2004), x.

12 Ibid.

During the Reformation, the English monarchy tended to bounce back and forth between Catholicism and Protestantism, depending on who held the reins of power. Henry VIII's split with Rome is well known (1534–1547),[13] but his children were no less controversial in English religious history. Henry was followed by the Protestant period of Edward VI (1547–1553), which was reversed by Mary Tudor who briefly reestablished Catholicism (1553–1558). Elizabeth I revived English Protestantism (1558–1603),[14] and was succeeded by Scotland's James I (1603–1625). Ultimately, James produced an heir in Charles I, who leaned toward the Episcopal Church and who was later beheaded by Oliver Cromwell's forces, ushering in a period of parliamentary control better known as the "Commonwealth" (1646–1658).[15]

Monarchs were not the only victims of the executioner's axe or the flames of the stake. Often beheaded or burned alive, England's religious martyrs fared no better during the Reformation.[16] To say the least, a cursory study of this period of English history reveals a tendency toward violent resolution to religious conflict and dissent, but the specific nature of the Puritan struggle in England is what gave rise to "New England " and is where we must turn to contextualize the sermons contained in the *Hartford Sermon Notebook.*

In general, if we think of the Puritans as Protestants, we can cautiously summarize their beliefs. Certain Protestant concepts were generally accepted by Puritans; that Rome and the Pope were the enemies of Christ, that the Catholic list of sacraments was too long, and that what was needed most was an end to the centuries of obedience to Catholic priests, who by the close of the sixteenth century were often less versed in scripture than the people they were preaching to. Puritans expressed their ire with certain ministers calling them "Dumme Dogs, Unskilful sacrificing priestes, Destroyeing Drones, or rather Catepillars of the Word."[17] In

---

13 As discussed by Edmund Morgan in *Visible Saints,* Henry VIII did something else that would have a tremendous impact on England's reformation when he allowed the translation of the Bible into English, thus spreading the "Word" to a wider audience on the island. Morgan, *Visible Saints,* 5.

14 Even though Elizabeth was a Protestant, she was also a shrewd politician, who constantly played Catholic and Protestant sympathies against one another to suit her needs. According to Edmund Morgan "In spite of Elizabeth's political skill, the Puritans increased their numbers steadily and continued to demand further reforms. But by the close of Elizabeth's reign they had made little headway." Morgan, *Visible Saints,* 5–6.

15 Tracy, *Europe's Reformations,* 186.

16 In his essay, "Contesting Control of Orthodoxy Among the Godly: William Pynchon Reexamined." *The William and Mary Quarterly* 54, no. 4 (October 1997), 796, Michael Winship reveals that the last English Burning of a Heretic, the Arian Edward Wightman, took place in 1612.

17 *Seconde Parte of a Register,* II, 211. As cited in Morgan, *Visible Saints,* 7. Included in Morgan's book are examples from the Registers of various "undesirable" men who had become preachers, including one "Mr Levit, parson of Leden Roding, a notorious swearer, a dicer, a carder,

his works, Perry Miller often uniquely describes "who" the Puritans were, and he describes them with a comfortable ease of familiarity unlike few other Puritan scholars. Writing in the 1930's, in response to other scholar's attempts at classification of the Puritans, Miller says:

> It is important to note that the Puritans were fully aware of the figure they cut. They did not, like some of their modern apologists, argue that a man can have a 'good time' even though a Puritan. Living was serious business, and those who took it gaily here would come to a reckoning hereafter. What made it supportable to them was not the incidental amusements along the way but the one engrossing joy of saints' communion with the God who had made them and had redeemed them (Miller, *The New England Mind*, 60).

By the end of the sixteenth century, Puritans had established much of their belief system, which, as James Tracy describes it, consisted of "a more general demand for purging the liturgy of a long list of "popish" elements, like saints'

days, candles, the exchange of rings at marriage, prayers at the graveside, and the religious celebration of Christmas."[18] Personal behavior, one's external qualities, mattered very much to the Puritan, as revealed by Edmund Morgan's example that Puritans "did not differ from their contemporaries in their views about the importance of salvation as much as they did in their views about behavior ... they wrote hundreds of books explaining the exact conduct demanded by God in every human situation."[19]

As the end of Elizabeth's monarchy approached, certain key elements of the Protestant ethos remained contentious, and one of the most important concepts prevailing was John Calvin's predestination.[20] When simplified, predestination is just about as it sounds, certain Christians were predestined for an afterlife in heaven, or conversely, damnation in hell. Calvin declared that predestination was "God's eternal decree, by which he compacted with himself what he willed to become of each man ... eternal life is foreordained for some, eternal damnation for others. Therefore, as any man has been created to one or

---

a hawker and hunter, a verie careless person, he had a childe by a maid since he was instituted and inducted ..." *Visible Saints*, 8.

18 Tracy, *Europe's Reformations*, 195.
19 Edmund S. Morgan, *The Puritan Family: Religion and Domestic Relations in Seventeenth-Century New England* (New York: Harper and Row Publishers, 1966), 2. The *Hartford Sermon Notebook* contains dozens of references to the internal and external man, and I believe these words are meant in the behavioral sense. It is this appearance of piety, which ties directly into Puritan concerns about the unknown hypocrites among them.
20 Tracy, *Europe's Reformations*, 195.

the other of these ends, we speak of him as predestined to life or death."[21]

The many implications of predestination are interesting. One might have asked the question, how do I know if I am predestined, and what might I be predestined for? These questions were born of Calvin's conception of predestination, and New England's Puritans searched for answers to them as they sought to create a community of the Elect. Predestination was also important to Reformed Theology because it went side by side with the doctrine of justification by grace alone.[22] In other words, grace and predestination are God's divine choice, and you could not have one without the other.

Perry Miller's definition of Puritans as Calvinists is helpful: "It is true, the Puritans were Calvinists, if we mean that they more or less agreed with the great theologian of Geneva."[23] Calvinism had an important influence on Puritan theology. The extreme exclusivity of the Puritan system, the church of the elect, was staggering, and even more so in the hands of New England's Puritans, who placed 3000 miles of ocean between themselves and any major competing forms. The Hartford Sermon Notebook contains many examples of this exclusivity, and its preachers make a clear

distinction between the regenerated elect, and the unregenerate damned.[24]

The historian David Hall points to a particular Calvinist doctrine known as Calvin's "middle way," and as it pertained to the ministry, it went roughly as follows: "Calvin warned that some Protestants erred in assigning no special privileges to the ministry, while others exaggerated its power beyond measure."[25] Calvin sought a structure for the ministry that was somewhere in between the poles, a "middle way." According to Hall, Calvin formulated this concept of the ministry from the apostle Paul, who believed his actions were a response to the Holy Spirit, independent of his own force of will. Calvin understood the ministry to be fuelled by God's Holy Spirit, without which ministers would simply be lecturers, rather

---

21 William Stacy Johnson ed., *Reformed Reader: A Sourcebook in Christian Theology* (Louisville, Kentucky: Westminster/John Knox Press, 1993), 93.
22 Ibid., 86.
23 Miller and Johnson, *The Puritan Source Book*, 56.

24 Article VII from the Synod of Dort defines the elect in Calvin's terms, making it clear that election comes before salvation, and only by the grace of God: "Election is the unchangeable purpose of God, whereby, before the foundation of the world, he hath, out of mere grace, according to the sovereign good pleasure of his own will, chosen, from the whole human race, which had fallen through their own fault, from their primitive state of rectitude, into sin and destruction, a certain number of persons to redemption in Christ, whom he from eternity appointed the Mediator and head of the elect, and the foundation of salvation." William Stacy Johnson ed., *Reformed Reader: A Sourcebook in Christian Theology* (Louisville, Kentucky: Westminster/John Knox Press, 1993), 98.
25 David D. Hall, *The Faithful Shepherd: A History of the New England Ministry in the Seventeenth Century* (Cambridge Massachusetts: Harvard University Press for Harvard Theological Studies, 2006), 9.

than men of God.[26] In other words, Calvin did not believe that the ministry possessed any special sacramental power, and that without the Holy Spirit, the word of God had no power to save.[27]

Calvin's theology includes much more than the nature of the ministry, but it is an important distinction here because of the nature of Hartford's ministry, circa 1679–1680. Calvin's concept of the ministry plays out in the *Hartford Sermon Notebook,* in Isaac Foster's ordination sermon, and in other sermons where Foster seemed to have been a mediator for God. Hartford's ministers, especially Foster, implored the congregation of Hartford to seek Christ for the assurance of eternal salvation that can only come from the son of God, but there are also many warnings in the sermons, whose general message is the exhortation that life without Christ is the surest way to damnation.

John Calvin influenced the Puritans as much as he did any other reformed church of the sixteenth and seventeenth centuries, but there were important differences between Calvin and the Puritans, especially concerning the covenant. The basic definition of the covenant as it relates to the Puritans in New England was a gathered church of voluntary believers, seeking perfection as visible saints under the watchful eye of God.

According to Edmund Morgan, after Mary's death, the church of England "Swept in Papist and Protestant alike in the wholesale conversion of the realm ... Elizabeth had swept the whole people of England into her so-called church just as Calvin had allegedly done with the people of Geneva. Every Englishman had been automatically transformed by government decree into a member of the new Anglican Church. There had been no voluntary gathering of believers."[28] The essential difference, and what was especially significant to the Puritans who settled and formed churches in New England, is the subtly important point of voluntary membership. Puritans were not interested in making everyone a member of the church, nor did they need to. Instead, Puritans in New England who were members of their church were able to make church attendance and ministerial upkeep mandatory for everyone, while keeping membership and sacramental benefits to themselves, the Elect, the "visible saints." In other words, the Puritans had created a much more exclusive system that did not seek a "middle way." The Puritan system was more orthodox, and in general, New England's Puritans did not believe in making concessions to those unfortunate souls among them not counted as members, though many of the sermons in the Hartford Sermon Notebook are exhortations to non-members.

---

26 Ibid.
27 Hall, *The Faithful Shepherd*, 10.

28 Morgan, *Visible Saints*, 24–25.

The often-prolonged process New England Puritans employed to "call" a minister seems very Calvinist given that the congregation decided the fate of their minister before, during, and after his ordination, instead of some distant bishopric. The account of Isaac Foster's call and ordination as it related to the ministers "call" is especially interesting. Harry Stout describes the power of New England's ministers as "awesome", yet he also explains that it was not arbitrary power, but rather, that New England's ministers simply possessed the formal education required, and via ordination, a kind of license to practice as preachers. The ministers were not necessarily any more inspired than most laymen were, they simply earned the right to be the preacher. Stout also points out that when these ministers abused their right to preach, they could be, and at times were, dismissed by the congregation.[29] The Thomas Cheever biography in chapter two, Cheever was harshly reprimanded and dismissed by his congregation, demonstrates the authority of New England's congregations. The point is simply that Puritan ministers were not untouchable, and the sermon notebook contains several examples where its ministers implore the congregation to support them.

The ministers of colonial New England were part of a large but mostly decentralized system of belief, whose ultimate goal was to guide God's elect to a final reunion with Christ. The ministers of the *Hartford Sermon Notebook* are commonly referred to as those of the second generation, and they functioned within a system that was very different from that of the Old World.[30]

David Hall's comparison of the relationship of church and state in the Old and New Worlds reveals some important differences among ministers on both sides of the Atlantic. The European model entailed a very close relationship between church and state. The church was everyone's church, with the king at the top. The church was closely associated with political and social functions, and many times, the church imposed its will through the civil courts. This dynamic tended to arouse a spirit of anti-clericalism, and general disdain for the clergy.[31]

The colonial experience in New England was quite different. Church courts were non-existent, and church membership was voluntary. There were no Inquisitions, and the civil magistrate imposed the penalties. The power of the clergy in New England was spiritual, and not part of the state apparatus. Hall asserts that these important differences created an environment that was less anti-clerical than that of Europe.[32]

New England's ministers may have been less likely to arouse anti-clericalism

---

29 Stout, *The New England Soul*, 19.

30 See Harry Stout's *The New England Soul* for a thorough description of the generational breakdown of New England's ministers.

31 David Hall, *World of Wonders, Days of Judgment*, 6.

32 Ibid.

than their counterparts in England, but the ordination day sermons of Isaac Foster contain an imploring element where he and Woodbridge seem to plead with the congregation to support Foster's ministry, as if support would not be forthcoming unless they did so. As a young preacher, Foster was very much in need of mutual acceptance on the part of his congregation; he knew they could send him packing, but given the chance, he could prove himself worthy.

Puritanism was a set of beliefs, it was a separate formulation of Protestantism with its own unique structure, but it was not yet a separate church.[33] Tracy tells us "Puritans had a distinctive tendency to personalize the doctrine of predestination, searching within their own experience for a moment of conversion at which God's grace had entered their lives."[34] Within this Puritan way there grew two very distinct systems that would later present many challenges to Puritans in New England, namely, Presbyterianism and Congregationalism. While Calvin influenced both systems, differences existed between them. The Presbyterian design consisted of a system of representative ecclesiastical bodies that functioned together as a larger church. This was in marked contrast to Congregationalism, which refused "to recognize any larger church body," and

was known as the Independent wing. Independents "believed decisions on all important matters must be made by each congregation."[35]

The social historian T.H. Breen provides a diversion from the specifically religious nature of the Reformation and its impact on the colonization of New England. Breen's book *Puritans and Adventurers: Change and Persistence in Early America* analyzes the forces in England that contributed to the New World exodus of the seventeenth century.[36] The book contains a series of essays that cover a geographic spectrum of immigration from New England to Virginia, and his description of the decay of the provincial localized villages of England is very interesting. Breen argues that forces other than religious zeal contributed greatly to patterns of immigration.[37] However, while Breen does not completely dismiss the impetus of religious independence, he argues that its role was secondary to that of the dynamic changes imposed on local loyalties by the English monarchy, and that the particularism that dominated so

---

33 Tracy, *Europe's Reformations*, 195.
34 Ibid.

35 Ibid., 196.
36 An excellent launching pad for Puritan social history begins with Edmund Morgan, and I would also suggest the works of David Hall. These historians do not easily classify into one methodological camp, and for my purposes, they do not need to. I would suggest that they both qualify as historians of many methods, and that their intellectual insights are second to none regarding New England in the seventeenth century.
37 T.H. Breen, *Puritans and Adventurers: Change and Persistence in Early America* (New York: Oxford University Press, 1980), 10.

much of the English countryside in the seventeenth century was under attack.[38]

While Breen offers a compelling argument for forces of immigration other than religion, there were several motivations at work, not the least of which was religious freedom. The historian David Weir suggests that we should be aware of many possible contributors to the immigrants of seventeenth century New England. "The complexity of the human psyche cannot simply be reduced to any one motivating force for migration: any individual could have numerous reasons for migrating to the new world ... Economic, political, and religious factors were certainly often public and primary ..."[39] Clearly, a variety of influences including religious preference, contributed to the complex migration of English people to New England.

Perhaps the most well known Puritans were the Separatists. This group includes the Pilgrims, who because of their views regarding baptism, they believed it was sacrilegious to baptize infants, were harassed by the Church of England. The Pilgrims separated from the Church of England and fled to Holland in 1607. Despite the relative freedom of worship the Pilgrims experienced in the Dutch Republic, the fear of Dutch acculturation provided much of the impetus for an Atlantic crossing and the famed voyage of the Mayflower.[40]

In 1620, the Pilgrims completed their Atlantic crossing and settled in Plymouth, but it is important to recognize that the Pilgrims were refugees from England, unlike the waves of English who followed them; non-separating Puritans like John Winthrop and John Cotton, who established the Massachusetts Bay colony at Boston, and Thomas Hooker's Hartford, Connecticut. The Bay Company was not running away from the problems of religious intolerance in England, rather, it was a "task force of Christians" whose goal was the completion of Europe's reformation in the Puritan image.[41]

Massachusetts Bay was a chartered colony of England that generally recognized the Church of England as a real church and enjoyed agreeable commerce with the mother country, but more importantly to its first settlers, the Bay Colony enjoyed a religious independence in the New World that simply was not possible had they remained in England. Under the leadership of Thomas Hooker, Hartford's earliest settlers found agreeable acreage and greater autonomy on the banks of the Connecticut River, but neither Massachusetts Bay nor Connecticut sought outward separation from the Church of England, they simply put an ocean between England's church and their own desired form of worship.

---

38 Ibid., 7.
39 David A. Weir, *Early New England: A Covenanted Society*, 28–29.
40 Tracy, *Europe's Reformations*, 196.

41 Perry Miller, *Errand Into the Wilderness* (Cambridge Massachusetts: The Belknap Press of the Harvard University Press, 1956), 11.

DISCUSSION QUESTIONS

1. According to the reading, what are the origins of the name Puritan?
2. Briefly summarize Perry Miller's characterization of Puritans.
3. What kinds of things did the Puritans wish to change about the Church?
4. Describe Calvin's "middle way."
5. Compare the Old World model of church and state with the Puritan's New World model.
6. Compare Presbyterianism and Congregationalism.
7. What did the Separatists believe about baptism?

CHAPTER THREE

Native Americans and the Problem of History, Part I

FROM *History's Shadow*

BY STEVEN CONN

INTRODUCTION

In December 1890 the Bureau of Indian Affairs (BIA) decided to round up some of the Sioux Indian chiefs in order to put an end to an Indian movement called the Ghost Dancers. Led by a prophet named Wovoka, the Ghost Dancers promised Indians a new beginning, free of white man's oppression. This had been interpreted as a possible insurrection by whites, and so the best thing to do, they reasoned, was to round up the leaders. Sitting Bull was probably the best known of the Sioux chiefs, having famously defeated George Custer at the Battle of Little Big Horn in 1876. The BIA sent a posse of forty Indian police to take Sitting Bull into custody. Upon arriving at Sitting Bull's house, they arrested him. A scuffle broke out when Sitting Bull resisted. Someone fired a shot and then people began firing indiscriminately. Within a few seconds, fifteen people were dead, including Sitting Bull.

After the terrible incident, 200 people from Sitting Bull's tribe joined a small band of Indians led by Chief Spotted Elk (a.k.a. Big Foot). This group of about 350 were making their way to a reservation where they could be protected. On December 28, just thirteen days after the death of Sitting Bull, they were encamped at Wounded Knee Creek. That morning, 500 US soldiers showed up to disarm the Indians. While they were in the process of doing that, a deaf Indian named Black Coyote did not understand what was going on and resisted having his gun taken from him. Someone fired a shot, and then the gunfire opened up. In the end, most of the Indians, and a few soldiers killed by friendly fire, lay dead. One estimate says that 300 Indians were killed, most of them unarmed, many of them women and children. Wounded Knee was the low point of the American

FIGURE 3.1.
Fig. 3.1: James Penny Boyd, "Ghost Dance," https://commons.wikimedia.org/wiki/File:Ghost_dance.jpg.
Copyright in the Public Domain.

FIGURE 3.2.
Fig 3.2: "Wounded Knee Massacre," https://commons.wikimedia.org/wiki/File:Wounded_Knee_1891.jpg.
Copyright in the Public Domain.

Indian experience in a land that had been taken away from them by whites.[1] The 1900 census recorded an American Indian population of around 250,000. It is estimated that there were as many as 30 million in North America when Columbus "discovered" America. The American Indian, most people believed, was doomed to extinction.

In the first chapter of his book *History's Shadow*, Steven Conn introduces us to a study of how whites in the nineteenth century imagined American Indians to be. White writers and intellectuals wondered about their origins, their languages, and generally tried to pin down exactly who these native people were. By the end of the nineteenth century these efforts had declined, as people assumed that the American Indian was no more.

But the American Indian did not go extinct. Instead, they rebounded in the twentieth century, their populations growing to ten times what they were in 1900. Wounded Knee became a point of pride for American Indians when, in 1973, the American Indian Movement took over Wounded Knee, South Dakota, in a standoff with federal authorities that lasted seventy-one days.[2] It is fair to say that in the twenty-first century, when non-white cultures are a bigger part of mainstream America, we aren't likely to think of the American Indian as lost. The American Indian today still faces many problems, but like other peoples who call themselves Americans, they aren't likely to go away.

* * *

---

1 Amy Ehrlich, *Wounded Knee: An Indian History of the American West* (New York: Henry Holt and Co., 1993).
2 James Adair, *History of the American Indians* (University of Alabama Press, 2005).

I regret with you, the want of zeal *among* our countrymen for collecting materials concerning the history of these people.

BENJAMIN SMITH BARTON, 1797

In 1903, W. E. B. DuBois wrote, "The problem of the twentieth century is the problem of the color line," and thus penned perhaps the most enduring pronouncement on the state of America ever made. By the time DuBois wrote, America's racial "problem" had become, on a host of levels, a matter of black and white. The color line, in DuBois's view, separated white from black. The contours of that line shaped the very essence of what America was in its soul, and the erasure of that line became DuBois's life work.

DuBois's famous statement needs to be seen as a prophecy—a remarkably prescient one at that—and as a summing up. We have become so accustomed to thinking of DuBois as a prophet of the key issues surrounding race in the twentieth century that it has been easy to forget that he came to maturity as much in the twilight of the nineteenth century as in the dawn of the twentieth. Among the developments he witnessed in the waning of Victorian America was the disappearance of a third race from the national consciousness. DuBois may have seen the world in black and white when he wrote in 1903, but when he was born in 1868, the nation's racial dynamic came in three colors: black, white, and red.

By the turn of the twentieth century, DuBois was already the nation's most profound thinker on matters of race. Yet it is not at all clear that he spent much time thinking about that third race. As his biographer David Levering Lewis remarks, DuBois recognized that in the United States there formally existed only two races—Asians had been "excluded" while Native Americans had become "invisible."[3] Invisible because by the time DuBois made his prediction about the color line the frontier had been "closed" for thirteen years, and the massacre at Wounded Knee had effectively ended a generation of continuous warfare between the federal government and native groups. Noting that most young people had never even seen an Indian, the author of an 1885 children's book about Indians pronounced: "With the exception of a few roving bands of Apaches and other wild tribes of the plains, the Indian pictured in these pages no longer exists."[4] The color line between black and white might well have become

the "problem" of the twentieth century, but only because for most Americans the "problem" of the Indian had been finally "solved."

In this outlook, DuBois was no different from most Americans, black or white, early in the twentieth century. My purpose is not to chide DuBois for his oversight. Rather, his relative silence on the question of Native Americans at the turn of the twentieth century underscores how thoroughly they had disappeared from Euro- and even African-American consciousness.

Three generations earlier such invisibility would have seemed nearly impossible. In a speech given to a New York City church congregation, Thomas McKenney, the first Superintendent of the Bureau of Indian Affairs (1824–1830), quoted a "distinguished citizen of Virginia" reminding his listeners of the nation's two part problem: "one of these relates to the black population which we carry in our bosom; the other to the red population which we carry on our back." In his *Notions of the Americans,* a collection of letters to Europeans about the United States James Fenimore Cooper published in 1827 as his version of Jefferson's *Notes on the State of Virginia,* Cooper put his comments about Native Americans immediately after his comments about slavery.

Alexis de Tocqueville, as astute an observer of antebellum society as DuBois was of the Gilded Age, certainly saw the United States as tri-colored. He paired Indians and African slaves

---

3 Lewis, *W. E. B. DuBois,* p. 72.

4 Drake, *Indian History for Young Folks,* pp. 5, 13.

almost metaphorically as polar opposites: "The Negro," he wrote in his classic *Democracy in America*, "has reached the ultimate limits of slavery, whereas the Indian lives on the extreme edge of freedom." Although they shared nothing of "birth, physique, language, nor mores," they did share "their misfortunes." The effects of slavery on Africans proved "not more fatal" than the effects of too much "independence" on Native Americans.[5]

For citizens of the United States in the late eighteenth and early nineteenth centuries, Indians were everywhere. They lived in a world, as Anthony Wallace put it recently, "in which Indians themselves were a constant presence."[6]

A presence and, as we have already hinted, a problem.

The diplomatic struggles and military encounters that characterized Euro-Native relations during the Revolutionary period are well known. American colonists found themselves fighting against Indians allied with the French, and then once more when other Indian groups became allies of the British during the Revolutionary War. Beyond the formalized violence of war, Euro-Americans clashed with Indians on numberless occasions, most often when tensions over land on the ever-expanding frontier came to a boil. When the revolutionaries established an independent republic, Indians may well have been a near-constant physical presence, but

they now found themselves in, but not of, the new nation. In Wallace's words, "native Americans fell outside the pole of the Jeffersonian republic, but inside the arena of Jeffersonian geo-politics."[7]

It makes sense to begin our considerations with Jefferson. Jefferson, in fact, was DuBois' predecessor as a philosopher of the nation's racial dilemma. None of the other founders spent as much time or intellectual energy thinking about Native Americans. Likewise, none of the others shaped policies that would prove so fateful to Native Americans. More than any other member of his circle, Jefferson recognized the increasingly intractable nature of relations between Euro-Americans and Indians. Writing to Benjamin Hawkins, Jefferson first commended him for "the attention which you pay to their rights ... the want of which is a principle source of dishonor to the American character." But then he turned more despairing: "the two principles on which our Conduct towards the Indians should be founded, are justice and fear. After the injuries we have done them they cannot love us, which leaves us no alternative but that of fear to keep them from attacking us, but justice is what we should never lose sight of."[8] Jefferson did not describe the relationship between white Americans and Indians with the famous metaphor he used to describe the institution of slavery, but he might as well have. Native

---

5 McKenney, *Memoirs,* p. 229; Tocqueville, *Democracy in America,* pp. 317–318.
6 Wallace, *Jefferson and the Indians,* p. 50.

7 Ibid., p. 19.
8 *Writings of Thomas Jefferson,* 5:390.

Americans represented another wolf held by its ears.

Yet, as Anthony Wallace has portrayed him, Jefferson, much as he struggled with the issue, could simply not envision a future for the United States that included a place for "Indians as Indians." As president, Jefferson tried to design an Indian policy that would humanely assimilate Native Americans into the new republic, but his vision of national expansion turned out not to have any room for Native Americans. Whatever uneasiness Jefferson felt about centralized power he lost to his "desire to obtain Indian land, at almost any cost." The buffer zone Jefferson tried to create between settlers and natives during his administration failed to prevent abuse of the latter by the Euro-Americans. By 1816, the policy was a "nullity, in Wallace's estimation."[9]

Most significantly, Jefferson's purchase of the Louisiana Territory in 1803 set in motion a sequence of events and forces that reached its antebellum conclusion in the Indian Removal Act of 1830. Jefferson's desultory policy of civilization and assimilation culminated, ironically but perhaps predictably, in Andrew Jackson's Trail of Tears. By the mid-nineteenth century, Indians remained a problem of national "geopolitics," but they no longer constituted the kind of presence they had been a scant fifty years earlier.

FOR JEFFERSON, Native Americans represented another kind of dilemma as well. Whatever agonizing he did over questions of geopolitics, Jefferson found in Native Americans an irresistible set of intellectual problems. As discussed in subsequent chapters, Jefferson the scholar pursued and encouraged the study of Native Americans with real enthusiasm and vigor. In his work emerge the beginnings of American linguistics, archaeology, and ethnology. In this respect, Jefferson was exemplary, but he was by no means alone. In the nineteenth century, Indians were the subjects and objects of all kinds of speculation, research, polemic, and jeremiad in the worlds of science and letters. By 1841, the anonymous author of *Events in Indian History* anticipated a certain weariness and impatience from the reading public when he began his short volume this way: "Another book upon the Aborigines of North America! Have we not volume upon volume of works on the Indians of this continent?"[10]

I should be clear at the outset that my book does not add to the "volume upon volume of works" written about Native Americans. Strictly speaking, this study is not really about Native Americans at all, and I am certainly no historian of Native America. The challenge of writing the history of Native Americans has been taken up by historians and anthropologists, both Native and non-Native, including Anthony Wallace, Vine

---

9   See Wallace, *Jefferson and the Indians*, pp. 11, 205, 218.

10   *Events in Indian History*, p. 9.

Deloria, Richard White, Daniel Richter, and Lucy Murphy, to name a few whose works stare down at me from my shelves. (Recently, historian Ellen Fitzpatrick has provided an excellent account of the rise of Native American historiography in the twentieth century.)[11] This book, I trust, would not cause further grimaces from the acerbic R. S. H. who wrote in 1848: "So much has of late been written upon the Indians that I tremble in approaching them.... [T]hey have suffered [at] innumerable hands, been bemoaned in lamentable prose, and wept over in most imaginative poetry: their fate has certainly been a hard one."[12]

Nor does this book belong exactly with those by scholars—most notably Robert Berkhofer, Anthony Pagden, Roy Harvey Pearce, and Bernard Sheehan—who have addressed the ways in which Europeans and Euro-Americans have imagined the American Indian. Berkhofer's landmark book *The White Man's Indian,* for example, demonstrated how the ways in which Native Americans were portrayed in popular culture served as blank screens upon which Euro-Americans could project their own fantasies and desires.

Rather this is a study of the volumes upon volumes of books like *Events in Indian History,* and of their authors. It examines Native Americans as objects of study and as subjects of intellectual discourse in the nineteenth

century. This study amounts to an intellectual history whose major actors are the Euro-American men (and occasionally women) who, for a variety of reasons and with a variety of motivations, took it upon themselves to study, record, and write about Native Americans. Neither intellectual historians nor historians of Native Americans have really considered fully how the curiosity that Indians aroused—and the ways that curiosity was pursued—shaped the nineteenth-century American mind. Studying Indians, I will assert, constituted a central, if now largely forgotten, part of the nation's intellectual discourse, defining American science and social science, and shaping conceptions of the nation's history. That is the story I have attempted to tell here.

In examining the study of Native Americans as a chapter in the nation's intellectual life, I make three, interrelated claims. First, the very existence of Native Americans posed fundamental challenges to the way Euro-Americans understood the world. They found themselves unable to answer basic questions: Who are these people, and where did they come from? How are they related to other human groups, past and present? Have they demonstrated historical progress, or are they doomed to extinction? Attempts to answer such questions lay at the heart of the way several intellectual genres developed in this country.

Second, as they attempted to answer these basic and fundamental questions,

---

11 See Fitzpatrick, *History's Memory,* chap. 3.
12 R. S. H. "Indian Women," pp. 401–402.

Euro-Americans relied first on the only explanatory apparatus they had available: biblical and classical texts. As the nineteenth century wore on, however, and more research accumulated, it became increasingly clear that Indians were descended neither from a lost tribe of Israel nor from any colony of displaced Etruscans—to name two of the more popular theories that circulated in the antebellum period. I suggest that the failure of biblical and classical texts to explain the questions posed by Native American language, culture, and history—along with more familiar phenomena like the arrival of German criticism and Darwinian natural science—shaped the transition from a sacred world view to a secular one. Although that shift occurred on both sides of the Atlantic, I suggest that the American intellectual encounters with Native Americans gave a particular cast to the way it happened here. As Samuel Drake put it in his 1851 *Biography and History of the Indians of North America,* "if we are to attribute everything to miracles, wherefore the necessity of investigation?"[13]

Finally, though, what troubled Euro-American scholars the most about Native Americans was their relationship to history. While people at all points in the past and at all points of the compass have had an interest in their own history, it is surely the case that history as a formalized practice and as an organized discipline only emerged during the course of the nineteenth century. That emergence had two components, each bound tightly to the other. On the one hand, the practice of history developed its own methodology during the nineteenth century, based on a set of rules that governed what historical questions should be asked, what constituted historical evidence, and in what form history should be written. On the other hand, Americans developed a new historical consciousness during the nineteenth century—a rough consensus shared by many about how the mechanisms of history worked, the exceptional place of the United States in the flow of history, and a sense, both reassuring and disquieting, that the distance that separated the present from the past grew almost daily. Method and consciousness reinforced each other, thereby drawing the boundaries of what constituted history.

This book argues that the attempts to study and understand Native Americans figured centrally in that process of definition. Trying to answer questions posed by the very presence of American Indians and the astonishing variety of their cultures forced Americans to confront the meaning of history, both their own history and the history of the Native Americans: How should history be studied? What drove its processes? Where might it ultimately lead? The change of American historical consciousness across the stretch of the nineteenth century meshed with attempts to figure out

---

13 Drake, *Biography and History of the Indians,* p. 33.

exactly where and how Indians fit into "history," as it was pursued and understood. Did Native Americans have a history? If so, how should it be recovered? More importantly, could "their" history be seen as part of "ours"? My sense is that the intellectual encounters with Native Americans made it possible for Euro-Americans to define history apart from myth, history apart from culture, and the realm of history as something quite different from the realm of the past. By the 1890s, Native Americans could very well have a past, but they did not, by and large, have a history. In this sense, Native Americans constituted history's shadow.

To get at this intellectual history, I have relied heavily on the discourse surrounding Indians that appeared in print during the nineteenth century. Vast as this literature is—the anonymous author of *Events in Indian History* did not exaggerate!—it comes as no surprise that it varies widely in a host of ways. Some of this variation stems from the wide variety of writers who turned their attention to Indians—from presidents and diplomats, to scholars and scientists, to ministers and poets. Then too, this immense body of writing, appearing in the form of books, magazine and journal articles, pamphlets, and lectures, was read by very different audiences as well. Writings about Native Americans in the nineteenth century traversed the full spectrum from the serious and learned, to the silly and laughable.

My purpose is not to sort out the serious from the trivial, to separate the scientific and scholarly wheat from the popularized, fantastical chaff, although some winnowing inevitably happens here. Rather, by treating these publications more or less as a single body I am attempting to demonstrate how pervasive Indians were in the intellectual life of nineteenth-century America. Further, I am arguing that the sheer volume and variety of this published material can reveal important things—not necessarily about the Indians themselves, but about the Euro-American culture that produced and read it.

Some years ago, when writing about the American 1930s, Warren Susman made a similar claim. One doesn't have to insist, he argued, that Superman comics are better than Shakespeare's plays to recognize that Superman might reveal a great deal about the culture of the 1930s. So it is here. Much of what got written, published, and read about Indians in the nineteenth century has been roundly and decisively dismissed by anthropologists, linguists, archaeologists, and others as useful or even legitimate science. After all, few among us take seriously the theory of the lost civilization of Atlantis, despite the currency it had in the mid-nineteenth century. Nonetheless, these writings remain important fragments of our intellectual and cultural history. In 1833, for example, Josiah Priest gave the reading public a ripping tale of the ancient and vanished races that once populated the American West. Not a word of his *American Antiquities and Discoveries in the West* is probably taken seriously today. By 1835, however, the book had sold 22,000 copies: serious sales even by today's standard. This book, and others like it, ought to command serious historical attention.

Yet at the same time, however, the trajectory I trace here describes the way in which discourse about Native Americans became increasingly professionalized. As in all other fields of intellectual life, the lines separating professional and respectable scholarship from mere popularizing were being drawn more sharply. The development of America's nineteenth-century intellectual life in many ways mirrors the delineations between "highbrow" and "lowbrow" that Lawrence Levine has charted in other areas of American culture. These realms interacted, to be sure, and the differences between the serious and the popular were never as sharp as many late nineteenth-century scientists and intellectuals insisted they were. One has only to think of the Barnumesque displays of Native Americans at the 1876 Centennial and at the 1893 World's Columbian Exposition—the former sponsored by the United States National Museum, the latter by the fair's department of anthropology—to remember that highbrow and lowbrow continued to intersect well into the last quarter of the nineteenth century. Nevertheless, the nature of intellectual discourse did change across the century. My concerns lie with how the study of Indians shaped what came to be considered the serious side of American intellectual life.

The next chapter begins by looking, in a literal sense, at these developments. In the nineteenth century, Native Americans filled the nation's visual culture in virtually every conceivable genre—from painting, to lithographs and mass-produced illustrations, to cigar store figures, and eventually to photographs. I make no attempt in the chapter at a full or complete evaluation of how Indians were represented visually. Instead, I want to focus on a few painters and photographers, to examine how their work was a historical documentation of Indians. We start with Benjamin West, arguably the first American to paint historical subjects in the grand manner. By the Civil War, history painting in the grand manner, once the apex of painterly achievement, had faded as a vital genre in both the United States and in Europe. I suggest, however, that the historical impulse did not disappear from American art, for American images of Indians, both on canvas and in photographs, created new conventions of how history could be represented. The shifting portrayal of Native Americans first in landscape paintings and finally in portraiture—both in paint and in photographs—charts the change from seeing Native Americans as part of a didactic and moral history to seeing them as part of an anthropology rooted in natural history. In this sense, the images examined in chapter 2 encapsulate our larger project. How did Euro-Americans construct a past for Indians? How did Euro-Americans construct a consciousness of their own history? And how did the two evolve quite apart from each other?

In chapter 3, we turn our attention to the study of Indian languages. In the early republic, the study of American Indian languages, by missionaries and others, was a thriving enterprise. Investigators compiled lengthy vocabularies, deciphered rules of grammar, and remarked on the rich, poetic and metaphorical quality of Indian speech. "Eloquent" was a commonplace description of how Indians used their language. Thomas Jefferson, in his *Notes on the State Virginia*, was only one of many writers who pointed to Chief Logan's speech to Lord Dunmore as evidence of the admirable quality of Indian eloquence.

Students of Indian languages believed their research would be the foundation for the new, scientific study of language, and therefore a field in which American scholars could out-do their European counterparts. They also believed that language was the key to understanding history—not just Indian history, but all human history—and that through the comparative study of languages, genealogical relationships between human groups could be established. The study of Indian languages, which had begun in the seventeenth century as part of the missionary impulse, had become a historical project by the turn of the nineteenth century.

By the end of the nineteenth century, however, the field of American Indian linguistics had not developed as those early nineteenth-century pioneers had envisioned. Instead, the study of Indian languages became one of several subfields of American anthropology. Language study developed as an essential part of the anthropological method, but not necessarily as a field unto itself and not necessarily with the same concerns about the relationship between language and history. The more autonomous work of philology and linguistics was still done primarily by the Europeans, and mostly on the dead and ancient languages being uncovered by archaeologists. When William Dwight Whitney, himself a professor of Sanskrit at Yale, wrote *The Life and Growth of Language* in 1875, he generalized Native American language as "cumbrous and time-wasting in its immense polysyllabism." What had once been seen as the key to understanding Indian history was now used primarily to create a system to classify Indian groups.

Whether or not American archaeology began with Jefferson when he sponsored excavations of Indian mounds, it is certainly true that archaeology in America began with investigations in American Indian sites. Chapter 4 explores the history of American archaeology and its relationship to the study of Indian history. By the middle of the nineteenth century, as the Ohio and Mississippi River valleys filled with settlers, Americans searched for Native American history by digging up what had been buried by past generations. These excavations, and their discoveries, were reported widely in both the American and English press.

The turn toward archaeology represented two important shifts in how American Indians were studied. The first was a new reliance on objects as the place where knowledge inhered. What I have called elsewhere an "object-based epistemology" defined the intellectual mission of excavators who dug for, collected, and classified American Indian objects.[14] Related to this was the conviction that objects constituted a permanent record of Native American history, while language disappeared with the speakers, and that by the middle of the nineteenth century, those speakers did indeed seem doomed to disappear.

This chapter examines how the field of American archaeology developed, how archaeologists defined their questions, and how ideas about archaeology intersected with ideas about history. As with the study of languages, by the end of the century American archaeology had assumed a secondary importance to the work going on in the Old World. As Bruce Kuklick has described in his book *Puritans in Babylon,* American excavations, especially in the Near East, made spectacular finds. Even more important, archaeologists were driven by a desire to prove the legitimacy of the Bible as an historical source. Ironically, questions that had been asked first and been left unanswered about American Indians

were now being asked halfway round the world.

By the end of the nineteenth century, nearly all the serious study of Native Americans fell within the purview of the newly emergent discipline of anthropology. This new field included four constituent parts: linguistics, archaeology, physical anthropology, and ethnology. Chapter 5 sketches how these four pursuits, once autonomous discourses, became subsidiaries of a new anthropology. It begins by examining the relationship between literature and the genre of ethnography. Indians filled the pages of American literature in the nineteenth century, most importantly perhaps in the work of James Fenimore Cooper. At the same time, ethnography was developing as another way of describing Indians in texts. By the end of the century, it was ethnography, not literature, that had become the single authoritative way of translating Indian culture into writing.

At the same time, physical anthropology developed as a way of addressing the questions of race and racial distinctions that were also central to the field of inquiry called ethnology. The story of how race was studied "scientifically" is well known to most students of nineteenth-century America, but my purpose in this chapter is to examine how it contributed to the formation of an American anthropology. Finally, this chapter considers the institutional matrix in which anthropology matured. It pays particular attention to the Bureau

---

14 Conn, *Museums and American Intellectual Life,* chap.1.

of American Ethnology, the growth of museums, and the emergence of university departments of anthropology. By the end of the nineteenth century, the study of Native Americans had become almost entirely anthropological. And as anthropology, the study of Native Americans, while interested to some extent in the Native American past, had become largely ahistorical.

The last chapter considers American historical writing proper. Having examined how the historical considerations of these other practices shrank, it looks at how Indians fared in the writing of history. I begin with romantic historians, particularly Francis Parkman, regarded by many as the last, greatest example of that school, and finish with Herbert Baxter Adams and Frederick Jackson Turner. In between, I pause to consider what I have called "the prehistoric revolution," the creation in the mid-nineteenth century of a conceptual space that existed before history. This, I believe, had an enormous effect on how Native American history was conceived. Having been removed from the mainstream narratives of histories being written in the nineteenth century, Indians could be put into this other, prehistoric category, and viewed as a people before and without a history.

The chapters in this book, like intellectual disciplines themselves, represent an artificial order and a categorization imposed on an otherwise messy situation. They are a convenience, and although I think that the choices I have made clarify a set of issues in America's nineteenth-century intellectual life, I should warn at the outset that there is considerable overlap between chapters—of people, of ideas, of events. I have done my best to disentangle them.

Each chapter of this book sketches a long arc, which begins with the founding of the republic, or thereabouts, and ends with the 1890s, approximately. Although Indians certainly drew the attention of writers and scholars before the late eighteenth century, the events of independence and nationhood, along with the shifts in knowledge and learning that took place as part of the American enlightenment, changed the context in which people asked questions about Indians. I end, roughly, in the 1890s, which may strike some readers as an almost perverse choice. After all, our understanding of Native Americans, both present and past, changed dramatically because of the Boasian revolution in anthropology and all that flowed from it in the first half of the twentieth century. I have made this choice because I remain convinced by John Higham's argument made some while ago that the decade of the 1890s witnesses a significant "reorientation" in American culture.[15] But whereas Higham, and others, see the 1890s as prefiguring many of the cultural struggles of the twentieth century, I want to view the decade as a culmination of a century-long process

15   Higham, "The Reorientation of American Culture in the 1890s," in *Writing American History.*

of thinking about history, and how that thinking was stalked by its shadow.

A note on usage: first, my considerations are confined geographically to the space we call the United States. There may well be a companion story here to tell about how the Indian civilizations of Central and South America were viewed, but that is for another time and another scholar. Likewise, it is a gross generalization to lump Canada in with the rest of North America. I refer to the United States, America, and North America almost interchangeably for style's sake, and because this usage reflects the way the terms were used in the nineteenth century. Likewise, I use "Indian," "Amerindian," and "Native American" in the same way. I recognize that for some academics these have become fighting words, but I have chosen not to engage in those fights here.

Studying the Noble Savage

Tocqueville's description of Native Americans is worth lingering over in some detail. He begins his observations by telling readers that, unlike the "vexatious contrast" of European societies where rich and poor confront each other daily, "the Indian, all poor and all ignorant, are also all equal and free." "Indifferent" to the trappings of European civilization now presented to them, "there was in their manners a habitual reserve and a sort of aristocratic courtesy." Tocqueville continues:

Gentle and hospitable in peace, in war merciless even beyond the known limits of human ferocity, the Indian would face starvation to succor the stranger who knocked in the evening on the door of his hut, but he would tear his prisoner's quivering limbs to pieces with his own hands. No famed republic of antiquity could record firmer courage, prouder spirit, or more obstinate love of freedom than lies concealed in the forests of the New World. The European made but little impression when they landed on the shore of North America; they were neither feared nor envied. What hold could they have on such men? The Indian knew how to live without wants, to suffer without complaint, and to die singing.[16]

The description weaves a marvelous tapestry of contradictory clichés: savagery and aristocracy; kindness and cruelty; peacefulness and war-mongering. And the paragraph resonates with familiarity: it is as succinct, indeed as breathless, a formulation of the idea of the noble savage as one is liable to find. That Tocqueville resorted to this trope,

---

16 Toqueville, *Democracy in America,* pp. 28–29.

borrowed from his fellow countryman Jean-Jacques Rousseau, should come as no surprise. One suspects, in fact, that this was the description of Native Americans Tocqueville already had in his head when he set sail for the United States.

In recalling the noble savage, however, in his welter of oppositions, Tocqueville implicitly admitted something else. No better or more persuasive understanding of Native Americans had emerged by the time Tocqueville toured the country. Simply stated, Indians largely remained a mystery for white Americans in the first half of the nineteenth century. As Isaac McCoy put it in 1829, almost exactly the moment when Tocqueville arrived for his visit, "it is remarkable that with the opportunities of more than two centuries to become acquainted with the Aborigines of our country, their character and condition should at all times have been so imperfectly understood by us."[17]

Remarkable to be sure, because the very nature of Native Americans had perplexed Europeans beginning in 1492. The misnomer by which they came to be known—Indians—reflects after all a fundamental misunderstanding about who these people were and what their relationship to the rest of the world was. As David Bidney pointed out some years ago, Indians posed both theoretical and practical problems for the colonists who came in growing numbers in the sixteenth, seventeenth, and eighteenth centuries.[18]

For much of this period, theory and practice intersected on the terrain of religion. For believing Christians, as Anthony Pagden has noted, it became crucial that non-Christians be brought into the fold, "indeed, cajoled or forced into entering it." For some Catholic Spaniards and Frenchmen, and for New England Puritans, the missionary encounter with Native Americans lay at the heart of their errand into the wilderness.[19] The missionary encounter, however, forced European colonists to confront a set of intellectual dilemmas. The first of these was language—how to communicate the word of God when Indians and Europeans understood not a word of each other's languages? The next set of problems revolved around figuring out just how Indians fit into the history and teleology of God's plan as revealed in the Bible. This, then, as Pagden points out, amounted to a problem of classification.[20] By the eighteenth century, this focus on classification enabled a shift in the study of Native Americans away from the theological to include the world of natural history. Late in the eighteenth century, Benjamin Smith Barton, one of

---

17 McCoy, *Indian Reform,* p. 9.

18 Bidney, "Idea of the Savage," p. 322.

19 There were, of course, all kinds of differences between the various religious groups proselytizing among Indians. As Edward Gray has noted, for the Puritans, unlike the Jesuits, "the first objective was not to administer the sacraments, but to make the Indians self-sufficient enquirers after grace." Gray, *New World Babel,* p. 50.

20 Pagden, *Fall of Natural Man,* pp. 2, 19.

the most important American natural-ists, titled his study of Native Americans, "An Essay towards a Natural History of the North American Indians."[21]

The study of natural history, and the particular way it emerged during the American eighteenth century, laid important foundations for how Native Americans would be studied and under-stood through much of the nineteenth. It was no accident that Tocqueville put his long description of the noble savage in the very first chapter, entitled "Physical Configuration of North America."

IN 1775, AFTER having "had them years standing before me," and having "lived with them as a friend and brother," James Adair published *The History of the American Indians*. In it, Adair argues that the Indians descended from the Jews, and he spends the vast bulk of the book proving this by examining "their religious rites, civil and marital customs, their marriages, funeral ceremonies, manners, language, traditions, and a variety of particulars." A quick sampling of his evidence: "Argument I, both have tribes.... Argument VI, they count time after the manner of the Hebrews.... Argument VII, they have prophets and high priests.... Argument XI, Mosaic law." And so it goes, through 23 argu-ments, for 200 pages.[22]

We won't bother to pause in order to figure out just exactly how Adair

deduced Mosaic law among the Indians with whom he had spent time. In fact, the theory that the Indians constituted a lost tribe of Israel circulated widely and persuasively in the late eighteenth century, and survived well into the nineteenth. Adair's book is remarkable only in the thoroughness with which he argued the theory, and in the authority with which he spoke, because, as he an-nounced at the outset, he had lived for some years with Indians.

Despite the weightiness of this tome, Adair did not put the question of origins to rest. In his essay, Barton reviews several major theories on the origin of Indians, an "almost endless list of hypotheses." He first considers the idea, put forth by a Mexican mathematician named Siguenra, that Indians descended from Nephtuhim, the grand nephew of Noah, and that they had journeyed to the New World "a short time after the confusion of Babel." Barton points out that some writers "have brought the Carthagenians across the Atlantic" and claimed them as the progenitors of the Indians. Others had attempted "to prove that the greater part of the world was peopled by the inhabitants of Scandinavia." Others still saw Wales or Ireland as the place from which the Indians first came. By the time he reached Adair and the theory of the Jewish origin, Barton quite dismisses what he calls this "strange opinion."

Barton ran through these theories in order to get to one he feels is, finally, right. After looking at the "conjectures" of Edward Brerewood, coupled with

---

21 Barton, "An Essay towards a Natural History of the North American Indians." The hand-written essay is undated.

22 See Adair, *History of the American Indians*.

the discoveries of Captains Bering and Cook in the North Pacific, Barton was convinced: "I imagine there can no longer be any doubt that America was principally peopled from Asia." He too offered a list of reasons to support the claim, and though it ran only to four items, rather than Adair's twenty-three, it included the fact that "the languages of the Tartars, and of other Asiatic nations, have a very considerable relation to those of the Americans."[23]

From our vantage, Barton's conclusion seems remarkably sharp, even if his claim about language is a more than a bit dubious. Most who have studied the question of how the New World was first populated agree that migration from northeast Asia via the Bering Strait is the most likely answer. In a well-known textbook on the archaeology of North America, Jesse Jennings, in the first line of the chapter on the "origins" of Native Americans, writes with a sense of finality on the subject: "At once the most important and the least dramatic event in American history was the passage of the first human from Asia into the New World 30,000 or more years ago."[24]

In the early republic and antebellum periods, however, Barton's sound reasoning failed to close the case. Caleb Atwater, the first person systematically to explore the intriguing and mysterious mounds that dotted the river valleys of Ohio, published the results of his surveys in 1820 (discussed further in chapter 4). Atwater virtually circled the globe searching for points of comparison. Looking for the "authors of our ancient works," Atwater found similar mounds not only in biblical lands, but in England, Wales, Scotland, Turkey, and across the Russian Empire. "Thus," he concluded, "we learn from the most authentick sources, that these ancient works existing in Europe, Asia, and America, are as similar in their construction, in the materials with which they were raised, and in the articles found in them, as it is possible for them to be."[25]

By 1837, M. M. Noah returned to the Israelites in an energetic book entitled *Discourse on the Evidence of the American Indians being the Descendants of the Lost Tribes of Israel*. He repeated some of what Adair had said over fifty years earlier, particularly about the similarities of language. "The number of Hebrew words in their religious services is incredible," he offered at one point and then elsewhere noted, "the Indians, like the Hebrews, speak in parables." However confidently Noah wrote about the topic, he did have to acknowledge that "it is a singular fact that history is exceedingly confused, or rather I may say dark, respecting the ultimate dispersion of the tribes among the cities of the Medes."[26]

---

23 Barton, "Natural History of the North American Indians."

24 Jennings, ed., *Ancient North Americans,* p. 25.

25 Atwater, "Eloquence of the North American Indians," p. 205.

26 Noah, *Discourse on ... Lost Tribes of Israel,* pp. 4, 11, 36.

By midcentury, then, the questions of who the Indians were and where they had come from remained open for debate. Evidence that the Welsh had sailed west to populate the New World, or that the Etruscans had done the same, continued to surface in the pages of books and magazines throughout the 1840s and 1850s. Superintendent McKenney summarized the state of the intellectual dilemma thoroughly, if a bit breathlessly, in 1846: "Who are the Indians? Whence they came? When and by What Route was their exodus from the land of their origin....Who were they, if any, that preceded them in the occupancy of this country?" Through no lack of trying, Americans seemed no closer to answering these questions in the middle of the nineteenth century than they had been at its beginning. In 1849 the author of *Peter Parley's Tales* for children had to confess to his young readers, "The origin of the aborigines of America is involved in mystery."[27]

That the basic question should still be a mystery, given the attention it had already received by 1849 from writers, scholars, and armchair speculators, would seem a stunning failure of America's intellectual community. Rather than indict them for that failure, however, or even poke fun at it, we ought to remember that Americans struggled to understand the Indians within the only historical frameworks available to them, those from the classical world, and, most importantly, the Bible. Indeed, Atwater began his exegesis on who built the mounds with reference to biblical history, and interspersed it with references like "The land of Ham, seems to have been the place where the arts were first nursed."[28]

Indeed, religious conviction more than anything else may have prevented Barton's Asian hypothesis from being more widely accepted. After all, one had to move quite far beyond the human history as revealed in the Bible to accept that theory. Or, as in the case of Caleb Atwater, who did seem to believe that Native Americans descended from the "tartars," one had to engage in extraordinary extrapolations to connect the corner of northeast Asia with "the land of Ham." As Superindendent McKenney put it emphatically: "There is, however, but one source whence information can be derived on this subject—and that is the Bible."[29] For Christian believers in the antebellum period, the origin of the Indians was an intellectual square peg, and writers worked with great if tortured vigor to jam it into the round hole of biblical and classical history.

The geographic origin of Native Americans was only one way in which the authority of the Bible was strained in the first half of the nineteenth century. As Benjamin Barton noted in 1797, those who debated the question of

---

27   McKenney, *Memoirs*, 2:11; *History of the Indians of North and South America by the Author of Peter Parley's Tales*, p. 10.

28   Atwater, "Eloquence of the North American Indians," p. 199.

29   McKenney, *Memoirs*, 2:14.

origins actually fell into two camps: the first of these speculated about which part of the Old World Indians had come from; the second "embraces those who suppose that the Americans are in strict language the aborigines of the soil, and not emigrants from other parts of the world." [30] Suggesting that Indians were autochthonous, that they had not come from anywhere else on the globe, was an even more radical proposition than arguing that they had arrived in the New World as a result of some set of historical events not described in the Bible. Genesis is quite clear about this: all human groups trace their lineage back to a single pair. As aborigines, "in strict language," Native Americans would fall outside the biblical genealogy.

Thomas McKenney minced no words as he drew the contours of this debate and hinted at its stakes. "If," he posited, "the garden of Eden is nowhere in America, Adam (the Adam of the Bible, and we have no authentic record of any other), could not have been created here." So far, so good. Then came the obvious conclusion: "The Indians cannot be, therefore, *indigenous* to America, but, being descendants of the original pair, they must have come of some one of the families that settled and peopled some one of the divisions of the globe. In other words, they must be of Asiatic, of African, or of European descent." McKenney sounds almost impatient at having to explain all this. After

all, "that the whole human family sprang from an original pair, that pair being the product of the power of God ... is a truth so universally admitted, as to render any elaborate argument in its support superfluous." Likewise, New York doctor Samuel Forry made the same point, although it took him over fifty pages to elaborate it. In assessing "the natural history of the American aborigines," he argued that "Revelation and Science are both beams of light emitted from the same Sun of Eternal Truth."[31]

But McKenney did have to make this point, despite the universality of its truth, because he wrote in the midst of a great debate over the nature of race, a debate in which the characteristics of the Native American figured prominently. On one side stood McKenney and other "monogenesists," who believed that all human beings had sprung from "an original pair," and thus believed in the essential unity of the human species. On the other side, the "polygenesists" argued that different races had different and separate origins, and thus had different capacities and destinies. Those in the mono-genesis camp derived their conviction and authority from the Bible's story of Genesis; polygenesists fancied themselves as empirical researchers, relying on the most current and sophisticated interpretation of scientific data.

In retrospect, this debate strikes us as so weighted with ideological baggage

---

30 Barton, *New Views,* p. iv.

31 McKenney, *Memoirs,* 2:15; Forry, "The Mosaic Account of the Unity of the Human Race," p. 30.

that it hardly seems worthwhile to evaluate it as science. Southerners, like Josiah Nott, bellowed loudly among those proponents of polygenesis, as a way of offering a thinly veiled defense of slavery. But polygenesists also claimed among their number some of the leading northern figures in American nineteenth-century science, most prominently Harvard University naturalist Louis Agassiz, probably the most celebrated scientist in the country during the mid-nineteenth century, and Samuel Morton, the Philadelphia physician who studied race by measuring skulls. Agassiz came to his views in part through his science and in part because of the physical revulsion the Swiss naturalist felt the first time he encountered black people on a trip to Philadelphia to visit Morton. When *De Bow's Review,* a southern magazine, ran a piece supporting polygenesis and denying a common origin of Caucasians and Africans, it quoted liberally from Nott, Morton, and Agassiz.[32]

The debate between the monogenesists and the polygenesists, and the relationship between that debate and the scientific construction of racial categories (not to mention racism) has been well documented.[33] In the racial schema devised by polygenesists, all races were not created equal, but existed in a hierarchy, which these scientists worked hard to define with precision.

As chapter 5 documents, in the scientific—ethnological—study of race, especially Morton's work with skulls, can be found the origins of the field we now call physical anthropology. What bears noticing here is just how much scientific energy was devoted to the study of race in the mid-nineteenth century. Once Americans set out looking for evidence of racial distinctions in earnest, they found it everywhere. Charles Pickering ventured forth with one of the United States Exploring Expeditions in the 1840s, convinced that five races inhabited the globe. By the time he returned his list had grown to eleven, "though I am hardly prepared to fix a positive limit to their number."[34]

Rather than review the racial ideologies that undergirded the science of race, I want to examine briefly the theological dimension of this discussion. We should be clear: both monogenesists and polygenesists maintained their belief in the divine creation and in most of the Christian tradition. Indeed, after 1859 Agassiz saw his life's work as defending religion from what he took to be the corrosive assaults of Darwinism. The critical difference between the two camps lay in the particular details of the Book of Genesis and the Hebrew Bible. Monogenesists believed that the story of creation as told in that text needed no revision. Polygenesists, however, weren't so sure. As Josiah Nott put it: "My main object ... is to cut loose the natural

---

32   "Is the African and Caucasian of Common Origin?" pp. 243–245.
33   See, for example, Stanton, *The Leopard's Spots,* and Gould, *The Mismeasure of Man.*

---

34   Pickering, *Races of Man,* p. 10.

history of mankind from the Bible, and to place each upon its own foundation, where it may remain without collision or molestation."

Nott understood the stakes when he entered the debate. In an essay for the *Southern Quarterly Review*, he offered that the Bible provided no "rational chronology" to explain "this wide spread and diversified population from a single pair." The scientific "facts" being accumulated about races and racial differences "cannot be explained ... without, in my humble opinion, doing violence to the Mosaic account." A few years later, he was more direct. "The unity of races," he told a lecture audience, "can only be deduced from forced constructions of the Old and New Testaments." Later, he asked his audience, "Where is the evidence of the descent of the black and red races from Adam, so clear as to upset the whole physical history of man?" Rejecting the details of the Old Testament need not mean, Nott assured readers, rejecting the Bible altogether. Indeed, denying the unity of the human race "so far from infringing on the veracity of scripture, will, I am satisfied, become one of the most solid grounds of its defense." The anonymous writer for *De Bow's* agreed: "The interests of sound and heaven-inspired theology are identical with those of physical truth. There is but one Author to the physical and moral universe, and every investigation tending to reconcile the two together of

which they must be capable, is a sacred and noble work."[35]

Monogenesists could be just as emphatic, though perhaps not as sanguine about how the debate between science and religion would resolve. M. M. Noah reminded his readers what they all ought to know already: "God that made man in his own image gave to the Indians an origin and parentage like unto the rest of the great family of mankind, the work of his own almighty hand." Dr. Forry undertook his review of the natural history of American Indians to demonstrate the unity of "the great family of the human race." He concluded by telling his readers, "On the one side, he has the conclusions of Dr. Morton ... and, on the other side, supported by the arguments of this paper, he has *the authoritative declaration of Moses that all human kind have descended from a single pair.*" Despite the proofs offered by Noah, Forry, and many others, James Southall, another monogenesist, understood that an epic battle had been joined. He wrote ominously that "there must be a trial of strength between the Bible and Science."[36]

The politics of this antebellum debate can be easily deduced. Polygenesists used science, first and foremost, as a defense of slavery; in addition, their conclusions about race could be used to justify the

---

35 Nott, "Unity of the Human Race," pp. 1–57; Nott, *Two Lectures*, p. 7; "Is the African and Caucasian of Common Origin?" p. 243.

36 Noah, *Discourse on ... Lost Tribes of Israel*, p. 31; Forry, "Unity of the Human Race," p. 80; Southall, *Recent Origin of Man*, p. 72.

treatment of Native Americans in the era of Removal and immediately after. For some monogenesists, the essential unity of the human species implied all sorts of moral and Christian duties toward Native Americans and enslaved Africans. As Herman Humphrey, the president of Amherst College, put it in an impassioned speech denouncing the removal plan, "if the people sit still and look calmly on while the Indian are abandoned to their fate, in violation of the most solemn compacts ... who in a foreign land will ever hereafter be willing to own that he is an American?"[37]

In the intellectual discourse that surrounded Native Americans during the first half of the nineteenth century, religion functioned in two ways. On the one hand, the intellectual constraints imposed by clinging to biblical frameworks of human history made it difficult to conceive of the history of Indians in other terms. As Noah put it, sounding almost exasperated: "If the Indians of America are not the descendants of the missing tribes [of Israel], again I ask, from whom *are* they descended?"[38] Whom indeed?

If commitment to biblical explanations retarded a more extensive understanding of Indian origins, then in the other direction biblical literalists did get it right on the question of monogenesis, even though evolutionary scientists today put that "original pair" not in a garden roughly five thousand years ago, but on the African savanna some several million years earlier. Resting their case only on the authority of scripture, rather than on the empirical weight of science, monogenesists insisted that the human family was a unity, and in this way they did nothing less than preserve, at least a little bit, the idea that Native Americans had a humanity.[39] For a believer like Indian Affairs Superintendent McKenney, the treatment of Indians at the hands of Euro-Americans caused a twitch in his faith. Looking back at what had happened in the wake of Indian removal, he wondered: "How are we to harmonize these conflicting events with our conceptions of the all wise, and good, and merciful God?" Asking whether all this destruction was a necessity, he concluded, "I think not."[40]

---

37 Humphrey, "Indian Rights and Our Duties," pp. 19–20.
38 Noah, *Discourse on ... Lost Tribes of Israel,* p. 33.

39 I should note that polygenesis survived well past Darwin. In a savagely racist screed published in 1891, for example, a southern writer found monogenesis a theory "so offensive to our natural instincts, and ... so absurd, and preposterous, that it never could have been entertained by intelligent minds, but from the apprehension that belief in it was required by the Bible." *Caucasian Anthropology,* p. 26. For more on this topic, see Stocking, "Polygenesist Thought in Post-Darwinian Anthropology," in *Culture and Evolution,* pp. 42–68. Curtis Hinsley has pointed out that the defense of monogenesism "lay at the religious core" of American anthropology well into the twentieth century. See Hinsley, *The Smithsonian and the American Indian,* p. 22.
40 McKenney, *Memoirs,* 2:61.

Searching for Indian History

James Adair understood the problem exactly in 1775. "In tracing the origin of a people," he wrote, "where there are no records of any kind either written or engraved, who rely solely on oral tradition for the support of their ancient usages, and have lost a great deal of them ... the undertaking [is] difficult."[41]

Difficult to be sure. For Americans in the early republic, the question of just how to study the history of Indians proved vexing and complicated. In fact, the late eighteenth and early nineteenth centuries witnessed the rise not only of a new historical consciousness among Americans, but new standards of historical practice and a growing formalization of how history could be studied. Indians and their history wound up at the center of these shifts.

Euro-Americans had known for some time that native groups did have an understanding of their own past, an indigenous set of historical traditions. For the more sympathetic among them, native creation stories corresponded closely enough with biblical ones to admit Indians to the fraternity of Christianity. Henry Schoolcraft, for example, found that "Cherokee tradition preserves an allegoric version of the deluge which is quite peculiar." One implication of this sympathy, as missionary John Heckewelder asserted, was that since "they have no historians among them,"

they thus had no one to plead their case to "a sympathizing world." Heckewelder took this sympathy to a logical conclusion: "Why, then, should not a white man, a Christian ... defend them as they would defend themselves."[42]

But as Adair observed, native histories existed entirely as "oral tradition," not as written texts. And as Schoolcraft, a remarkable student of native America, put it in 1830: "all unwritten tradition, extending beyond the era of Columbus, may be considered as entitled to little credit."[43] The distinction was central to this new conception of how history proper would be recovered. It would have several consequences for how Indian history was studied.

First, this definition of history's epistemology threatened to exclude Indian history altogether. As Alexander Bradford recognized in 1843: "The term history, in its usual acceptation, is somewhat restrictive in its scope. If its extent were strictly limited to authentic narratives and records ... only a small portion of the human race has preserved any very ancient written memorials; and with the exception of the historical facts contained in the Sacred Volume, we should be left in ignorance of the most important occurrences of the early ages of the world." This recognition underscored that Indian history needed to be recovered and understood outside the boundaries of history proper, as it had

---

41   Adair, *History of the American Indians,* p. 10.

42   Heckewelder, "An Account," p. 327; Schoolcraft, *Notes on the Iroquois,* p. 358.
43   Schoolcraft, "Discourse," pp. 8–9.

come to be defined. By the end of the eighteenth century, as Pamela Regis has observed, people without writing could not have a history.[44]

As a consequence, anthropologist Clark Wissler noted some years ago, echoing Benjamin Barton, "almost from the first, it was recognized that the recovery of this lost history must be achieved, if at all, by natural history methods." And as Regis has demonstrated in her study of eighteenth-century American natural history, natural historical representations of America tended to depict the country as existing outside the flow of historical time.[45] Subsumed under this ahistorical mode of representation, and without "any ancient written memorials," Indian history would have to be natural history, not quite human history. Indians became, in the eyes of Euro-Americans, a people with a past, but without a history.

Additionally, the definition of history as a text-based enterprise meant not only that Indians could not have a history, as it was coming to be defined, but it also meant that they could not function as their own historians. William Moore, writing in 1855 as John Frost, put the dilemma succinctly. In attempting to study Indian history, "the Indians can give us no assistance; for of their own history, beyond the traditionary records of two

or three generations, they know nothing; and the strange notions which some of them entertain of their origin need not to surprise us." Likewise, in his 1862 study of the Cree, F. V. Hayden echoed the now familiar historical conundrum when he wrote, "Among people where no written records exist, and whose only method of preserving their national histories is oral tradition ... little can be extracted worthy to be considered of historical value." But he went on to be quite specific: "In regard to the Crees, all appears obscure farther back than 1760.... From 1760 down to the present time the history of the Crees can be traced with a fair degree of certainty."[46] If Indians were to have any history at all, they would require as their champions interlocutors like John Heckewelder.

Indians in the nineteenth century told their own history to be sure, though in ways that went largely unrecognized and misunderstood by white Americans. Some, like the Ojibway chief Kah-Ge-Gah Bowh, tried to bridge these cultural divides. Known to the white world as George Copway, he brought out *Copway's American Indian* in 1851 with supporting testimonials from people like Thomas McKenney, Washington Irving, William Gilmore Simms, Henry Schoolcraft, and James Fenimore Cooper. In the prospectus, Copway, who identified himself as a "Christianized Indian," announced that the journal

---

44 Bradford, *American Antiquities*, p. 9; Regis, *Describing America*, p. 37.

45 Wissler, "American Indian and the American Philosophical Society," p. 189; Regis, *Describing America*, p. 25.

46 Frost, *Indian Wars*, p. 4; Hayden, *Contributions to Ethnography and Philology*, pp. 234–235.

FIGURE 3.3.

Thomas Cole, The Course of Empire: The Savage State, ca. 1836. In a five-part series, Cole presented a "gloomy" view of history's progress.

FIGURE 3.4.

Thomas Cole, The Course of Empire: The Arcadian State, ca. 1836.

FIGURE 3.5.
Thomas Cole, The Course of Empire: The Consummation of Empire, ca. 1836.

FIGURE 3.6.
Thomas Cole, The Course of Empire: Destruction, ca. 1836.

FIGURE 3.7.
Thomas Cole, The Course of Empire: Desolation, ca. 1836.

would be "devoted entirely to subjects connected with the past and present history and condition of the people of his own race." Copway acknowledged that the publication was "certainly a novelty in the literary history of the United States, that an Indian should propose to conduct a paper devoted to the cause of the Indian." Copway recognized that "the inquisitiveness of the Anglo-Saxon Races is very large"; his publication endeavored "to answer questions, which have been put to us in every part of the country … for the benefit of our 'paleface' friends." *Copway's American Indian* did not survive beyond its first year, and few Indian voices contributed to the writing of mainstream history in the nineteenth century.[47]

Locating history only in written records meant that those indigenous oral traditions must be something other—less—than history. By and large, that something became "myth." History moved, it evolved, it existed in the flow of time; myth, on the other hand, was understood to be static and to have no relation, therefore, to history. This opposition of history and myth in the first half of the nineteenth century became a central foundation, as Joshua Bellin has argued, upon which ethnology was built.[48] Indeed, "myth" as a term came into common usage only in the early

---

47   *Copway's American Indian* 1 (1851).
48   Bellin, *Demon of the Continent,* p. 134.

nineteenth century. At the same time, as Lionel Gossman has noted, only by the end of the eighteenth century did history emerge as something distinct and apart from literature.[49] Thus the modern conception of myth and the modern practice of history may well have grown up as mirror images of each other. In the United States, at least, the process of removing Native Americans from the realm of history helped define what was meant by myth. In fact, as this book illustrates, in the early years of the nineteenth century history developed in relation to several other fields. Many in the early republic attempted to understand history in different ways by relying on different sources—grammars, vocabularies, artifacts. This book, in part, tells the story of how boundaries of historical studies hardened across the span of the nineteenth century to exclude much of this nontextual material.

Chapter 5 explores in more detail how the Indians moved from the realm of history, to natural history, and finally to ethnology and anthropology—all of which treated Indians largely ahistorically, or outside the boundaries of any specific chronology. For the moment, it is enough to keep in mind the observation of Josiah Nott: "*Chronology* [] may be regarded as the touchstone of history." This development tracks another shift in which the scientific study of race we touched on earlier was deeply

implicated. As race emerged as the "scientific" category into which Native Americans were put, they could be more easily removed from the category of nation. As Benedict Anderson has observed, nations have histories, while race has been conceived of as largely a fixed and unchanging category.[50]

As American intellectuals confronted the questions posed by Native Americans in the first half of the nineteenth century, they helped shape a definition of history that simultaneously excluded Indians, and made relying on Indian sources intellectually illegitimate. As Samuel Drake reminded readers, "their notions ... can no more be relied upon than the fabled stories of the gods in ancient mythology."[51]

The study of Indians, and the search for Indian history, also helped drive the shift from speculation to empiricism, from the armchair theorizing of the colonial era to the science of the new republic. This shift, of course, occurred across the intellectual landscape in the Western world, but it is worth remembering how much the encounter with the New World, and with its puzzling inhabitants, drove this shift. As Anthony Padgen has pointed out in his tracing of these developments in the Spanish new world, by the eighteenth century texts about Indians written by people with actual first-hand experience replaced

---

49 Gossman, *Between History and Literature,* p. 227.

50 Nott, *Two Lectures,* p. 68; see Anderson, *Imagined Communities,* p. 149.

51 Drake, *Biography and History of the Indians,* p. 29.

those written from an intellectual and actual distance. What's more, these writers insisted that only this kind of research could guarantee the accuracy of the findings.[52]

Over and over again, as later chapters will demonstrate, American scholars and others who wrote about Native Americans stressed that they had done the investigations themselves. Artists like Charles Bird King and George Catlin; linguists like John Heckewelder; archaeologists like Caleb Atwater and Ephraim Squier—all extolled the virtue of their own empirical research. In his 1847 synopsis of Indian research, John Russell Bartlett made the point with satisfied confidence: "Out of confusion, system began to develop ... what seemed accidents, were found to be characteristics. What was regarded as anomalous, was recognized as a type and feature of a class."[53] For people like these, any remaining confusions would only be resolved by more of the same.

This new empirical, scientific positivism had a complicated side. More research might well help answer questions that had thus far eluded Americans, but there was a risk for those who did this research, who immersed themselves in the lives, languages, and cultures of native peoples. They might develop a sympathy for those they studied, which could lead

them to portray Indians as something other than obstacles to white progress. Thomas McKenney, for example, concluded from his experiences that Native Americans possessed "the capacity ... for the highest attainments in civilization," and even more provocatively he claimed that, "the Indian in his intellectual and moral structures [is] *our equal.*" Even the historian of Indians might run this risk. Army surgeon Edwin James wrote in his own history of Indians that the historian "will find many instances of generous feeling, of dignified and manly conduct ... and genius; which require only the 'purchased page' of history to make them admired." Lewis Henry Morgan, regarded by many as the father of American anthropology, wrote to William Stone about the need for a vast "repository" of Indian material, not simply for study or preservation: "another of the leading objects should be to ... encourage a kinder feeling toward the Red Man."[54]

Sentiments like these, needless to say, flew in the face of prevailing prejudices and ideologies. Although few would argue today that scientific inquiry takes place wholly outside the world of values and ideologies, the study of Native Americans was a particularly charged enterprise in the nineteenth century.

---

52 Pagden, *Fall of Natural Man,* p. 200.
53 Bartlett, *Progress of Ethnology,* p. 4.

54 McKenney, *Memoirs,* p. 34; Edwin James, "Contributions towards a History of Indian Languages"; Morgan to Stone, June 10, 1844, New York Historical Society.

Indians and the Cycles of History

In defining their notion of history as a textual study, rooted in chronology, and thus locating Native Americans outside the boundaries of that history, Americans underwent a shift in the nature of their historical consciousness and in their understanding of how history worked. This shift capped a nearly four-hundred-year process of reversal in the way time itself was perceived in the West, what Anthony Kemp has charted as the shift from "an image of syncretic unity and essential sameness" to one of "dynamic change."[55] By the eighteenth century, many perceived history to work in ever-repeating, ever-oscillating cycles of rise and fall. The writings of classical antiquity, of course, had expounded on this theme, but these were rediscovered with a new enthusiasm in eighteenth-century Europe. From there, this notion followed so many other European exports across the Atlantic to become, by the time of the Revolution, what Stow Persons described some years ago as "the distinctive historical conception of the dominant social group in America."

Benjamin Smith Barton, a member of that founding generation, certainly believed "that civilization has been constantly preceded by barbarity and rudeness." History also taught, he cautioned, "a mortifying truth, that nation may relapse into rudeness again; all their proud monuments crumbled to dust ...

it may be our lot to fall into rudeness once more." In 1820, the members of the American Antiquarian Society echoed that view of history when they commented on the origins of their new group: "The decline as well as the rise of nations is in the course of nature—like causes will produce like effects; and, in some distant period, a decline may be the state of our country."[56]

Americans in the early republic manifested their connection to this sense of the classical past in all sorts of ways—from the creation of a national senate to the founding of towns called "Athens" from Georgia, to West Virginia, to Ohio; from filling up those towns with examples of "Greek Revival" architecture to clothing George Washington—our own Cincinnatus—in a Roman toga. Yet even in the midst of this extended homage to the classical past and its ideals, a cyclical notion of history disturbed increasing numbers of Americans. In the early years of the nineteenth century, Americans could certainly tell themselves that they existed in a "youthful" stage of history's great cycle. Even so, a cyclical view of history's motion meant that even this new nation must age and fall eventually and inevitably—the victim of some exogenous force or of its own corruption.

Perhaps, some Americans began to reason, the very act of establishing the nation itself represented a break from

---

55 Kemp, *Estrangement of the Past,* p. vi.

56 "Origins of the American Antiquarian Society," p. 30.

the inexorable cycle of history's rise and fall. And in that break, as Dorothy Ross has argued, they began to replace the cyclical view of history with one in which "perpetual life" might be possible.

Linear progress—with all that it implied of improvement, perfection, and distance from an oppressive past—rather than a cycle with its decline and decay. This could be both America's historical fate and the way Americans would come to understand their history. With each passing year of the nineteenth century, scientific discovery and technological innovation only underscored the distance between the present and the quickly receding past. By the mid-nineteenth century, a dominant view had come to prevail that the Greek and Roman past, far from being models to emulate, represented examples to be avoided. By the Gilded Age, as Dorothy Ross believes, Americans were surely and mostly a progressive people.[57]

Still, like any shift in intellectual life, this one was neither complete nor abrupt, and the older view of how history operated lingered even as a new one emerged. As we will see in chapter 5, James Fenimore Cooper grounded his Leatherstocking Tales in a cyclical view of history. This view of history also appears in the work of the landscape painter Thomas Cole, whose painting Cooper

admired—"one of the very first geniuses of the age" according to Cooper. Most dramatically perhaps in his ambitious five-painting series *The Course of Empire,* which Cooper thought of as "a great epic poem," Cole used landscape painting as a way to comment both on history and on the state of American society.[58]

Cole received the commission that became *The Course of Empire* from New York businessman Luman Reed, and completed the cycle in 1836. At first glance, the five paintings trace a straightforward rise and fall, not of a particular empire, but of some generic one, in some indeterminate past. All five are set in the same, equally indeterminate place: a natural harbor with a dramatic rock outcropping towering over it in the background. Across the series, nature remains constant amidst the comings and goings of human activity.

The first painting, *The Savage State,* shows swirling clouds at daybreak. The scene is thick with trees and vegetation, and dark with shadow. In this rough, untamed wilderness a few equally wild hunters, clad in skins, chase a deer. These men inhabit the circle of teepees on the far right of the painting, occupying the only human-made clearing in the scene.

In the second painting, *The Pastoral or Arcadian State,* the light has brightened and softened. Nature here, its trees and clouds and rock features, is decidedly gentle, pleasant, and without

---

57 For this discussion I have drawn particularly from Persons, "Cyclical Theory of History," pp. 147–163; Ross, "Historical Consciousness," pp. 909–928; and Miles, "The Young American Nation," pp. 259–274.

58 Cooper to Louis Legrand Noble, January 6, 1849, in *Letters and Journals of James Fenimore Cooper,* 5:396–400.

threat. The figures seem more or less Greek—especially the bearded old man seated in the left foreground. But these Greeks have built something that looks remarkably like Stonehenge in the center of the canvas. Religion, in one form or another, has arrived.

By the time we arrive at *The Consummation of Empire,* the third and largest in the series, nature has disappeared entirely, save for that one outcrop. It has been buried under a Greco-Roman architectural fantasy of columns, pediments, and sculpture. These buildings serve as the set for a bewildering number of figures and a dizzying activity. Boats arrive in the harbor; a hero marches triumphantly across a bridge, all under the glare of a midday sun.

The architecture of *Empire* might be indiscriminately classical, but the decadence and corruption implied in *The Consummation of Empire* were surely Roman. By painting four, *Destruction,* it has all gone bad. Back are the swirling, ominous clouds, giving an atmospheric echo to the scene of catastrophe playing out in the harbor city. Flames leap into the air, engulfing boat and building; helpless people tumble from a collapsing bridge into the water; the survivors risk death at the hands of invaders.

As the sun goes down on *Desolation,* nature has returned, creeping literally over the ruins of Empire. Gone are the human beings, replaced by new trees, vines, and a family of birds nesting on top of a Corinthian column in the foreground. The series ends, therefore, just before its beginning, as the scene reverts to its original nature, awaiting the next cycle of human ascension. So goes the course of empire.

The setting for this series is generic both in time and place because Cole wanted it to serve as a historical allegory. So goes the course of all empires. In this sense, the series presents what art historian Alan Wallach has called Cole's essentially "pessimistic philosophy of history." Cole was also convinced that viewers would miss the point of the series when it went on display in fall of 1836. In a letter to his patron Luman Reed, he complained: "very few will understand the scheme of [the paintings]—the philosophy that may be in them." To some extent he was right. The critic for the New York *Mirror* saw in the paintings "*that* which *has been* in all past times," not what was presaged in the United States where "the perfection which man is hereafter to attain, will be based upon a more stable foundation: political equality; the rights of man; the democratick principle; the *sovereignty of the people.*"[59] Two views of history collided with the exhibition of *The Course of Empire.* By 1836, Cole's was already on the wane.

---

59 For more on *The Course of Empire,* see Miller, "Thomas Cole and Jacksonian America," pp. 65–92; and Miller, *Empire of the Eye*; Powell, *Thomas Cole;* and Truettner and Wallach, eds., *Thomas Cole.* Quotes from Wallach, "Thomas Cole: Landscape and the Course of American Empire," in *Thomas Cole: Landscape Into History,* p. 95.

There is much of contemporary politics too in *The Course of Empire,* of the debates between Whig federalists and Jacksonian democrats.[60] Cole's pessimism wasn't simply about the past and the course of history, but about the present and future of American society as well. How could it have been otherwise, given his essential historical sensibility? But like his view of history, Cole's political allegiances were to principles and ideals that were disappearing fast.

It comes as no surprise that a progressive view of history should find a congenial reception in Jackson's America. In an age of greater democracy and more fluid class lines, the ideal of progress must have resonated with Americans who wanted to believe in their own abilities to rise in society. Indeed, Persons suggests that for most of the founders, "the notion of progress was repugnant," because at some level it rejected both social hierarchies and Enlightenment thinking. Cole, for his part, had no use for Jacksonianism either.

But to root this change in historical consciousness entirely in the politics of Jacksonian America, or to see a progressive view of history as incipient in eighteenth-century republican ideology as it grew in the nineteenth-century United States, right though I think those explanations are, misses another force behind this change of historical attitude. The first painting in Cole's series, with its

teepees and reference to savages, returns us to the question of Native Americans, even if the figures in the painting look approximately European and not native.

By the 1830s when they were so brutally "removed," the perceived fate of Native Americans, I suspect, was shaping American ideas about history. Whatever the debate over their past, American scholars who studied Indians in the antebellum period found themselves in virtually unanimous agreement about the future. That fate seemed self-evident to Americans: extinction. This consensus of opinion itself reflects the way in which Indians were increasingly viewed as part of natural, rather than human, history. The notion that species could disappear from the earth as a result of natural processes and quite apart from any biblical flood was one of the remarkable developments of late eighteenth and early nineteenth-century natural science, straining the relationship between science and religion. So novel and difficult was the idea of natural extinction that no less a scientist than Thomas Jefferson believed that there might still be herds of mastodons roaming the continent somewhere. Indians were not simply animals in the view of most Americans in the nineteenth century, but they were surely headed down the same road as the iguanadon and the giant sloth.

Indeed, the only real disagreement took place over whether individual Indians might assimilate into Euro-American society or whether, unwilling or unable to do this, they were indeed

60 See especially Miller, "Thomas Cole and Jacksonian America."

headed for extinction in a biological sense. Either way, "Indianness" was doomed. Even Ojibway chief George Copway believed that the Indians' days were numbered. Plaintively, poignantly he wrote about the purpose of his journal: "That race is fast vanishing away; a few years more and its existence will be found only in the history of the past: may not an Indian, then, hope for countenance and support in a modest and unambitious effort to preserve ... the still lingering memorials of his own people, once numerous and strong?"[61]

This was not necessarily the consensus of the founding generation, who, as Bernard Sheehan has noted, believed that Indians would see the obvious desirability of civilization, and thus that they would give up their own savagery happily and voluntarily.[62] That hope had largely faded by the early national period. Indeed, extinction became such a constant and familiar refrain in the literature of the nineteenth century that it is almost not worth quoting. It was a conviction, rather than a prediction, and it was such a ubiquitous belief that it did not exist so much in the realm of empirical observation as in the world of unquestioned assumption. A quick sampling can stand for a whole literature: for L. Bliss, the task of recording the history of this "ill-fated" race would be "of mournful interest," and amounted to "something almost holy"; an anonymous writer for the *Southern Literary Messenger* managed to kill off the noble savage when he wrote, "this wild, but noble and unhappy race, is rapidly becoming extinct," and as a consequence, the historian faced a "melancholy task." He might well find himself "weeping over the final extinction of the aboriginal natives of America." William Pidgeon hoped that Americans would "value researches which have been made with a view to perpetuate the memory of nations that have preceded those that are now falling into ruin."[63]

Pidgeon's use of the word "ruin" gives us a striking, if altogether inadvertent, connection to Cole. Cole had described his concept for *The Course of Empire* to Reed by saying that he would illustrate "how nations have risen" and how they all "become extinct."[64] In Cole's view of history, of course, ruin is what empires fall into. Ruins remain to dot the landscape, serving as "melancholy" if evocative reminders of that process. But by the mid-nineteenth century, Indians were so clearly falling into ruin that Euro-Americans need not worry that they themselves might suffer the same fate. White Americans were fruitful and multiplying; Indians were all on the verge of extinction.

---

61 It was not until 1954 that the American Anthropological Association acknowledged officially that the assimilation of Native America into Euro-America was perhaps not "inevitable."
62 Sheehan, *Seeds of Extinction,* pp. 4–5.

63 Bliss, "Drake's Indian History," p. 301; "American Indians," pp. 333, 337; Pidgeon, *Traditions of De-Coo-Dah,* p. 21.
64 Cole quoted in Powell, *Thomas Cole,* p. 64.

American scholars did not generally give Native Americans credit for having risen much on the scale of civilization, but they certainly agreed about their fall. Euro-Americans thus shifted the inevitability of decline, with all its attendant anxiety and gloominess, onto the people progress was displacing. In this way, they created the imaginative space to conceive of their own history as the unfolding of linear progress.[65] As an American historical consciousness took shape in the antebellum period, its definition located Indians outside of the progressive, chronologically marked time whose ticking clock measured the history of Euro-Americans alone.

Several scholars have examined the relationship between conceptions of Indians and the formation of American identity: Elise Marienstras, for example, sees popular images of the vanquished Indian as helping Americans conceive of themselves "as a collective entity." Philip Deloria, in fact, observing the ritual and practice of "playing Indian," believes that it has been impossible to conceive of an American identity without Indians.[66] Equally important, however, it is impossible to create a national identity without first creating historical narratives around which a collective sense can draw legitimacy and sustenance. In the new United States, that historical understanding was shaped by the ways scholars and intellectuals defined the history of Native America.

This may also explain a secondary debate among those who studied Native America in the first half of the nineteenth century. Did those tribes and groups who currently inhabited the continent represent the denegerate, degraded descendants of earlier more civilized Indians—Aztecs perhaps? Or was the continent first populated by a more enigmatic people called Mound Builders, whom we will meet in chapter 3, who were quite distinct from contemporary Indians and who had already disappeared entirely?

Most who considered the issue ultimately came down on the side of the latter. As John Bartlett put it in 1847, it "has been developed to show that a people, radically different from the existing race of Indians, once occupied the valley of the Mississippi ... they were to a certain extent advanced in the arts of civilization."[67] To admit Indians into a great cycle of history meant that, while they were currently in decline, they might rise again. For expansion-minded and increasingly progress-minded Americans, this thought proved too uncomfortable. Writing in 1872, J. D. Baldwin made the

---

65 Pearce makes a related point in his classic work *The Savages of America*. See especially p. 160. David Bidney dates this shift to 1795, after which point he says "Americans come to believe that the savages in their midst could have no share in the progress of their civilization." Bidney, "Idea of the Savage," p. 325.

66 Marienstras, "The Common Man's Indian: The Image of the Indian as a Promoter of National Identity in the Early National Era," in Hoxie et al., eds., *Native Americans and the Early Republic*, pp. 261–262; Deloria, *Playing Indian*, p. 37.

---

67 Bartlett, *Progress of Ethnology*, p. 7.

point quite clearly. Although it might be true that "the history of the world shows that civilized communities may lose their enlightenment, and sink to a condition of barbarism," the Indians of North America demonstrated no such thing. Theirs "was original barbarism. There was nothing to indicate that ... the Indians inhabiting our part of the continent ... had ever been civilized even to the extent of becoming capable of settled life and organized industry."[68] Thus, such American scholars moved Indians out of progressive history and into cyclical history incompletely. Indians could experience decline, without ever having experienced a reciprocal rise.

From our vantage, the consequences of this seem nothing short of vicious and destructive. As anthropologist Johannes Fabian has pointed out in his examination of the relationship between anthropology and colonialism, "expansive, aggressive, and oppressive" societies require both space in which to expand, and "Time to accommodate the schemes of a one-way history: progress ... in short, *geopolitics* had its ideological foundations in *chronopolitics*."[69]

The widespread (again, almost ubiquitous) belief that savage Indians and civilized whites simply could not coexist may have been a consequence of this "chronopolitics." Beyond the now-obvious inability to coexist in the same physical space, they could not inhabit

the same historical space and likewise could not share the same present. As a reviewer wrote in the *North American Review* in 1830, "year after year, the cultivated border advanced bearing before it the primitive people, who would not mingle with their invaders, and who could not stop their progress." What else to conclude but that "a barbarous people ... cannot live in contact with a civilized community."[70]

It is surely right that, in this sense, American intellectuals in the first half of the nineteenth century participated in a colonial enterprise. And yet, just as we need to take more seriously the strained, almost desperate attempts to fit Indian history into a biblical framework, we ought to acknowledge just how difficult and daunting it must have been in the first half of the nineteenth century to conceive of a history for Native Americans. At a moment when the power of writing as a preserver of history—Greek, Roman, Egyptian—was growing more and more potent, how could scholars study people who had no writing and had left no texts? In an age when the differences between past and present grew not only more pronounced with each passing year, but could even be measured along that chronology, how could historians understand people who did not fit onto that timeline?

Earlier in this chapter we turned to Alexander Bradford, who in 1843 recognized that the emerging practice of

---

68   Baldwin, *Ancient America*, pp. 58–59.
69   Fabian, *Time and the Other*, p. 144.

70   "Removal of the Indians," pp. 64, 107.

history would necessarily exclude "most important occurrences of the early ages of the world." Undaunted, he went on to suggest just how Native American history could be studied: "Thus of necessity are mankind impelled ... to examine other channels by which the events of remote antiquity may have been transmitted, and to study and compare the languages, customs, traditions, science, religion and monuments of nations."[71]

The rest of this book will examine just how American scholars, across several different intellectual pursuits, tried to answer Bradford's challenge, and how American intellectual life and an American sense of history during the nineteenth century was shaped in the process.

---

71   Bradford, *American Antiquities*, p. 9.

DISCUSSION QUESTIONS

1. What had happened by 1903 to make the American Indian "invisible"?
2. What were Thomas Jefferson's thoughts on the "Indian problem"?
3. How does the author distinguish his book from the many books on the history of the American Indian?
4. The name of the book is *History's Shadow*, which refers to American Indians. Why does the author call them "History's Shadow"?
5. The author lays out the various topics covered in his book. What is the topic of Chapter 3 and what does he say about it?
6. How about Chapter 4?
7. How about Chapter 5?
8. How about the last chapter?
9. Under the subtitle "Studying the Noble Savage," how does Tocqueville describe American Indians?
10. What French philosopher coined the phrase "noble savage"?
11. For Europeans, what problems did Indians pose for their religion?
12. Describe a popular theory in the eighteenth and nineteenth century for how American Indians fit into biblical stories.
13. What was the difference between the "monogenists" and the "polygenists?"
14. Under the subtitle "Searching for Indian History," Indian history as told by the Indians themselves was rejected. Why?
15. Under the subtitle "Indians and the Cycles of History," the author describes which conflict among nineteenth-century historians?

CHAPTER FOUR

Labors of Love

FROM *War Stories: Suffering and Sacrifice in the Civil War North*
BY FRANCES M. CLARKE

INTRODUCTION

In the 1960s there was a new movement in history called Cliometrics (named after Greek mythology's historical muse, Clio). It was an attempt to study economic history in a more analytical and statistical way. Thinking that traditional historians had become too subjective, the "Cliometricians" hoped to find a more objective, empirical approach (think historians in white lab coats). This movement generated lots of criticism over the claim that it didn't take into account specific political and economic factors that differ over time; one critic, Howard Zinn, claimed that it simply failed to take into account the human element that is central to history. Nevertheless, the Cliometricians did do something quite interesting with the American Civil War. They decided to collect all the data necessary to come to an exact dollar cost of the war. They collected data on the destruction of buildings, of the cost of the war itself (for both sides), and even developed formulas for determining the cost of each dead soldier (something like projected earnings during his lifetime minus food, clothing, and shelter). And they came up with a figure: $20,000,000,000. Yes that's right, 20 billion dollars. That's in 1860s monetary terms. Adjust for inflation over time and it comes to a gargantuan amount. But the Cliometricians didn't stop there. Instead they went on to play the historical game of counterfactual hypothesis. This is where you ask, "What if?" What if something else had happened instead of what did happen? So the question the Cliometricians asked was, what if we had ended slavery peacefully like they did in Europe, where slavery was outlawed and all the slave owners paid fair market value for the loss of their slaves? Their answer was startling. If we had taken the European approach to the abolition of slavery, for one-tenth of that $20 billion we could have paid all slave owners fair market value for their slaves and given each freed slave twenty acres,

FIGURE 4.1.

Fig. 5.3: "Women in the Civil War," http://civilwar.eastlymehistoricalsociety.org/index_files/photopages/Page1491.htm. Copyright in the Public Domain.

a mule, and a two-year supply of food to help them become independent farmers. All the blood spilled and all the treasure lost could have been averted.[1] Of course there are numerous reasons why it didn't happen that way, not least of which the deeply rooted racism in the North and South going back two centuries. European conflict was historically more along nationalist than racist lines. Despite it being a rather broad hypothetical, and despite the Cliometricians having since become history themselves, it does give us something to think about.

Frances M. Clarke, it is fair to say, is not a Cliometrician. Her book of war stories set in the Civil War, as well as her approach to the role of women in the Civil War, is deeply personal. By scouring letters and diaries she has found not only the role women played in the war, but how women perceived their role. The story she tells is one of sympathy, love, and compassion winning out over scientific methods and professionalism. It is a story that is as human as a story can get.

* * *

1   John Lyons et al., eds., *Reflections on the Cliometrics Revolution: Conversations with Economic Historians* (New York: Routledge, 2008). Reprinted interviews from the *Newsletter of the Cliometric Society.*

We will make them one great home to take the place of the many they have left.... As they fight we will build this great house ... it shall be stocked with everything that home can give and its love shall clothe and feed and tend them; wherever they are ... in one form or other our love shall reach them.

S. G. Cary, "Thirty Third Report of the New England Women's Auxiliary Association" (1865)

Writing for the *Atlantic Monthly* in 1865, a Northern volunteer suggested that the government could easily have provided the sick and wounded with all of the services offered by volunteers throughout the war. What the government could *not* do, he argued, was to provide "so many bonds of love and kindness to bind the soldier to his home, and to keep him always a loyal citizen." "If our army is ... more pure, more clement, more patriotic than other armies,—if our soldier is everywhere and always a true-hearted citizen," he proclaimed, "it is because the army and soldier have not been cast off from public sympathy, but cherished and bound to every free institution and every peaceful association by golden cords of love."[2] By sustaining men's attachments to the home front, women had saved the republic from militarism's corrupting potential: despondency on one hand and brutality on the other.

When Unionists told stories about civilian efforts to alleviate wartime suffering, they typically emphasized the personal, heartfelt nature of their labors, telling tales in which soldiers' ability to suffer well inspired volunteers' deepest love, and volunteers' love, in turn, aroused soldiers' noblest suffering. Whether they portrayed young soldiers turning from apathy or despair after receiving homefront donations, or hardened troops morally transformed through sympathetic nursing, stories about wartime voluntarism insisted that women's most important war-work lay in extending "golden cords of love" to the war zone.

Much like the stories examined in previous chapters, these ones drew from a wealth of enduring imagery. Emphasizing women's selfless devotion to soldiers, they shared themes in common with ancient and modern war narratives, from a stress on women's innate selflessness and compassion to a focus on their role in inspiring men's bravery, both as recipients of their protection and spectators for their deeds.[3] Yet as with stories of exemplary sufferers or heroic officers, these tales of civilian voluntarism also reverberated in ways specific to their time and place, lending a particular urgency to women's actions and a distinctive shape to their voluntarism. Unlike earlier and later conflicts, the Civil War took place at a time when

2 Reynolds, "Fortnight with the Sanitary," 246–47.

3 Jean Bethke Elshtain, *Women and War* (New York: Basic Books, 1987).

many Unionists believed that women's moral influence over men was not just socially valuable but politically essential. Without such influence, America's republic would degenerate just as surely as its many failed antecedents. It was no trivial afterthought to extend "golden chords of love" to the war zone in such a context, for doing so complemented men's work on the battlefields in the most literal sense, with men fighting to protect republican democracy, and women working to preserve republican virtues. Moreover, home and family were the wellspring of patriotism according to most middle-class Unionists, such that the best soldiers were those who thought most often of home. Preserving men's domestic attachments thus had crucial military implications. Not only did women's love safeguard the character of the nation's citizenry, it also mobilized men for service and secured their lasting allegiance. Most important, the mass of Northern volunteers were true believers, convinced that this conflict had to be fought on two fronts at once: the first against the enemy, the second against the myriad temptations that drew soldiers away from God. Believing in the power of feminine influence to rouse men's better natures and transform their souls, most viewed women's efforts to keep home in men's thoughts as a sacred duty, at once serving political, military, and religious ends.

Northern voluntary efforts were fundamentally shaped by middle-class convictions about the significance of home and maternal influence. That is, volunteers did not just tell stories about the importance of preserving emotional connections with men, they formed efforts designed to do exactly that. Personalizing the goods they sent to the front, women broadcast the love they bore for Union soldiers. Working to domesticate the war zone, they adorned all the spaces that came under their control with homelike touches, from floral arrangements to well-laid tables. Indeed, practically every aspect of Northern voluntary work was directed at shoring up men's links to families and evoking memories of home, from women's manner of conducting battlefield relief and hospital work to their creation of soldiers' homes and lodges.[4]

The bulk of the historiography on Civil War voluntarism concentrates less on the voluntary movement as a whole than on the United States Sanitary Commission (USSC), the North's largest voluntary group. Historians diverge in their understandings of this organization's purpose and long-term implications. In George Fredrickson's much-cited study, USSC leaders appear as self-interested elites, concerned not so much with alleviating suffering as with demonstrating the benefits of

---

4 Patricia L. Richardson, *Busy Hands: Images of the Family in the Northern Civil War Effort* (New York: Fordham University Press, 2003), supports the general arguments made in this chapter regarding the significance of domesticity to Civil War Northerners and their interest in shaping voluntary efforts in ways that facilitated ties between soldiers and the home front.

bureaucratic management. Their organization marks the point at which amateur do-gooders, motivated by piety, paternalism, and zeal, began making way for experienced professionals who promoted the standards of centralization, order, and efficiency.[5] In contrast, more recent studies by historians Judith Giesberg and Jeanie Attie stress the divergent agendas of male and female USSC workers. Refuting the idea that women accepted male colleagues' methods, Giesberg depicts the war years as a time when USSC women honed their organizational skills and built alliances that would bear fruit in the post-bellum era, giving rise to a more militant, sex-specific brand of benevolent activism.[6] Pointing to the gender conflicts that plagued the USSC, Attie similarly notes that its female leaders resisted efforts to undermine their authority, while women donors thwarted attempts to systematize and nationalize their voluntarism. By demonstrating the endurance of traditional forms of female voluntarism, and exploring the gender conflicts that shaped relationships among volunteers, this scholarship suggests that the Civil War did not cause a thoroughgoing or uniform transformation in civilian benevolence.

Nevertheless, this recent scholarship continues to treat tales depicting voluntarism as a labor of love as mere cant. As Giesberg points out, male volunteers used sentimental tales of voluntarism to deny the value of women's labor. Bent on ignoring the fact that their female colleagues administered large and complex organizations, she argues, USSC men instead portrayed women as ministering angels, their work a product of their feminine natures and thus not really work at all. Adopting a similar perspective, Attie argues that these sentimental narratives helped men to depoliticize women's war-work, thereby circumventing the challenge this work posed to the ideology of separate spheres. Since USSC men were conservative elites interested in expanding state power, she notes, tales of women's spontaneous benevolence furthered nationalist aims as well, demonstrating that the Union had the support of women, supposedly "the least partisan and most virtuous members of the community."[7]

It is indisputable that stories of women's devotion to the troops helped to buttress an existing gender ideology and further nationalist ends. But it should also be acknowledged that middle-class women themselves were largely responsible for creating and broadcasting tales portraying their voluntarism as a labor of love. In light of their unprecedented mobilization and the multifaceted nature of

---

5 Fredrickson, *Inner Civil War*, chap. 7; see also Ginzberg, *Women and the Work of Benevolence*, chap. 5; and Bremner, *The Public Good*.

6 Attie, *Patriotic Toil*; Giesberg, *Civil War Sisterhood: The U.S. Sanitary Commission and Women's Politics in Transition* (Boston: Northeastern University Press, 2000).

---

7 Giesberg, *Civil War Sisterhood*, ix–xi; Attie, *Patriotic Toil*, 3–4.

their war-work, it is worthwhile asking why these particular stories maintained their appeal throughout this war. The answer lies not just in the obvious fact that women, like men, were deeply influenced by their culture's norms and values. This chapter suggests that sentimental stories about women's war-work resonated because they demonstrated the power of female influence and served as a vehicle for extending that influence. Long schooled in the transformative power of feminine emotion, many women sought to mobilize this power during the war, convinced that their efforts were vital in assisting the war effort and ensuring a stable polity. For large numbers of middle-class women, these sentimental stories did not mystify the "real" nature of their voluntarism. Rather, they helped to remind Americans just how crucial it was to extend women's moral authority into the public domain.

The Civil War North represents a high-water mark in wartime voluntarism. In no subsequent conflict were civilians so directly engaged in alleviating suffering. In later wars, the state would assume most of the auxiliary functions that volunteers took on at this time, narrowing the terrain on which civilians operated. In the Civil War, however, Unionists did not necessarily *want* the state to accept complete responsibility for soldiers. Imagining the war as a "people's contest," they chose to rely on a volunteer force rather than a professional army, just as they elected to depend on civilian volunteers to fill many support roles vital

to the war effort. According to most benevolent women, the state simply could not provide the crucial emotional work their labor accomplished. No matter how efficient the Medical Department became, it could never remind soldiers of their homes and thereby save them from being transformed into mercenaries. Nor could it convince soldiers that the war was a mutual quest, engaged in by the entire community, thus countering daily reports of war profiteering, declining enlistments, or battlefield losses. Most crucially, nothing but personalized relief efforts could hope to counteract the increasingly inhumane, bureaucratic nature of the war itself. In the midst of what some scholars have dubbed the first "modern war," middle-class women determinedly sought to extend the felt connections between people on an intimate, local, and individual level.

***

Northern voluntarism initially grew out of dire necessity, springing from the chaos that existed in the early months of the war. Shortly after the fall of Fort Sumter in April 1861, troops had come flooding into the capital in response to a government appeal for 75,000 three-month militiamen. Several hundred thousand additional men were called service over the next few months, almost none arriving fully equipped with uniforms, weapons, and other necessities. Unable to deal with their requirements, the federal government looked to the states not just to raise but also to outfit regiments. State and local governments, in turn, called on civilians. In Pennsylvania, the Quartermaster General of Militia requested that women immediately "form associations in each county" to provide stockings and blankets for the troops.[8] Tens of thousands of women responded to similar requests sent out across the North, often by converting existing sewing clubs, church, and reform groups into soldiers' aid societies. In the war's first few weeks, according to one estimate, there were already 20,000 voluntary organizations catering to soldiers at work around the country.[9]

Scope for benevolent work remained even after the government increased its responsibility for provisioning the army. Privation in the ranks was widespread, despite the fact that Northern farms generated enough to feed the troops, and manufacturers were soon capable of equipping them without relying on foreign imports.[10] Insufficient or defective goods might still be caused by unscrupulous contractors, unforeseen

disruptions to the supply lines, or officers' faulty paperwork. Whatever the cause, the results were the same: food arrived late or spoiled; shoes wore out on the march; uniforms made of "shoddy" disintegrated at the first sign of rain; and army rations remained woefully inadequate, especially for the sick and injured.[11]

Civilians worked to fill the many holes in the military's supply system and to furnish the needs of hospitalized men. Across the loyal states, voluntary organizations set up hundreds of soldiers' homes, private hospitals, and refreshment saloons. They created their own systems for supplying these institutions and ran their own hospital steamers and

---

8 Order issued by R. C. Hale, September 10, 1861, newspaper clipping contained in Minute Book of the Richmond (later Mansfield) Soldiers' Aid Society, 1861–1864, MG-211, Pennsylvania Historical and Museum Commission, Harrisburg. This aid society formed in response to this order, as did dozens of others in the vicinity.

9 Mary Elizabeth Massey, *Women in the Civil War* (Lincoln: University of Nebraska Press, 1994), 32; originally published as *Bonnet Brigades* (New York: Knopf, 1966).

10 See Emerson David Fite, *Social and Industrial Conditions in the North During the Civil War* (1910; Williamstown, Mass.: Corner House Publishers, 1976), chaps. 1 and 4, for a discussion of agricultural and manufacturing output in the Civil War North.

11 According to William Quentin Maxwell, *Lincoln's Fifth Wheel: The Political History of the United States Sanitary Commission* (New York: Longmans, Green and Co., 1956), 35, a basic ration in 1861 consisted of a pound of hard bread, one and a quarter pounds of fresh or salt meat or three-quarters of a pound of bacon. Added to this, for every hundred men the army provided eight gallons of beans, ten pounds of rice or hominy, ten pounds of coffee, fifteen pounds of sugar, four gallons of vinegar, and two pounds of salt. The typical ration was supplemented later in the war with a slight increase in hard bread and the addition of three pounds of potatoes. Many companies also pooled funds to purchase fresh produce, such as vegetables, eggs, and milk, and hospital administrators did the same. By war's end, the Medical Department had created special diet lists, which itemized the type and amount of particular foods that army doctors were supposed to give to men suffering from specific ailments. Nonetheless, soldiers' diets tended to be nutritionally deficient. And poor hospital management, sudden influxes of patients, or lack of nearby resources meant that physicians continued to rely on volunteers to supply fresh food and other necessities.

railroad carriages to help ferry injured men from the front.[12] They concocted dozens of fundraising ventures—ranging from the immense fortnight-long "sanitary fairs" held in Northern cities, to tens of thousands of smaller social events—the proceeds of which mostly funded hospital stores.[13] Volunteers

---

12   In the West and East, the USSC ran thirty-nine hospital railway carriages that transported 225,000 soldiers over the course of the war, while tens of thousands more were carried north in USSC-managed hospital ships. Discovering that the government was liable to commandeer trains in the event of military necessity, the USSC also purchased its own engine for use in the West. Other voluntary organizations, such as the Western Sanitary Commission (mentioned below), similarly sponsored their own hospital cars. The government took over the management of hospital cars and boats in the war's last year, although voluntary agencies generally retained agents on board these transports to dispense food and supplies. George A. Otis and D. L. Huntington, *The Medical and Surgical History of the War of the Rebellion*, 2d issue, pt. 3 (Washington, D.C.: Government Printing Office, 1883), 2:957–71, details these arrangements. See also Ralph C. Gordon, "Hospital Trains of the Army of the Cumberland," *Tennessee Historical Quarterly* 51 (1992): 147–56.

13   These events raised millions of dollars, mostly in support of the USSC. Details can be found in J. Matthew Gallman, "Voluntarism in Wartime: Philadelphia's Great Central Fair," in *Toward a Social History of the American Civil War*, ed. Maris A. Vinovskis (Cambridge: Cambridge University Press, 1990), 93–116; J. Christopher Schnell, "Mary Livermore and the Great Northwestern Fair," *Chicago History* 4 (1975): 34–43; Robert W. Schoeberlein, "A Fair to Remember: Maryland Women in Aid of the Union," *Maryland Historical Society* 90 (1995): 467–88; Harriet Mott Stryker-Rodda, "Brooklyn and Long Island Sanitary Fair, 1864," *Journal of Long Island History* 4 (1964): 1–17; and William

tracked the fate of soldiers, following them into camp with Bibles, onto the battlefield with supplies, and into hospitals as nurses and visitors. They formed committees to lobby the government for an ambulance corps and to improve the army Medical Department, as well as raising money for soldiers' families, among a host of other activities.

Despite the claims of wartime propagandists, this flourishing of benevolence was neither unified nor harmonious. Volunteer groups mobilized simultaneously in thousands of different locations, drawing members from diverse backgrounds with varying, sometimes conflicting, aims and methods. They vied for official support, public largesse, and social prestige, such that the movement was riven by ideological conflicts and personal animosities. At the center of these conflicts was the USSC, a group whose male leaders had pretensions to unite all volunteers under a central hierarchy, national in scope and geared toward the efficient management of army health. Sanitary Commission leaders repeated the same mantra throughout the war: a centralized system for distributing voluntary supplies would aid military efficiency. Anything less would usurp official prerogatives, undermine discipline, and injure soldiers. If there was no check on women's benevolence, a few men would receive too much, burdening themselves with useless goods or eating

---

Y. Thompson, "Sanitary Fairs of the Civil War," *Civil War History* 4 (1958): 51–67.

themselves sick. Others would go with-out, and no stockpiles would exist for times of greatest need.[14] Failure to create a national organization of volunteers, moreover, would play straight into the enemy's hands, fostering "in contributor, agent and beneficiary alike, the very spirit of sectionalism and '*State-ish-ness*' to which we owe all our troubles."[15] Eager to centralize all voluntary efforts under their auspices, the USSC's male executive persistently underscored the connection between an orderly effort led by experienced men and triumphant nationalism, criticizing their competi-tors in the process.

Scholars have lavished considerable attention on the USSC's male leader-ship, using their perspective to discuss the nature of wartime voluntarism. In thinking about the shape of voluntarism overall, this emphasis is misplaced for three reasons. First, although the USSC's executive committee presented a relatively uniform outlook, the men and women active throughout this organization—whether as special relief agents, sanitary inspectors, associate secretaries, or nurses—held diverse viewpoints.[16] Some were "cosmopolitan rationalists," to use Jeanie Attie's phrase, that is, representatives of a New England, urban, mostly Unitarian social elite who supported scientific inquiry, elite-led institutions, and an expan-sion of state power. But many others spoke with noticeable religious and sentimental accents. Second, as recent scholarship points out, USSC men did not have a free hand to implement their agenda. They dealt with a largely female constituency, who had to be appeased lest they throw their support behind rival groups or stop donating entirely.[17] Finally, the USSC always competed with a host of other voluntary groups

---

14   See, for example, "What They Have to Do Who Stay at Home," no. 50, *Documents*, 1:1–10.

15   "Statement of the Object and Methods of the Sanitary Commission, 7 December 1863," no. 69, *Documents*, 2:7 (emphasis in original).

16   The USSC's board eventually included twenty-four members who met quarterly in Washington. To cope with an enormous work-load, the organization formed a Standing Committee that gathered in New York five or six days a week. Frederick Law Olmsted held greatest responsibility, filling the position of executive secretary until 1863. This role was then filled by Dr. J. Foster Jenkins, who, in turn, was succeeded by Johnathan S. Blatchford in April 1865. Most of the USSC's work was channeled through associate secretaries and chief sanitary inspectors. Until 1864, there were three associate secretaries: one responsible for work east of the Alleghenies plus New Orleans, another in charge of work in the West, and one designated Chief of Sanitary Inspection. In addition, the USSC appointed a chief sanitary inspector for each large division of the army. On the USSC's organiza-tion, see "Statement of the Object and Methods," *Documents*, 2:1–58; and William Y. Thompson, "The U.S. Sanitary Commission," *Civil War History* 2 (1956): 41–63. The USSC employed around 200 additional workers by 1864, many of whom held salaried positions. Biographical information on the USSC leadership is contained in an appendix to Maxwell, *Lincoln's Fifth Wheel*, 317–50. For similar details on the USSC's women leaders, see Attie, *Patriotic Toil*, chaps 1–2; and Giesberg, *Civil War Sisterhood*, chaps. 2–3.

17   Attie, *Patriotic Toil*, 70. On this point, see Attie, *Patriotic Toil*; and Giesberg, *Civil War Sisterhood*, in particular.

that, taken together, outnumbered and outspent this single organization. Examining the evolution of Northern voluntarism as a whole, it is possible to see that however much USSC men desired to create a fully professionalized, hierarchically ordered voluntary system, the mass of volunteers had their own ideas. Overwhelmingly, they supported forms of voluntarism that allowed them to reach soldiers directly, to display their affection, and to shore up the strength of men's relationships to the home front.

Much to the consternation of Sanitary Commission leaders, hundreds of organizations, both large and small, simply ignored their appeals, determined to conduct their own affairs on a local or state level. West of the Mississippi, a rival Western Sanitary Commission (WSC) supplied the majority of aid to soldiers and refugees in that area. Ignoring repeated entreaties from the USSC, this group refused to merge the two organizations. Instead, the prominent St. Louis business leaders and philanthropists in charge of the WSC established their own system of soldiers' homes and hospitals, employing a corps of around 300 female nurses to work in hospitals and on WSC hospital-steamers. With an extensive supply system roughly one-quarter the size of its larger rival, the WSC maintained its own agents

for distributing goods at the front, in hospitals, and among Union refugees and former slaves.[18]

Elsewhere, sizable aid organizations also remained aloof from the USSC. The state of Indiana opted for an independent Sanitary Commission, created in March 1862 under the leadership of a local businessman. Iowa followed Indiana's lead, eventually adopting a compromise in response to lobbying from the rival associations: it established one depot at Chicago to funnel donations to the USSC and another at St. Louis, to supply the WSC. In Pennsylvania, the Philadelphia Ladies Aid Society and the Penn Relief Association retained their autonomy throughout the war, maintaining control over their supplies and frequently sending local women to assure their distribution at the front, as did the Union Relief Association of Baltimore

---

18 William E. Parrish, in "The Western Sanitary Commission," *Civil War History* 36 (1990): 17–35, notes that the WSC raised almost $780,000 and distributed stores valued at $3,500,000. See also J. G. Forman, *The Western Sanitary Commission: A Sketch of Its Origin, History, Labors for the Sick and Wounded of the Western Armies and Aid Given to Freedman and Union Refugees* (St. Louis: R. P. Studley and Co., 1864); W. R. Hodges, *The Western Sanitary Commission and What It Did for the Sick and Wounded of the Union Armies from 1861 to 1865* ([St. Louis]; privately printed, 1906); and Frank B. Goodrich, *The Tribute Book: A Record of the Munificence, Self-Sacrifice and Patriotism of the American People During the War for the Union* (New York: Derby and Miller, 1865), chap. 7. For a discussion of the acrimonious relationship between the WSC and the USSC see Maxwell, *Lincoln's Fifth Wheel*, 97–106.

and the New England Soldiers' Relief Association of New York.[19]

Countless civilians and smaller local groups likewise opted to direct their benevolence as they saw fit. It is impossible to know how many women's groups sent donations straight to local companies, for such ad hoc initiatives had no need for recordkeeping. But soldiers' letters make clear that the mails were filled with packages of homemade food and clothing making their way directly to friends and family at the front. It is just as difficult to determine the precise number of civilians who volunteered in the many initiatives that catered to soldiers passing through towns and urban centers. Judging by the scale of their work, their numbers were substantial. Almost all of the regiments making their way through Philadelphia stopped to partake of the free meals, bathing facilities, and reading rooms at the Cooper Shop Refreshment Saloon or the neighboring Union Volunteer Refreshment Saloon, privately funded ventures that were imitated in Baltimore, Pittsburgh, and elsewhere.[20] Local citizens also set up soldiers' rests or small hospitals throughout Union-held territory that were staffed by volunteers to care for furloughed or discharged soldiers too debilitated to make their way home.

One of the primary attractions of these autonomous ventures was that they enabled civilians to track the precise destination of their voluntary offerings, and often to receive direct thanks from the individual regiments, men, or hospitals that received them. In contrast, the USSC centralized and stockpiled donations, distributing them only after receiving an official request. Under the direction of a Department of General Relief, contributions of hospital supplies, clothing, medicines, and food were collected by twelve USSC branches that formed clearing depots for donations sent in by thousands of affiliated aid societies operating in villages and towns. At these branch depots, goods were unpacked, resorted, stamped with the USSC's seal, and then forwarded to central supply rooms in the West or East, where army medical officers or USSC representatives in the field could request them.[21]

This centralized system generated growing controversy by the war's second year, leading to increased competition among voluntary organizations. As the USSC expanded in size, charges of fraud and mismanagement plagued the organization. Soldiers returned from hospitals claiming to have purchased clothes donated to the Sanitary Commission or to have starved while hospital staff gorged on the food sent for their benefit. Critics

---

19 Goodrich, *Tribute Book*, chap. 8.
20 James Moore, *History of the Cooper Shop Volunteer Refreshment Saloon* (Philadelphia: James B. Rodgers, 1866).

21 "Statement of Object and Methods," *Documents*, 2:22–30; and Charles J. Stillé, *History of the United States Sanitary Commission: Being the General Report of Its Work During the War of the Rebellion* (Philadelphia: J. B. Lippincott and Co., 1866), 248–51.

began to denounce the salaries of USSC leaders and to decry its system of paid agents.[22] This anxiety coalesced midway through the war into support for the U.S. Christian Commission, a group formed in 1861 that drew together Protestant ministers and leaders of the YMCA, the American Tract Society, and a number of other evangelical religious groups. Having initially limited its work to the distribution of religious literature at the front, the Christian Commission began moving into the USSC's domain in late 1862, doling out hospital stores and supplies along with its Bibles and tracts.

Christian Commission publications touted their organization as a purely voluntary effort that reached out to soldiers directly. Contrasting their system with that of the Sanitary Commission, they initially eschewed paid employees, instead recruiting ministers to undertake short-term, unpaid tours at the front. Over a thousand Christian Commission ministers had been sent to the field by the end of 1862, a number that increased fivefold before fighting ceased. Busily campaigning for public support, Christian Commission publicists emphasized that goods donated to their organization went straight into soldiers' hands without mediation from officials,

while the Sanitary Commission's system "destroyed the individuality of [women's] boxes by scattering their contents." Undertaking to make every local church organization a fee-paying auxiliary, the Christian Commission rapidly attracted the allegiance of several hundred women's groups.[23]

Because the USSC relied on public support, the organization had little choice but to personalize its mission in response to this challenge. While historians have noted this fact, few have appreciated just how extensive the changes were to the Sanitary Commission's initial program. Indeed, by the war's end, the USSC barely resembled the original plans of its male founders. These men had set out to demonstrate that individuals of the highest intelligence could assist the government in conducting the war on a firm "scientific basis." With this aim in mind they spent the war's first year focusing on preventative sanitary measures, such as monitoring hygienic conditions in camps and hospitals, conducting physical inspections to weed out unfit troops, and appraising army physicians of developments in medicine,

---

22 Attie, *Patriotic Toil*, chap. 4, deals with these charges. As she notes, these suspicions of USSC fraud and profiteering grew from a longstanding constellation of anxieties concerning the expansion of the market and concentrations of power (144). See also Maxwell, *Lincoln's Fifth Wheel*, 191–93.

23 On the formation of the Christian Commission and its support among women's groups, see Moss, *Annals of the United States Christian Commission*, 63–110, 356–58. Although this organization initially adopted a system of recruiting ministers on a voluntary basis to undertake six-week tours at the front, it later relied on paid field agents. Eventually, the organization employed 5,000 agents, in addition to 157 lady managers of Diet Kitchens, 108 army agents, and 53 agents on the home front. The quote is from Maxwell, *Lincoln's Fifth Wheel*, 192.

surgery and disease prevention.[24] They certainly did not envision their organization serving mainly as a conduit between civilians and soldiers.[25] Women's collection of clothing, hospital stores, and food was to be merely a stopgap measure, a temporary expedient to mitigate soldiers' suffering while the government established its supply systems on a more stable basis. This is not what transpired. In order to appeal to the public and to respond to the needs of the moment, the USSC was compelled to shift its focus decisively over time, away from disease prevention and toward the personal ministry and monitoring of Union soldiers. By 1865 the Department of General Relief encompassed more than three-quarters of the USSC's workload, making the organization wholly dependent on women's efforts for their success. As this dependence increased, USSC activities grew ever more similar to the modes of benevolent activism they had initially belittled as overly sentimental and overtly pious.

Almost every aspect of the USSC's original design was modified in order to personalize relief efforts. Even before the Christian Commission began making serious inroads into their support, Sanitary Commission leaders set out to alter their system of battlefield relief to furnish the wounded with individual attention. Having first established a single depot near the headquarters of each army through which to dispense supplies, they altered this system in 1862 by introducing a Field Relief Corps. Under the direction of Lewis H. Steiner, each army corps was now provided with its own permanent field relief agent, supplied with government-owned horses and wagons stocked with the USSC's medical supplies, food, and stores.[26] Nevertheless, Steiner's men continued to act at a remove from the wounded, dis-

---

24   Maxwell, *Lincoln's Fifth Wheel*, 10; "Plan of Organization for 'The Commission of Inquiry and Advice in Respect of the Sanitary Interests of the United States Forces,'" dated June 21, 1861, reprinted in Stillé, *History of the United States Sanitary Commission*, 533–38. Early USSC publications reiterated that the "chief object" initially contemplated by the organization was that of sanitary inspection and disease prevention. See, for instance, "Statement of Object and Methods," *Documents*, 2:15.

25   While women's groups around the country were busy collecting supplies for the troops, the business of systematizing voluntary contributions formed no part of the USSC's original design. In fact, the executive did not draw up plans to engage in such work until several months after beginning operations. See Frederick Law Olmsted, "A Report to the Secretary of War of the Operations of the Sanitary Commission and upon the Sanitary Condition of the Volunteer Army," December 9, 1861, no. 40, *Documents*, 1:75.

26   Stillé, *History of the Sanitary Commission*, 251–56. If this initiative was originally undertaken without thought of rival organizations, USSC agents were soon conscious of the need to present themselves in a manner designed to win favor among the Northern public. Advising a subordinate to ensure that field relief agents maintained morally upright and sensitive behavior, Steiner cautioned that a "scrutinizing fa[u]lt-finding eye is upon us all the while." Lewis H. Steiner to "Capt. Isaac Harris," August 20, 1863, Lewis H. Steiner, Letterbook 1863–1864, Box 2, MS1430, Maryland Historical Society, Baltimore (hereafter Steiner Letterbook).

tributing supplies only after the request of army medical officers.[27] To close this remaining gap, a further innovation took place in mid-1864 with the formation of an Auxiliary Relief Corps led by Frank B. Fay, a Christian minister and former major of Chelsea, Massachusetts. Given charge of fifty men (mostly theological students), Fay organized his volunteers into small teams and placed them in direct relation to wounded soldiers. His men "understood that the corps was organized for personal ministry, and that this was to be provided with all the sympathy and devotion they would give a patient at home," Fay noted in his wartime diary.[28] Elaborating on the tasks undertaken by his men, one of their number explained that he would meet the wounded as they were carried from the field, providing them with food, bathing their wounds, and dispensing clean clothes. After conveying the wounded to hospitals or performing last rites for the dying, agents would then undertake nursing duties, such as cleaning the wards, writing letters, and reading to patients. The Sanitary Commission typically acclaimed this

work as a way for families to establish a proxy on the battlefield, someone to provide "a sister's or a mother's care," as this agent expressed it.[29] Clearly, they worried about their image as a soulless bureaucracy more concerned with procedures than with individual soldiers, and they tailored their battlefield relief accordingly.

The USSC's message likewise took on increased sentimental and religious overtones as the war continued. Early in the conflict, commission publicists sometimes relied on rational appeals rather than emotion to make their case, as was evident in one plea they sent to insurance companies, which emphasized the monetary value of each soldier. Calculating the cost of his enlistment, outfit, training, bounty, pay, and rations, potential donors were advised that USSC efforts "saved the country ten times its cost by what it has done to economize the life, health, and efficiency of the army." Historians have used these pragmatic arguments to portray the USSC as a thoroughly bureaucratic venture that eschewed sentimentality.[30] But appeals to fiscal prudence mostly targeted the business community. When

---

27 Steiner advised his field relief agents to "see every medical officer in the Corps, find out the wants of his Hospital and courteously offer assistance, not obtruding this or interfering with his plans." Lewis H. Steiner to David S. Pope, n.d. [August 1863], Steiner Letterbook.

28 William Howell Reed, ed., *War Papers of Frank B. Fay: With Reminiscences of Services in the Camps and Hospitals of the Army of the Potomac, 1861–1865* ([Boston:] privately printed, 1911), 95.

29 Reed, *Hospital Life*, 72–73; Stillé, *History of the Sanitary Commission*, 274–77. The number of auxiliary relief agents was augmented with civilian volunteers during major battles.

30 "Statement of the Object and Methods," *Documents*, 2:56–57. Bremner (*The Public Good*, 55), for instance, argues that the USSC "discharged its tasks with acumen rather than sentiment"; see also Fredrickson, *Inner Civil War*, 104 and passim.

addressing women donors, USSC publications differed little from those of their rivals, typically offering lists of the number and type of goods distributed alongside heartrending tales of suffering men saved by well-timed supplies.

Much like other organizations, the USSC made heavy use of testimony from field agents bearing witness to the physical and emotional effects of women's goods on soldiers.[31] Quick to recognize the importance of first-hand evidence, branch society leaders solicited letters acknowledging the receipt of women's donations from surgeons and soldiers, which they published in city papers and reprinted in circulars mailed regularly to each of their auxiliaries.[32] Via such personal exhortations, the Sanitary Commission increasingly framed its message in terms popularized by evangelical revivals, such as when the Commission petitioned clergy through-out the Northwest "in Humanity's name and for the Redeemer's sake" to seek contributions and public support. Terming the results of these efforts a "great awakening," one USSC publicist noted that during the first months of 1863, the number of aid societies auxiliary to the Northwestern Branch increased from 250 to more than 2,000.[33] It did not take long for the Sanitary Commission leaders to comprehend that if they wanted their message to appeal, they had no choice but to frame their work as a religious mission directly affecting particular soldiers.

A host of additional initiatives catering to individual men reveal even more pointedly the USSC's growing concern with personalizing its services. In August 1861 the USSC established a Department of Special Relief in Washing-ton, D.C., under the direction of Frederick Knapp, a Unitarian minister and cousin to USSC president Henry Bellows.[34] As Knapp explained in his first report, his mission was to supply

31 Henshaw, *Our Branch and Its Tributaries*, 98–99. In addition, the USSC employed "travelling missionary agents" to tour the country and hold public meetings about their work, information on which can be found in Box 883, U.S. Sanitary Commission Records, New York Public Library, Rare Books and Manuscripts Division, New York (hereafter USSC Records).

32 [Mary Clark Brayton and Ellen F. Terry], *Our Acre and Its Harvest: Historical Sketch of the Soldiers' Aid Society of Northern Ohio* (Cleveland: Fairbanks, Benedict and Co., 1869), 33, 58–59, 67–68. The USSC also requested family members to forward letters from soldiers in order to inspire their contributors, some of which were later published in Lydia Minturn Post, *Soldiers' Letters from Camp, Battle-Field and Prison* (New York: Bunce and Huntington, published for the U.S. Sanitary Commission, 1865).

33 Henshaw, *Our Branch and Its Tributaries*, 95, 103.

34 Knapp was born in New Hampshire in 1821. He graduated from Harvard Divinity School in the 1840s, before setting up a parish in Brookline, Massachusetts, which he left to join the USSC. After the war, he continued his guardianship over young men, first as principal of the Engleswood Military Academy in New Jersey until 1867, thereafter by founding a home school for boys in Plymouth, Massachusetts. An obituary, taken from the *Old Colony Memorial* (Walpole, N.H.), can be found in Frederick Newman Knapp Papers, Box 1, Massachusetts Historical Society, Boston (hereafter Knapp Papers).

food, shelter, and medical attention to soldiers arriving in the capital but too ill to continue to the front, as well as those waiting on army pay or discharges. He would go on to evolve a remarkably extensive system for monitoring these stray men. Some of Knapp's team of Special Relief Agents set themselves up at railway stations to keep a lookout for needy soldiers, whom they carried back to one of the numerous soldiers' homes that the USSC administered. Others concentrated on intercepting troops before they could fall in with bad company, visiting the paymaster's office twice daily to inquire after anyone submitting papers.[35] To deal with "sharpers," Knapp stationed detectives at railroad depots who handed out tens of thousands of small manuals (called "Soldier's Friends") filled with dire warnings about schemes for robbing the unwary, alongside information on USSC Homes and Lodges.[36] Next, he pioneered a system of "Sanitary Relief Couriers" to assist soldiers in reaching their homes. Any man showing up without means of leaving the city was given clean clothes, escorted to the nearest station, and provided with a ticket. For incapacitated men, Knapp offered personal escorts, responsible for obtaining their tickets, seeing to their needs on the train, and delivering them to their front doors. His agents were on hand at each railroad terminus to take soldiers to the next station or to transport the sick to nearby Commission Homes.[37] Here

---

35 Frederick N. Knapp, "Two Reports Concerning the Aid and Comfort Given by the Sanitary Commission to Sick Soldiers Passing Through Washington," September 23, 1861, no. 35, *Documents*, 1:1–2; Frederick N. Knapp, "Third Report Concerning the Aid and Comfort Given by the Sanitary Commission to Sick Soldiers Passing through Washington," March 21, 1862, no. 39, *Documents*, 1:5. Large numbers of men arrived at the paymaster's too late in the day to submit claims, while many more had irregular documents that might require weeks, even months, of investigation. Slow-moving officials were not solely to blame. Commanding officers sometimes listed as deserters men who had in fact been wounded in battle or taken ill on a march. Once these men had been transferred from one hospital to another, it was often tricky for them to procure records detailing their movements, making it extremely difficult to obtain discharge papers or refute charges of desertion. Likewise, it was common for volunteer doctors who lacked experience with military regulations to incorrectly fill out discharge or transfer papers, thus stranding soldiers in bureaucratic limbo. Volunteers like Knapp—highly literate and well

versed in official procedures—were essential in navigating military bureaucracy for these men.

36 To Knapp's mind, these stranded troops were easy prey for the corrupting influences of the city. His official reports were replete with apprehension that soldiers would drink or gamble away their money, or become prey to confidence men, ever ready "like evil birds of prey," to rob the unwary. Knapp, "Third Report," 3. See also Knapp, "Fourth Report Concerning the Aid and Comfort Given by the Sanitary Commission to Sick Soldiers Passing Through Washington," December 15, 1862, no. 59, *Documents*, 1:7–9. Knapp handed out to such men a USSC publication titled *The Soldier's Friend* (Philadelphia: Perkinpine and Higgins, 1865).

37 Knapp, "Third Report," 5. Fearing that some might still fall through the cracks in places where the Commission had established no Lodges or Homes, Knapp drew up a circular in May 1864, which he sent to communities near all of the principal railroad stations in Union-held territory, pleading with civilians to aid disabled soldiers as trains stopped in their areas. Frederick N. Knapp,

was voluntarism at its most intimate level, conveying Union soldiers directly from the war zone back to their waiting families.

As the conflict expanded in size, encompassing ever-larger numbers of men and ever-expanding death tolls, the USSC responded by creating an aid network that was ever more individualized. There were five Sanitary Commission Homes and Lodges in and around the capital by war's end, in addition to dozens of others established in Cleveland, Ohio, Memphis, Nashville, Louisville, Cairo (Ill.), Cincinnati, Alexandria (Va.), Boston, Chicago, and elsewhere, as well as a Home for Nurses and Soldiers' Wives and Mothers in Washington, D.C., and a Home for Nurses in Annapolis.[38] Claiming that military bureaucracy could only deal with armies in the aggregate, the organization worked to particularize each soldier so that family members could track his location and fate, setting up a special committee to ensure that reliable records would exist

to document deaths in general hospitals; instituting a system for marking graves; and developing printed forms with space to list deceased soldiers' family members, place of burial, cause of death, and "dying requests"—a scheme clearly designed to minimize the anonymity of soldiers' deaths.[39] Constantly beset by worried family members searching for missing relatives, they also established a hospital directory in Washington, D.C., in late 1862, which recorded the names, locations, and medical conditions of soldiers in army hospitals. Branch offices were soon operating in Philadelphia, Louisville, and New York, tabulating daily reports from hundreds of army hospitals and responding to the flood of inquiries.[40] Concerning itself equally with the financial stability of Northern families, the USSC set up a Pension Bureau and War Claim Agency early the following year, which eventually encompassed a hundred subagencies dedicated to completing pension applications and providing free legal advice to invalid veterans or deceased soldiers' family

"Report Concerning the Aid and Comfort Given by the Sanitary Commission to Sick and Invalid Soldiers, for the Quarter Ending June 30, 1865," July 1, 1865, no. 94, *Documents,* 2:17–19.

38 Stillé, *History of the Sanitary Commission,* 290. These homes and lodges cumulatively provided 4.5 million meals and more than a million night's lodgings. The USSC also claimed that on a daily basis its Department of Special Relief catered to 2,300 soldiers. Anon., *The Sanitary Commission of the United States Army: A Succinct Narrative of Its Works and Purposes* (New York: n.p., 1864; repr., New York: Arno Press, 1972), 230; see also Knapp, "Report for the Quarter Ending 30 June 1865," 44–45.

39 The War Department later took up this more detailed method for recording soldiers' deaths, according to *Sanitary Commission of the United States Army,* 105.

40 Details relating to this massive undertaking can be found in the Washington Hospital Directory Archives, 1862–1866, RG 12, USSC Records. Summaries are contained in Stillé, *History of the Sanitary Commission,* 307–11; and J. S. Newberry, *The U.S. Sanitary Commission in the Valley of the Mississippi, During the War of the Rebellion, 1861–1866* (Cleveland: Fairbanks, Benedict and Co., 1871), 428–45, 503–9.

members.[41] As these activities suggest, rather than moving away from modes of benevolence focused on mitigating suffering, USSC efforts evolved in the opposite direction—toward a personalized ministry that reached out to donors on an emotional level while offering individualized support for soldiers and their kin.

Voluntary organizations that operated outside of the USSC's purview provided a range of similar services that extended personalized care to those subsumed by a homogenizing army bureaucracy. Most major cities across the loyal states had soldiers' homes and lodges or sizable hospitals funded and managed by civilian donors. The Soldiers' Depot in New York, for instance, was originally designed to seek out and protect stray soldiers from that state. In April 1863 the newly appointed civilian managers rented several adjoining premises on the corner of Howard and Mercer streets, just off Broadway and not far from the docks and railroad depots that formed soldiers' entry point to the city. Fitting out these buildings with space for 650 men, they added a barbershop, dining and reception halls, a reading room, private apartments, and multiple dormitories and hospitals. Their operation had

soon expanded across the country to encompass a system of "Military Couriers and Station Agents" who traveled on trains conveying soldiers between Washington and New York, performing a role similar to that of Knapp's couriers. Throughout Union-occupied territories, the Soldiers' Depot set up additional agencies, employing dozens of men to visit army hospitals and battlefields.[42] Likewise, the Citizens' Volunteer Hospital in Philadelphia began small and expanded quickly, accommodating approximately 200,000 soldiers during its three years of operation.[43] These substantial undertakings were designed not just to supplement government medical care but also to block the paths leading soldiers to vice or despair.

The managers and volunteers who staffed these ventures usually saw themselves as surrogate parents, dedicated to ensuring that troops returned to their families with their money and "self respect" intact, as Frederick Knapp put

---

41 Other voluntary agencies, even small ones, offered similar services, according to [Linus P. Brockett], *The Philanthropic Results of the War in America*, expanded reprint (New York: Sheldon and Co., 1864), 53. The New England Soldiers' Relief Association, for example, provided soldiers with help in obtaining back pay, pensions and discharges.

42 *Report of the Board of Managers of the New York State Soldiers' Depot, and the Fund for the Relief of Sick, Wounded, Furloughed, and Discharged Soldiers* (Albany, N.Y.: Van Benthuysen's Steam Printing House, 1864), 9–11. Public and private funds kept this venture running, with the New York legislature providing an initial grant of $300,000. The annual reports of agencies are appended to ibid., 47–137.

43 *History and Annual Reports of the Citizens' Volunteer Hospital Association* (Philadelphia: Burk and McFetridge, 1889). Like many other wartime ventures, this one kept minimal records, which were mostly destroyed upon disbanding. In the late 1880s, however, sixteen of the former male board members met and decided to print these remaining annual reports.

it. He described the USSC as akin to "the father of a home" seeking to ensure "the comfort and good of his children."[44] Like many wartime voluntary workers, he was an unswerving sentimentalist and a committed Christian, devoted to a belief that social unity and moral virtue could only come through emotional interactions between citizens (albeit paternalistic ones that supported his authority as a surrogate father). Evidence from Knapp's internal reports underscores this point, for they differed little from those he wrote for public consumption. Virtually every document he sent to the USSC's executive board stressed his heartfelt connections to the troops by highlighting his dealings with specific men. "He is a mere boy, of about eighteen, from a New Jersey regiment," he wrote of one soldier:

> He evidently struggles to be manly and brave, but his homesickness ... masters him. We have thus frequent opportunity here in the Home to make note of what in the general excitement is almost unavoidably overlooked ... namely, what a vast amount there is in the hearts of these soldiers of personal sacrifice, daily struggle to put down anxious feelings ... tender thoughts of home checked

in their utterance and hope silently waiting.[45]

Demonstrating his emotional connections to needy men, Knapp eagerly sought to plumb the depths of soldiers' "hearts." It may be true, as some scholars claim, that over time a number of male and female volunteers came to rely on a more detached, "masculine" language of scientific professionalism in describing their war-work.[46] But most continued to view benevolence as a Christian service, best administered by those who were earnestly committed to their charges.

Maintaining men's connections to home and emphasizing the sentiments animating benevolence was a central preoccupation of all voluntary groups, no matter how big or small. If some USSC leaders began the war with plans to institute a centralized, bureaucratic system that would demonstrate to the Northern public the virtues of efficiency and order, their donors had other ideas. Forced to recognize that most voluntary workers desired intimate connections with soldiers and a system that allowed them to frame voluntarism as a personal exchange, the Sanitary Commission helped to facilitate the maintenance of emotional bonds between soldiers and

---

44 Knapp, "Report for the Quarter Ending 30 June 1865," 4.

45 Knapp, "Third Report," 7. His reports were often written in the form of first-hand testimony, purportedly taken straight from his daily journal, as if to emphasize the way his writing offered unmediated access to his innermost feelings.

46 Ginzberg, *Women and the Work of Benevolence*, 134.

the home front as much as did their competitors. Only by looking at the meanings that middle-class Northerners invested in domesticity is it possible to understand why so many sought to characterize their voluntarism as a labor of love.

***

While recovering in a Philadelphia army hospital in 1864 one Union soldier perfectly captured the significance of home for middling Northerners. Publishing "A Soldier's Thoughts of Home," in a newspaper produced on the premises, he enthused:

> Home! How the sound of that word flies through the portals of the soldier's ear, and finds a lodgement in the soldier's heart, illuminating its darkest recesses with the light [of] love and affection, inspiring him with nobler thoughts and better impulses, kindling anew the fires of patriotism and ambition, and animating him to deeds of bravery and daring.[47]

For this writer and countless others, home was the site of selfless emotions, and these emotions had clear civic and military effects. Merely to mention the word "home" produced a transformation, immediately bringing to mind an

earlier schooling in "nobler thoughts and better impulses," as well as stimulating a desire to represent country and family on the battlefield.

This soldier's assumptions about the meaning of home were of recent origin, dating back only to the late eighteenth century. Assertions of patriarchal privilege had lost favor around this time, as revolutionary leaders embraced the principle of individual rights. Putting forth a new rationale for women's dependent status, Revolutionary-era thinkers revised negative judgments of feminine irrationality, carnality, and emotional excess, instead depicting women as the more morally virtuous sex, their tenderness and passivity unfitting them for political life. From their position in the private sphere, however, women were now granted new political responsibilities. Relying on a blend of liberalism, republicanism, and sensationalist psychology, social commentators invested novel importance in affection as "the glue of civil society," explains historian Jan Lewis. Through their natural affection, women would cultivate the ties that bound society together. And through their maternal roles, they would plant the seeds of civic virtue in their offspring.[48]

Concern over the republic's volatility made women's new roles especially crucial in the antebellum North. Until

---

47 "A Soldier's Thoughts of Home," *Hospital Register* (Satterlee Hospital, West Philadelphia), 2, no. 42 (June 11, 1864): 1.

48 Lewis, "Mother's Love," 210. See also Ruth H. Bloch, "The Gendered Meanings of Virtue in Revolutionary America," *Signs* 13 (1987): 37–58; and Richardson, *Busy Hands*, 96–98.

the end of the Civil War, people typically referred to the Union as an "experiment," pointing to an uncertain future in which the republic's survival was by no means assured. Widespread anxiety over the possibility of social disintegration had grown apace with increases in industrial production, social conflict, and political discord, forming a veritable cacophony by mid-century.[49] According to middle-class spokespeople, it was up to women to act as a vital counterbalance to an ever more amoral public sphere. While men engaged in the cutthroat pursuit of self-interest and the hurly-burly of politics, women were expected to safeguard cherished values, instilling self-control, moral purity, and civic mindedness in their children, and opening up a space for the expression of altruism, selflessness, and affection.

The links between motherhood and the survival of the republic elevated childrearing to a high-level concern. Self-proclaimed experts on the subject agreed by mid-century that children's characters were malleable. Drawing from sensationalist psychology and an evangelical concern with youthful conversion, they saw the first years of life as especially important in shaping future dispositions. Almost universally, they granted mothers the primary role in children's moral education. Women were expected to educate children through appeals to emotion rather than

reason. And a vast body of child-rearing literature and sentimental writing told mothers how to acquire emotional influence over their offspring. First, they had to recognize that children learned by their mother's example: they would imitate her affections, her qualities, and her actions. It was therefore up to mothers to watch carefully their own behavior, "not ... to teach virtue but to inspire it," as one advisor put it. Second, mothers had to ensure that children grasped the depth of their feelings, such that they appeared utterly devoted and yet entirely self-effacing. Describing the way women were enjoined to display selfless emotion, Lewis points to the fictional mother who arose early each morning to deliver her prayers "almost—but not quite—eluding the watchful eye of her child." Leading by example rather than stern enforcement (which might be construed as willful), the mother was supposed to craft a self overflowing with a deep emotion that escaped only inadvertently, in spite of her "extraordinary efforts [at] self-suppression."[50]

Women were promised immense power in exchange for their maternal self-denial. In line with the evangelical belief that social change could only come from individual conversions, mothers were constantly told that their influence held limitless potential to transform society. As Reverend John Abbott put it:

---

49   On the many manifestations of antebellum anxiety, see the preface to Paludan, "A People's Contest."

50   Lewis, "Mother's Love," 211, 220; Mary Ryan, *The Empire of the Mother: American Writing about Domesticity 1830–1860* (New York: Harrington Park Press, 1985), 144.

"Mothers have as powerful an influence over the welfare of future generations, as all other earthly causes combined." Moreover, they were offered a form of immortality, an assurance of living forever within their children. Ultimately, the message underlying all maternal advice literature was that "women, like Christ," could be "instruments of someone else's salvation."[51]

Psychological theories and scientific developments in the first half of the century seemed to confirm the power of early impressions and maternal influence to shape the social order. Nineteenth-century understandings of the mind held that imagination was "essentially passive and mechanistic." Thoughts traveled along channels carved out by earlier memories, such that new viewpoints were formed via older associations, with the mind linking particular thoughts not just to an original association but also to the emotions attached to that association.[52] It was thus believed that the mere mention of particular words—especially emotionally charged ones like "mother" or "home"—could immediately conjure up the powerful feelings with which they were connected. The soldier quoted earlier waxing lyrical about home vividly expressed these beliefs. Picturing a mind comprised of distinct passageways, he described the term "home" speeding "through the portals" of his ear and finding "lodgement" in his heart,

automatically unleashing a flood of associations strong enough to transform his behavior.

Whereas particular words held almost magical power to recreate emotional and moral states, powerful feelings were also thought capable of influencing from afar. Victorian commentators often described emotions as unbounded, seamlessly moving from one person to another via a mysterious process more often assumed than explained. It seemed to many by mid-century that there was an invisible connective force enigmatically at work in the world. Mesmerists by the 1840s were positing the existence of a "universal fluid" or electrical current that connected all matter, seen and unseen. Allegedly able to tap into this force, they staged spectacular displays that healed at a distance simply by moving their hands over patients' bodies. In equally impressive fashion, spirit mediums began accessing the supernatural realm around the same time. Claiming an ability to bring back messages from beyond the grave, they gained mass adherents by mid-century.[53]

Not coincidentally, widespread interest in invisible forms of communication arose just as a range of new scientific inventions began connecting people across

---

51   Lewis, "Mother's Love," 211, 221.
52   Forgie, *Patricide in the House Divided*, 195.

53   On the enormous popularity of mesmerism and spiritualism, see Laurence R. Moore, *In Search of White Crows: Spiritualism, Parapsychology, and American Culture* (New York: Oxford University Press, 1997); and Fred Kaplan, " 'The Mesmeric Mania': The Early Victorians and Animal Magnetism," *Journal of the History of Ideas* 35, no. 4 (1974): 691–702.

space and time in novel ways: from the camera's ability to capture the past to the telegraph's capacity for relaying messages across vast distances.[54] Doubtless, for many nineteenth-century people, the idea that one's emotional or moral state could jump across space, involuntarily communicating itself to others, seemed just as plausible as the act of sending a telegraph or taking a photograph. Thus did one wartime volunteer identify women's moral influence as "electric currents [running] along the invisible wires of sympathy," while another described voluntarism as "an irresistible moral contagion from heart to heart" that had "taught the value of liberty" and wove "a strong network of alliance between civil and military life."[55]

Of course, at the beginning of the war there was no guarantee that women's influence would extend to the army. Concerns were voiced as soon as the conflict began over how military life would affect the thousands of young soldiers streaming into army camps. What would happen to these men, many for the first time separated from parental oversight, compelled to associate with the wicked or corrupt, and obliged to adjust to military discipline and the infliction of violence? Would they return home brutalized by their experiences? Would they come back inured to vice or habituated to the subservience

required of them as soldiers? From the perspective of middle-class civilians, war threatened not just the dissolution of the Union but also the moral corruption of its defenders.

Civilian volunteers immediately acknowledged that retaining men's family connections had critical military and social implications. Visiting Union soldiers' encampments in Washington, D.C., a few days after their disastrous rout at the first battle of Bull Run, one USSC official attributed the dejection of a New York regiment to the fact that nearby troops had been "feted and toasted" while they had been "neglected," indeed "positively maltreated," by the home front. "Let the New York women remember these boys," he told his brother. "If they continue to be badly used, they will discourage other of their fellows from adventuring in the cause of their country." In a similar vein, a volunteer working at the Volunteer Refreshment Saloon worried about a regiment of farmers' sons "who had had a considerable amount of moral training at home." Fearing these men would become "dispirited," if they believed "no one cared for them except as food for powder," he justified his own work as a means of demonstrating "that they were the cherished soldiers of the nation."[56] In a period when men represented their

---

54 Nudelman makes a similar point (*John Brown's Body*, 117).

55 Reed, *Hospital Life*, 73; Reynolds, "Fortnight with the Sanitary," 247.

56 John Hancock Douglas to "My Dear Brother," July 28, 1861, John Hancock Douglas Collection, Library of Congress, Manuscript Division, Washington D.C.; S. B. Fales quoted in Goodrich, *Tribute Book*, 419.

families in every sense—legally, socially, and politically—no one doubted that a lack of homefront support could have devastating implications for soldiers' morale.

The threat that divided families posed to the social order also greatly concerned middle-class volunteers. Never far from USSC leaders' minds was a lurking fear that alienated soldiers and their impoverished kin could become a rebellious mob. One of their first orders of business was thus to ensure that troops maintained financial links with the home front. For months they tossed around proposals to garnishee soldiers' wages on behalf of families, informing the secretary of war that they stood ready to act as a trustee to collect and allot men's pay (an offer ultimately declined as impractical).[57] Troops should be encouraged "in every possible way" to send home half to three-quarters of their army wages, they went on to warn the government, for ensuring a soldier's "continuing relation with his family" would preserve his "moral tone," keeping him from "the vices of camp, and from becoming a mere mercenary man-at-arms." Equally important, the government had to ensure timely payment of wages, lest soldiers' families become dependent on charity. "There is the danger of a great pauper class being thus created, especially in our large cities," cautioned one USSC report.[58] With an eye on the war's potential effects on social cohesion and class relations, voluntary organizations set out to strengthen Northern families and reinforce soldiers' domestic ties.

Middle-class women had their own stake in encouraging emotional links with the army. Most saw it as their responsibility to promote morality and work for men's salvation. Their claim to moral superiority rested on fulfilling this responsibility. The war offered an extended test of whether women's influence could reach beyond the confines of the home at a time of national crisis. Every story of a man saved from temptation by women's donations, and every tale of a cheerful sufferer whose moral fortitude triumphed over injury, demonstrated men's susceptibility to women's influence and affirmed the durability of domestic bonds. Encouraging soldiers to keep home at the forefront of their minds, women upheld their roles as moral guardians and confirmed the importance of the domestic sphere over which they presided.

Voluntary organizations quickly intuited that the best way to attract women's support was to emphasize their ability to nourish emotional attachments between soldiers and civilians. The Christian Commission was particularly

---

57 The USSC Standing Committee's Minutes from June through September 1861, contained in USSC Records, Series 32, Box 971, reveal constant discussions of this issue, with Olmsted favoring an allotment system whereby families would be authorized to draw on soldiers' pay. See also Maxwell, *Lincoln's Fifth Wheel*, 46–48.

---

58 Olmsted, "Report to the Secretary of War," 30–32.

masterful on this score. Its first public statement described the "gratuitous personal labor" of religious agents as a conduit through which "small packages of clothing, books, and medicines can be forwarded, and momentoes of social affection can be interchanged."[59] Identifying voluntary contributions as intimate gifts embodying home-front affection, it promised to act as a direct channel to soldiers, implicitly contrasting its small-scale, idiosyncratic distribution methods with the USSC's more remote and orderly system.[60]

Capitalizing on public anxiety with army life's corrupting influence, the Christian Commission also promoted itself as a way for civilians to exert moral guardianship over soldiers. To encourage religiosity in the ranks, the organization promised to circulate religious literature in camp; to create "religious associations" in each regiment; and to put "such associations in correspondence with the Christian public." True to its word, Christian Commission agents deluged troops with religious material and instruction. In 1864 alone, they distributed roughly one and a half million Bibles, almost the same number of hymn and psalm books, eight million "knapsack books" containing prayers and scripture, eighteen million religious newspapers, and over thirty-nine million pages of tracts. Fanning out across the war zone, agents conducted religious services and prayer meetings, many of which took place in the spacious Christian Commission chapels donated to many regiments by war's end.[61] The organization's publicity invariably imagined soldiers who were eager, even desperate, for such personal attention. Asserting the importance of individual ministry, they depicted young men surrounded by temptations, standing on the precipice of sin with nothing to stop them falling but the warm hand of the Christian Commission agent, extended in earnest sympathy.[62] To a home front keen to keep a watchful eye on the army, this message reassured that oversight was possible and that soldiers welcomed the effort.

Seeking to bolster this reassurance, voluntary organizations constantly reminding troops that they would one day return to civilian lives. "You are not regular soldiers; this is not your trade,"

---

59 "Address," January 13, 1862, reprinted in Moss, *Annals of the Christian Commission*, 111.
60 Quoted in Maxwell, *Lincoln's Fifth Wheel*, 192–93. In fact, the Christian Commission sometimes represented its work as the very antithesis of orderly processes, claiming that its central office kept no record of expenditures, being too busy in the work of actual distribution.

61 "Address," reprinted in Moss, *Annals of the Christian Commission*, 111; Moss, *Annals of the Christian Commission*, 729, 181. The USCC supplied canvas roofs and stoves for the construction of these chapels, which went to any regiment that had agreed to construct the necessary log walls.
62 Material of this nature can be found in the five scrapbooks containing annual reports, circulars, printed documents, and newspaper articles relating to the USCC contained in "Records Relating to the United States Christian Commission, 1861–1866," RG 94, Records of the Adjutant General's Office, National Archives and Records Administration, Washington, D.C.

reminded one tract addressed from "The Home to the Camp," by the American Unitarian Association. Assuring men that they were central to family life, this tract pictured time on the home front suspended as loving kin held their breath waiting for soldiers' return:

> We gather at our meals, or around the evening table, and your place is vacant.... There are great gaps in our hearts and our homes, which cannot be closed because of you.... The old places are kept open and warm for you. You are only absent, and we wait and watch; daily and nightly we pray for you.[63]

Working to strengthen men's emotional attachments to former lives at every turn, voluntary organizations rarely missed an opportunity to lend poignancy to their work, as did the Christian Commission when sending to the army tens of thousands of "comfort-bags" constructed by children's Sunday school classes and containing cheerful notes written in juvenile hands, along with articles for mending clothes and writing letters.[64]

Individual volunteers just as eagerly framed their message in ways designed to recall soldiers' memories of home and prepare them for a return to domestic life. Notes attached to women's offerings underscored the emotions behind their gifts, appealing for reciprocity. In a note pinned to her contribution, one volunteer wrote: "My son is in the army. Whoever is made warm by this quilt ... let him remember his own mother's love." Another popular message slipped into hand-made socks evoked an image of domesticity restored:

Brave sentry, on your lonely beat,
May these blue stockings warm your feet,
And when from wars and camps you part,
May some fair knitter warm your heart.[65]

Just as often women drew attention to their own losses in their notes, merging soldiers and civilians together in sympathetic communion. Troops received articles with labels such as: "A pillow and sheet on which my wounded son was brought home from Cross Lanes," or "Three pairs of socks, sent home in the knapsack of a dear brother who fell at Antietam." Others reminded men of women's exertions on their behalf: "This blanket was carried by Milly Aldrich, who is ninety-three years old, down hill and up hill, one and a half miles, to be given to some soldier," explained one message.[66]

Alternatively, there were more insistent urgings for soldiers to recall former

---

63   John F. W. Ware, "The Home to the Camp: Addressed to the Soldiers of the Union," Army Series No. 3, *Tracts of the American Unitarian Association* (Boston: American Unitarian Association [1861], repr. 1865), 1.

64   Moss, *Annals of the Christian Commission*, 651.

65   Goodrich, *Tribute Book*, 153.

66   [Brayton and Terry], *Our Acre and Its Harvest*, 63.

lives, as was the case with the volunteer who stitched a poem into the front of a hospital shirt, headed "To the Boy Who Don't Drink, Lie, or Steal":

Soldier, brave, will it brighten the day,
And shorten the march on the weary way, To know that at home the loving and true Are knitting and sewing and praying for you?
Soft are the voices when speaking your name;
Proud is their glory when hearing your fame;
And the gladdest hours of their lives will be
When they greet you after the victory.[67]

Emphasizing that the home front remained "loving and true," this woman offered domestic support as a reward for men of principled conduct. Like all the notes sent to soldiers, she designed hers to elicit their emotions. Using a sentimental image of women so devoted they thought only of men's return, so emotionally burdened they could only whisper loved ones' names; she personalized her offering in an effort to awaken soldiers' better natures.

To focus soldiers' attention on the affection embodied in their goods, volunteers used a range of additional methods. Some stitched their own names onto clothing or bedding. Others helped to construct "album quilts," consisting of patchwork squares made from the scraps of women's dresses, often adorned with the donor's name or "a patriotic sentiment or cheering

couplet." Recognizing civilians' desire to personalize their goods, one enterprising Vermont surgeon informed residents of that state that anyone fitting out a hospital bed could have his or her name inscribed on the bedstead, while hospital wards would be renamed after towns or counties that donated at least three dozen beds.[68] It was not enough for many volunteers simply to donate goods; they wanted to mark those goods as the product of a particular individual or township's care and affection to symbolize the emotion behind efforts to minister to the troops.[69]

Voluntary organizations were well aware that donors wanted evidence of their goods affecting soldiers. Their promotional literature tapped into this desire by repeating stories of men powerfully reminded of families on receiving even the smallest token from home. One voluntary worker appealed for donations by describing troops' reactions to the handmade gingerbread she was distributing, which "always brought the gushing tears and was, without fail, just like wife or mother's."[70] Equally common were tales of men astonished to discover that seemingly anonymous

---

67 M. A. Newcomb, *Four Years of Personal Reminiscences of the War* (Chicago: H. S. Mills and Co., 1893), 101.

68 [Brayton and Terry], *Our Acre and Its Harvest*, 61–62; circular headed "To the Ladies of Vermont," January 5, 1863, by Ed E. Phelps, Surg. U.S.V. Surgeon in Charles and Medical Director for Vermont, newspaper clipping contained in New England Women's Auxiliary Association Records.

69 Richardson, *Busy Hands*, 109–15, makes a similar point.

70 [Hoge], "Address Delivered by Mrs. Hoge."

goods had, in fact, come straight from their families. Sanitary Commission official Alfred Bloor related one such incident in which a soldier uttered "quite a shriek of delight" upon being given a new handkerchief, exclaiming that it had been embroidered by the ladies' aid society in his hometown and was almost certainly the work of his sister.[71] Imagining a nation that retained its intimate connections despite the great distances separating men from their families, tales like these allowed the Sanitary Commission to downplay their anonymous methods, while offering donors a chance to imagine their goods going straight to friends in the army.

Occasional stories about miraculous coincidences only went so far in convincing donors that their goods had affected men. Seeking more concrete evidence of soldiers' appreciation, women often slipped notes into the goods they sent to the army in hopes of making a personal connection with recipients. After writing such a note, one woman was overjoyed at receiving a response from the soldier who now wore her hand-knitted socks. "It will be one of the oasis of my life, that letter of yours," she confided, "for it will remind me that I am doing a little."[72] Obviously this woman had an interest in seeing that her donation reached a worthy beneficiary in light of the many

allegations of goods being misused. Yet, her fervid language—which not only depicted a thank you note as "the oasis of my life," but went on to discuss her devotion to soldiers and her longing to help them—implies that something more was at stake than a simple assurance that a package had reached its goal. The soldier who answered her letter not only confirmed the receipt of goods, he testified that an emotional exchange had taken place, one that he cared enough about to write to a stranger. For countless volunteers, imagined or actual emotional exchanges like this one were the currency that rewarded them for their efforts.

Given that hospital work was one of the most visible ways that women demonstrated devotion to the troops, nursing offered critical evidence of their ability to influence men emotionally. Most middle-class nurses structured hospital relationships along domestic lines, imagining themselves as maternal surrogates caring for affectionate boys. This allowed them to verify the importance of domesticity, while also presenting their relationship with male patients as familial, and thus asexual. At the same time, middle-class nurses could disassociate their work from wage labor by linking it to the domestic sphere, supposedly a realm of pure emotion, free from the taint of commerce. Just as important, in depicting their hospital

---

71 Bloor, *Letters from the Army of the Potomac*, 51. See also [Brayton and Terry], *Our Acre and Its Harvest*, 61–62.

72 "Serg't Bancroft" to Rebecca F. Doane, September 19, 1864, Box 2, Knapp Papers.

work as a labor of love nurses gave their work meaning and value.[73]

Most women working in Civil War hospitals relied on patients for affirmation and support. Lacking professional training, they labored alongside sizable numbers of male officers who viewed them as intrusive or ineffectual. The only way they had to confirm their usefulness was through patients' responses. Nurses often said as much in their diaries and letters, as did one who told her sister: "I feel all the time of failure, of not coming up to the mark," later adding, "I think my poor men care for me."[74] For such women, the justification for their presence in hospitals lay in its emotional impact. Pointing to the healing power of feminine sympathy, they contrasted women's intuitive compassion and gentleness with the insensitivity bred by professionalism.[75] "Apothecary and medicine chest might be dispensed with," confidently asserted one nurse, "if an equal amount of genuine sympathy could be brought home to our stricken men."[76] Only men's acknowledgment of their abilities could support these claims about the healing power of women's ministrations.

The majority of enlisted men accepted nurses' attempts to create familial relationships and responded accordingly. In more than a hundred letters sent to nurse Sarah Ogden, her patients fondly reminisced about the care they received at her hospital on Broad and Cherry streets, Philadelphia. "I feel that I never can repay you for the kindness you showed towards me when I was suffering from my wounds down thare in my old Broad & Cherry home," wrote one soldier. Another noted, "often Due I think of the times that I had when I was in the city of Philadelphia it was just like a home to me."[77] These men both

---

73   Schultz, *Women at the Front*, chaps. 3–4.

74   Emily Elizabeth Parsons, *Memoir of Emily Elizabeth Parsons* (Boston: Little, Brown, 1880), reprinted as *Civil War Nursing* (New York: Garland Publishing, 1984). This memoir consists of letters sent to family members during the war (23, 89). Nina Bennett Smith also describes the way women nurses compensated for their lack of formal authority by advancing claims about women's right and duty to extend domestic care to soldiers (see the introduction to Smith's "The Women Who Went to the War: The Union Army Nurse in the Civil War," Ph.D. diss., Northwestern University, 1981).

75   Jane E. Schultz, "The Inhospitable Hospital: Gender and Professionalism in Civil War Medicine," *Signs* 17 (1992): 363–92, notes that women nurses' rejection of medical models of professionalism was not an indiscriminate protest against men in general. Allying themselves with enlisted men, women nurses instead criticized what they viewed as bureaucratic inhumanity and a detached professionalism that treated soldiers as "medical specimens." The aim of their critique was not to replace male authority, she argues, but to individualize patient care. On official resistance to women nurses and the hostile relationships that sometimes developed between them and medical men, see also Leonard, *Yankee Women*, chap. 1; Smith, "Women Who Went to the War," chap. 3; and Ann Douglas Wood, "The War Within a War: Women Nurses in the Union Army," *Civil War History* 18 (1972): 206–7.

76   Quoted in John R. Brumgardt, ed., *The Diary and Letters of Hannah Ropes* (Knoxville: University of Tennessee Press, 1980), 71.

77   Egbert Sinsabaugh to Sarah Ogden, April 6, 1864, and Christopher Keslar to "Respected Friend," February 16, 1864, Sarah Ogden Papers,

acknowledged and endorsed Ogden's attempts to create "a home." She loaned patients money, helped them obtain furloughs, and exchanged correspondence that, in a few instances, lasted through the war. Men responded by writing to Ogden, imploring her to visit their families, or making plans to call on her in the future.[78] "Home" for these soldiers and their nurses was not so much a physical space as a set of relationships based on emotional reciprocity.

There were a number of practical incentives for the sick and wounded to accept women nurses as maternal surrogates. Most men understood that gaining nurses' regard earned them added attention and sometimes extra food. "Visited my pet patients in the evening," wrote one nurse in her diary, adding later: "Played dominoes with two of my pet boys, after giving a number of them a nice relish at supper of dried beef and a can of ... cherries."[79] Such attentions were no small matter for men languishing in hospital for months on end with few distractions and a bland diet. Just as important, patients sought emotional relationships with nurses because they recognized that these women were

some of their most ardent supporters. Whereas army physicians tended to treat patients as "medical specimens," explains scholar Jane Schultz, nurses worked to "individualise suffering," remembering men's names, noting their personal details, and recording their dietary preferences. Sometimes they circumvented hospital rules in order to ally themselves with enlistees, such as by sneaking food to men against doctors' orders, or lavishing affection on those surgeons had given up for dead. Given that soldiers often felt themselves to be victims of insensitive doctors or bureaucratic red tape, Schultz argues, women nurses and their patients possessed "a solidarity born of a shared sense of oppression."[80] Picturing their modesty as opposed to physicians' conceit, their disinterestedness contrasting with men's selfish political and professional ambitions, nurses figured their presence as a vital corrective to a sometimes corrupt and arbitrary medical system.

Reinforcing their efforts at creating emotional relationships with their patients, women worked to make hospitals as homelike as possible. In virtually every general hospital, volunteer nurses decorated their wards and provided a range of diversions for their patients. Describing a visit to one field hospital close to the front, a male aid worker noted that the nurses had cut pictures from magazines

---

GLC6559, Gilder Lehrman Institute (hereafter Ogden Papers).

78   See, for example, Ira P. Jones dated 1863 and Allen T. Richards to Sarah Ogden, February 5, 1864, James Chase to Sarah Ogden, January 24, 1863 and John Groaner to "Most noble & Kind Lady," October 15, 1862, Ogden Papers.

79   Stearns, *The Lady Nurse of Ward E*, 221, 227. This memoir consists of wartime diary entries and letters written by the author to her sisters.

80   Schultz, "Inhospitable Hospital," 378–80; Jane E. Schultz, " 'Are We Not All Soldiers?': Northern Women in the Civil War Hospital Service," *Prospects* 20 (1995): 45.

and pasted them to the walls. Using colored cloth, they also decorated all of the tent poles, as well as pinning sprigs of evergreen over each bed in order, he wrote, to add a "home-like feeling to the wards."[81] Similar scenes greeted the wounded in most of the hundreds of wards in which women labored. Some planted gardens and flowerbeds outside their windows, soliciting "delicacies" for their patients and organizing festivals or other activities for their amusement. In Rebecca Pomroy's ward at Columbian College Hospital in Washington, D.C., the bay windows were filled with plants, the walls were adorned with pictures and moral mottoes spelled out in foliage, and Pomroy's workbox lay in the center of the room, prominently displayed on a large table. Nurses at Hammond Hospital at Point Lookout, Maryland, similarly vied with each other in beautifying their work spaces: festooning them with cedar and holly wreathes; decorating furniture and walls; and creating artful arrangements of seaweed, pebbles, and shells collected from the nearby beach.[82]

Outside and around hospital wards, civilian volunteers also worked to erase the signs of war and remind men of home. Women planted gardens near the front lines to provide soldiers with fresh produce and to beautify the landscape.

They sent canvassing committees into towns and villages, exhorting local farmers and gardeners to lay a "soldier's acre." Always, they described these efforts as a powerful reminder of civilians' emotional attachments to their soldiers. Putting his finger on the purpose behind these decorative touches, one volunteer noted the way homelike images quickly reached the "tender spot" in soldiers, instantly driving away the influences of camp.[83]

Nurses were not the only ones working to domesticate the war zone. Civilian donors did what they could to mitigate the anonymity of Civil War medicine. Tens of thousands of sick and wounded soldiers spent long periods recuperating in general hospitals—typically large complexes of buildings that resembled small towns rather than private spaces. While nurses personalized their wards, volunteers furnished equipment and funds to recall patients to civilian lives and past times. At the Armory Square Hospital in Washington, D.C., they appointed and staffed a library, a reading room, and a business college that trained soldiers for clerical work. Next, they raised money for a new hospital chapel where patients gathered for religious services, temperance meetings, and social events, or listened to local

81   Reed, *Hospital Life*, 95, 120. On these efforts, see also Richardson, *Busy Hands*, 246–50.

82   Mrs. H. [Anna Morris Holstein], *Three Years in Field Hospitals of the Army of the Potomac*, 30–31; Smith, "The Women Who Went to the War", 58; *Hammond Gazette* (Point Lookout, Md.), March 13, 1863.

83   [Brayton and Terry], *Our Acre and Its Harvest*, 122–24; Newberry, *USSC in the Valley of the Mississippi*, 314–22; Reed, *Hospital Life*, 153.

women serenade them.[84] Most general hospitals were equally well appointed, few going without lecture halls, libraries, reading rooms, night schools, bowling alleys, landscaped gardens, or other improvements, paid for by volunteers determined in their quest to remind soldiers of homefront solicitude.

From the perspective of hospitalized men, one of the most important reminders of home lay in the food that civilians provided. Swapping bland hospital diets for "home-cooked" meals, volunteers set up "specialized diet kitchens" to prepare a range of menus for men suffering particular ailments. This initiative eventually received endorsement from the War Department, with Christian Commission agent Annie Wittenmyer directing its implementation.[85] By 1864 she had appointed 157 "lady managers" who consulted with surgeons to determine the dietary preferences of men in approximately sixty of the military's general hospitals. Evidencing the way women aimed to individualize patient care and imbue spartan hospital surrounds with

a measure of domestic comfort, one Christian Commission agent described the work as a way of bringing "to the bedside of every patient, in home-like preparation, such delicate food as might be prescribed." Activities like these demonstrated women's indisputable right "to the sphere which includes housekeeping, cooking and nursing," argued fellow aid worker Jane Hoge. Even in hospitals well managed by men there was "the same lack of homelike air, and indefinable tone of domestic comfort, that is seen in bachelors' mansions, no matter how lordly," she argued, going on to note: "A comfortable, home-like meal, after thorough ablution, had a magical effect," which "in many instances ... effected a cure."[86] Such comments suggest women's stake in domesticating military life. Men might be able to build the hospitals and shoulder the guns, but only women could create a home with its "magical" ability to comfort and cure. As volunteers like Hoge repeated throughout the war, the only way to limit militarism's corrupting potential was by extending women's domestic influence throughout the army.

Middle-class voluntary workers were not only interested in using feminine influence as a counterbalance to the roughness of army life, they also sought to model a properly ordered domesticity for the mass of ordinary enlistees. As soon as a man entered the Soldiers' Depot in New York, for instance, he was

---

84 *Armory Square Hospital Gazette* (Washington, D.C.), March 26, April 2 and 16, and May 7, 1864.

85 Moss, *Annals of the Christian Commission*, 663–70. Wittenmyer initially worked as a sanitary agent for the state of Iowa and president of the Keokuk Soldiers' Aid Society, but she resigned these positions in 1863 to work for the Christian Commission after a series of battles with the male-dominated Iowa State Sanitary Commission. See Leonard, *Yankee Women*, chap. 2; and Noah Zaring, "Competition in Benevolence: Civil War Soldiers' Aid in Iowa," *Iowa Heritage Illustrated* 77 (1996): 10–23.

86 Moss, *Annals of the Christian Commission*, 666; Hoge, *Boys in Blue*, 111, 158.

required to take a bath, have his head cleansed, and change into a clean set of clothes. This was not an unreasonable demand given that body lice infected most soldiers. But the intent went beyond sanitary considerations. "The strict attention to cleanliness, combined with the neatness, order and discipline of the building," wrote the Depot superintendent, will awaken "a feeling of self-respect in the men." He clearly felt that many enlisted men could do with such a lesson. Sarah Woodbridge, one of the managers of the USSC's Hartford Soldiers' Rest in Connecticut, shared his belief. She hoped that her neat and tidy institution—with its warm fireplace and tables covered in fresh white linen—would have a salutary "moral influence" over all who entered.[87] Neither writer singled out working-class soldiers as the specific group they were trying to reach, but the tone of their reports—which emphasized teaching men the need for discipline, cleanliness, and order—suggests that they imagined their lessons benefiting those who presumably had no prior knowledge of a well-managed home life. Their writings leave a distinct impression that middle-class volunteers saw the war as an opportunity to reach out to masses of working-class men—to instruct them in the intrinsic worth of bourgeois domesticity and build

emotional connections that could demonstrate their worthy intent and fitness to act as men's moral guardians.

Casting themselves as parental substitutes, middle-class volunteers viewed it as their right to exert dominance over soldiers imagined as innocent children. When troops refused to exhibit the decorum these home-like spaces required, their managers' paternalism could easily shade into coercion. James Grimbs, a fourteen-year-old bugler, discovered this fact when he arrived at the Soldiers' Depot in New York in mid-1863 after receiving a discharge from the army. During a meeting with the superintendent, he mentioned that he had no friends in America and was thinking of using his remaining money to pay the fare back to his native Ireland. He then left for the evening in the company of an older male friend, entrusting his bags and most of this money to the Depot's staff. But when he returned the following day with his breath smelling strongly of alcohol, the superintendent refused to hand over his possessions. After Grimbs absconded again, the superintendent dispatched a police officer who tracked him to a "disreputable house," brought him back to the Depot, and forced him into bed. He was escorted straight to the harbor the next morning where the *Albert Gallatin* lay docked. Depot staff paid his fare home, changed the remainder of his money into British currency, and handed it over to the captain for safekeeping. The fact that Grimbs was underage probably added

---

87 "Report of the Board of Managers of the New York State Soldiers' Depot," 25; "Report of Hartford Soldiers' Rest," reprinted in Knapp, "Report for the Quarter Ending June 30, 1865," 24–25.

to this superintendent's heavy-handed paternalism. But it was also common for voluntary workers to pass judgments on soldiers' moral behavior or characters whatever their age, and to deny them assistance if they failed to measure up to invisible standards of respectability.[88]

Middle-class volunteers hoped their paternalism would result in a nation of morally virtuous men. Given their widespread belief in mother-love as the strongest and purest of feelings, capable of tapping into the goodness at the core of even the most depraved individual, it seemed obvious to them that reintroducing soldiers to homely environments held transformative power. At war's end they congratulated themselves on the success of their efforts. Union soldiers had not been corrupted, they proclaimed. Instead, they had emerged victorious and melted seamlessly back into civilian life. And the thanks for this outcome rested squarely with the emotional bonds that volunteers had established with soldiers throughout the war. As Thomas Gifford, secretary of the Citizens' Volunteer Hospital Association of Philadelphia, put it, his members had been motivated

by pure love for their soldier-patients: "*Love* was the beacon light that guided us," he explained in his final report. And in future years, young soldiers would remember a time when they had been saved "from death's yawning abyss through *Love's* instrumentality."[89] Applauding its membership in similar terms, the final report of the USSC's New England Women's Auxiliary Association asked rhetorically what women had done to aid the war effort. They had built a "great house, spreading far and wide, sheltering all ... stocked with everything that home can give," they answered. And wherever soldiers went, "in one form or other our love ... reach[ed] them."[90] Like most Northern voluntary workers, they emphasized not the efficiency of their work but its emotional impact on men and its unparalleled ability to extend domestic influence even in the midst of war.

***

In September 1862, having just crossed into Ohio after fighting in the South, Union enlistee William Garrett described the impact of female benevolence in a letter to his sister. Portraying himself as a man made callous by his time among a hostile population, he told of entering the Union "dirty ragged without shoes and broke down for want of sleep,"

---

88 "Report of the Board of Managers of the New York State Soldiers' Depot," 27– 28; Knapp, "Fifth Report Concerning the Aid and Comfort Given by the Sanitary Commission to Sick and Invalid Soldiers, October 1, 1863," no. 77, *Documents*, 2:8–9, for instance, discusses his vigilance in turning possible deserters over to military authorities. He also barred from USSC homes any soldier caught drinking and inquired into soldiers' characters before distributing emergency monies to fund their journeys home.

---

89 Third Annual Report, December 20, 1865, in *History and Annual Reports of the Citizens' Volunteer Hospital Association*.

90 S. G. Cary, "Thirty Third Report of the New England Women's Auxiliary Association," January 16, 1865, New England Women's Auxiliary Association Records, Massachusetts Historical Society, Boston.

wandering about town "not caring for any body," and expecting no one to care for him in return. "[W]hat do you think was the first remark I heard made," he asked. "[I]t was from a lady," exclaiming, "look at that poor soldier with no shoes I expect he was in the fight in Charlston." Further down the road, a "young lady" pressed him to accept a meal: "she invited me in and set me the best in town." Recounting the transformative effects of this sympathy, and identifying himself as a man susceptible to transformation and thus worthy of women's regard, he exclaimed: "I had to eat three times before I could get back on the boat. I felt ashamed of myself to think what I was started out for and then was treated by the ladies the way I was."[91] This was the impact women volunteers aimed for with their voluntarism: not simply to provide for men, but to convince them of an abiding attachment that would guarantee their moral transformation and eventual return to family life.

By gearing their voluntarism toward achieving such transformations, the mass of Northern volunteers believed they were performing vital political work. Only too well aware of the Union's fragility, they feared the war's potential to destabilize the social order, weaken soldiers' independence, and spread immorality. They imagined that by extending home care to the war zone, they had displayed the virtues of middle-class domesticity, helping to limit social conflict and offset the war's brutalizing impact on men. Convinced of the moral benefits of domesticity and mother love, they viewed even the simplest traces of home—a hand-sewn shirt, a piece of gingerbread, a comforting word—as a force that could immediately recall a man to an earlier state, no matter how dreadful his surroundings. Their emotions had acted as a "moral contagion" that spread throughout the Union armies, they believed, providing a bulwark against a fragmented and immoral society and guaranteeing a unity that was necessary both for victory and for a stable peace. Paying more than lip service to this belief, the majority of women volunteers structured their work around facilitating emotional exchanges with soldiers and reminding them that they would soon return to civilian life.

Arguably, the most important consequence of Civil War voluntarism on women's social activism lay in the conviction that women had, in fact, helped to save the nation by expanding their influence at a time of crisis. This belief led not in the direction of women's rights, but toward more militant efforts at moral suasion.

The Civil War produced no significant upsurge in support for female suffrage. Nor did it fundamentally alter beliefs about women's moral superiority.[92] In the immediate postwar era,

---

91 William Garrett to his sister, September 27, 1862, William Garrett Papers, HCWRC.

92 Attie suggests that the Civil War was "the first modern war in which masses of women participated with expectations that their home front

the majority of socially active women remained committed to religious-based volunteer work that emphasized the importance of their influence and example.[93] They joined voluntary groups like the Woman's Christian Temperance Union, an organization that differed from its antecedents in admitting only women members. Participating in militant crusades against the purveyors of alcohol, such women smashed open barrels of liquor and directly challenged publicans and their customers.[94] Taking seriously the belief that women could remake the social order, they set out on a new mission to transform men's behavior.

The Civil War would not be the last conflict in which women were honored in sentimental terms. But the tides had shifted by the twentieth century, significantly altering the way people conceived of home and female influence.[95] Consider, for instance, one of the most popular tunes of World War I, "Keep the Home Fires Burning," which urged women:

Keep the Home Fires burning,
While your hearts are yearning.
Though your lads are far away
They dream of home.

There's a silver lining
Through the dark clouds shining,
Turn the dark cloud inside out
'Til the boys come home.[96]

contributions would translate into expanded political rights" (*Patriotic Toil*, 46). Yet as Silber, in *Daughters of the Union*, 125, notes, this conflict hardly acted as a catalyst for feminism. Most of those active in the women's rights movement had staked out their positions prior to the war. And although a number of prominent women volunteers used their wartime experiences as a springboard to professional careers as social workers, they were in a tiny minority. Most female reformers in the 1860s and 1870s continued to view themselves as guardians of a domestic sphere that safeguarded society's most cherished values, rejecting suffrage as a threat to the division of public and private life. Yet activist women in these years also broke with the antebellum tradition of participating in male-led voluntary organizations, instead joining a wide variety of separatist groups dedicated to much more assertive attempts to bring the values of motherhood and domesticity into the public sphere, shifts highlighted in Sarah M. Evans, *Born for Liberty: A History of Women in America* (New York: Simon and Schuster, 1997), chap. 6.

93 The three organizations that held greatest appeal among women in the postwar years—the home and foreign missionary societies of the Protestant churches, the Woman's Christian Temperance Union, and the Young Women's Christian Association—were all explicitly religious, notes Anne Firor Scott in "Women's Voluntary Associations: From Charity to Reform," in *Lady Bountiful Revisited: Women, Philanthropy, and Power*, ed., Kathleen D. McCarthy (New Brunswick, N.J.: Rutgers University Press, 1990), 42.

94 The militancy that temperance women displayed in the postwar years had roots that lie in the 1850s, as detailed by Jed Dannenbaum in "The Origins of Temperance Activism and Militancy Among American Women," *Journal of Social History* 15 (Winter 1981): 235–52.

95 Rebecca Jo Plant, *Mom: The Transformation of Motherhood in Modern America* (Chicago: University of Chicago Press, 2010), deals at length with this transition.

96 "Keep the Home Fires Burning," arranged by British composer Ivor Novello with words by American poet Lena Guilbert Ford, was popular in both Britain and the United States during

This sentimental refrain appealed to women to act as soldiers' mainstay—to embody a home front that men were fighting to protect. But home by this time was no longer conceived as holding supreme power to influence men and ward off their corruption. A wide range of experts and specialized professions by the twentieth century now competed with women as guardians of social order and morality. And women themselves were no longer isolated from the formal political realm, given mass movements in favor of women's rights.

World War I, notes Barbara L. Tishler, in "One Hundred Percent Americanism and Music in Boston During World War I," *American Music* 4, no. 2 (Summer 1986). 164–76.

Most important, no matter how much conservative commentators implored women to set society's moral tone, the stakes were necessarily lower. For it was clear to all after the Union's victory that the republic was in no danger of collapse. This success ensured not just national unity, but a stronger, more organic nationalism that made the dissolution of the United States virtually inconceivable. In keeping the home fires burning, twentieth-century women sustained homefront morale. But their Civil War predecessors imagined themselves doing much more: saving men from becoming mercenaries, upholding social order, preserving the republic from disintegration, and extending their domestic influence far and wide.

DISCUSSION QUESTIONS

1. What does the author mean by "golden chords of love"?
2. When women "personalized" the goods they sent to the front, what exactly were they doing?
3. The USSC was the largest government operated volunteer organization during the Civil War. How have historians differed in their assessments of it?
4. According to the author, how were sentimental stories about women's roles in war zones used by the women themselves?
5. The author wishes to de-emphasize the role of male elites in the USSC. Why?
6. The US Christian Commission gained much support during the war. Why?
7. How did attitudes toward women change with the American Revolution? How did this change play out in the years between the Revolution and the Civil War?
8. Women working in Civil War hospitals relied on patients for affirmation and support. Why?

CHAPTER FIVE

Death at the Machine

Critiques of industrial capitalism in the fiction of labor activist Lizzy Holmes

BY RUTH PERCY

INTRODUCTION

Emma Goldman is possibly the most outrageous woman in US history. As an anarchist in the late nineteenth and early twentieth centuries, she not only preached against the evils of capitalism, but also condemned marriage as an oppression of women. She claimed that women and men had the right to love anyone they pleased, and as many as they pleased. She did not fight for the right of women to vote because voting was a sham. She once said in a speech, "If voting changed anything they'd make it illegal." For Goldman, voting, democracy, and wage labor simply perpetuated the same broken capitalist system. What all humans deserved was self-governing communities founded on cooperation and free love. Nothing less than that would do. Her many speaking tours were popular attractions simply because she was so outrageous and uncompromising.

FIGURE 5.1.
"Lizzie Holmes," https://commons.wikimedia.org/wiki/File:Lizzie_Holmes.jpg. Copyright in the Public Domain.

Perhaps Goldman's most outrageous act was her involvement in the plot to assassinate industrialist Henry Frick. She and her then-lover, Alexander Berkman, thought that by committing this so-called "propaganda by the deed" they would spark a nationwide revolution against the capitalist system. The assassination attempt failed, and there was no revolution. Goldman and Berkman, both immigrants from Russia, had not understood the mindset of the American worker, who wanted better wages and working conditions, not revolution. Berkman went to prison for a very long time, while Goldman's role in the crime remained hidden.

Goldman's other brush with violent insurrection came in 1901 when a would-be anarchist, inspired by her speeches, shot and killed President McKinley. Goldman then had the audacity to defend the assassin, thus alienating her from many of her own radical contemporaries. They didn't call her "Red Emma" for nothing.[1]

In contrast to Emma Goldman's story, Ruth Percy tells us of another radical woman who was a contemporary of Goldman. Lizzy Holmes knew Emma Goldman, and they were from the same radical anarchist movement. But Holmes's radical career was very different from Goldman's. By looking at Lizzy Holmes and her fictional stories that were published in the conservative *American Federationist*,

FIGURE 5.2.
Chicago Police Department, "Emma Goldman Mugshot," https://commons.wikimedia. org/wiki/File:Emma_ Goldman_-_mugshot_from_ Chicago,_Sept_10,_1901.jpeg. Copyright in the Public Domain.

Percy shows us another side of the story. While Emma Goldman was the woman who defined the radical labor movement at the beginning of the twentieth century, Lizzy Holmes provides us with a more nuanced look at the roles of women in the movement.

* * *

1   Vivian Gornick, *Emma Goldman: Revolution as a Way of Life* (New Haven, CT: Yale University Press, 2011).

Introduction

As the journal of the mainstream—and politically conservative—American Federation of Labor (AFL), the *American Federationist* provided its readers with a predictable mix of articles on trade union issues and disputes, reports on the fate of the organization's fortunes, and political editorials. From the time of its inaugural issue in March 1894, the journal served as a useful source of information and opinion for its members but, on a literary front, made for a dry read. However, between the late summer of 1901 and the spring of 1903, the *American Federationist* published a series of fictional stories penned by Lizzie M. Holmes, a radical journalist of anarchist and socialist background and a labor activist who had been involved in various campaigns to organize women workers in Chicago's heavily immigrant and multi-ethnic workforce.

Holmes's fictional stories stood out in the pages of the *American Federationist* for several reasons. In contrast to other labor journals (most notably those of the Knights of Labor, which by the late 1880s regularly included serialized fiction), the *American Federationist* very rarely published fictional stories.[2] The journal routinely published poems, but in the years before the appearance of Holmes's first story in 1901, only two fictional pieces had been published (in the first and fourth issues of the third volume in 1896), which were both written by newspaper owner–turned–unionist J. W. Sullivan. Because Holmes's pieces were short stories with melodramatic plots, they offered a sharp departure from the dry reportage and bread-and-butter unionism and instead connected to an earlier tradition of fiction in the labor press. Holmes further departed from the journal's usual content by including women protagonists. The stories' subjects included young working-class women and men broken by industrial capitalism and middle-class female reformers supporting their working-class "sisters" alongside enthusiastic and virile young male unionists.

Written when Holmes appears to have been in dire financial straits a decade after her involvement in Chicago's socialist and anarchist circles, the stories in the journal also stand out because her background did not make her a likely contributor. Indeed, she appears to

have been more suited to the anarchist and free-love press, and she continued to write for those journals after she accepted a contract from the *American Federationist*. Although generally described as a minor figure in the history of anarchist, socialist, and left-wing labor movements in the United States, Holmes played an important role in Chicago's radical scene.[3] Her association with the Hay-market martyrs and her defiance when delivering her testimony during the trial that followed the Haymarket

---

2 The Knights of Labor's *Journal of United Labor* included the odd story throughout the early 1880s. In July 1887, it adopted a new format and began to publish serialized stories in almost every issue. Interestingly, most of these stories were taken from other sources, many of them British publications.

3 Holmes has a marginal place in the historiography of the labor, socialist, and anarchist movements. Aside from Meredith Tax, Bruce C. Nelson, Carolyn Ashburgh, and Blaine McKinley, few scholars have paid any attention to her. The lack of any personal papers aside from those published may explain this, as does the ambiguous place she occupied between the socialist and anarchist movements and the mainstream, relatively conservative AFL. Meredith Tax, *The Rising of the Women: Feminist Solidarity and Class Conflict, 1880–1917* (1980; repr., Urbana: University of Illinois Press, 2001); Bruce C. Nelson, *Beyond the Martyrs: A Social History of Chicago's Anarchists, 1870–1900* (New Brunswick, NJ: Rutgers University Press, 1988); Blaine McKinley, "Free Love and Domesticity: Lizzie M. Holmes, *Hagar Lyndon* (1893), and the Anarchist-Feminist Imagination," *Journal of American Culture* 13, no. 1 (1990): 55–62; Carolyn Ashbaugh, *Lucy Parsons: American Revolutionary* (Chicago: Charles H. Kerr, 1976). Margaret S. Marsh mentions her very briefly in relation to the aftermath of the Haymarket bombing: Marsh, *Anarchist Women, 1870–1920* (Philadelphia: Temple University Press, 1981), 109–10. Roseanne Currarino analyzes one of Holmes's stories, "Economy That Proved Disastrous," in "The Politics of 'More': The Labor Question and the Idea of Economic Liberty in Industrial America," *Journal of American History* 93, no. 1 (2006): 27–30.

massacre made her a notorious figure, particularly within the antiradical milieu of the AFL.

That the fiction of a radical female activist should appear at all in the organ of the mainstream American labor movement makes these stories notable, both then and now. In addition, Holmes had lived and worked within the multiethnic world of Chicago anarchists, socialists, and immigrant workers, yet her fictional characters, both male and female, were exclusively white Anglo Americans. The inconsistencies among Holmes's fiction, her personal history, and the standard fare of the *American Federationist* suggest the stories require some further scrutiny. How best can we read these stories? What can we learn from them? These stories seem to represent a line of continuity with an earlier labor movement, that of the Knights of Labor, which began regularly publishing serialized fiction in an attempt to increase its membership; the AFL followed suit eleven years later.[4] As such, the presence of fiction in these journals suggests that labor culture was heavily influenced by the popularity of melodramatic dime novels that characterized turn-of-the-century working-class culture.[5] In addition, and of more interest to the readers of *Labor*, these stories demonstrate the complexity of an individual's participation in the labor movement. Recent feminist labor history examining labor journalists and writings has done much to point out the complex, rather than linear, relationship between a subject's radical or labor politics and her journalistic or literary production.[6] In this article, I argue that Holmes's life and writings for the *American Federationist* show us a transient and flexible labor activist who at times adapted her work to suit her audience out of economic necessity.

As a work in labor history, this article aims to bring more attention not only to the short fiction of an understudied U.S.

---

4 Robert E. Weir, *Beyond Labor's Veil: The Culture of the Knights of Labor* (University Park: Pennsylvania State University Press, 1996), 195.
5 Michael Denning, *Mechanic Accents: Dime Novels and Working-Class Culture in America* (London: Verso, 1987).

6 See, for example, Robert Ventresca and Franca Iacovetta, "Vigilia D'Andrea: The Politics of Protest and the Poetry of Exile," in *Women, Gender, and Transnational Lives: Italian Workers of the World*, ed. Donna Gabaccia and Franca Iacovetta (Toronto: University of Toronto Press, 2002), 299–326; Elizabeth Faue, *Writing the Wrongs: Eva Valesh and the Rise of Labor Journalism* (Ithaca, NY: Cornell University Press, 2002). See also Barbara Foley, *Radical Representations: Politics and Form in U.S. Proletarian Fiction, 1929–1941* (Durham, NC: Duke University Press, 1993); Constance Coiner, *Better Red: The Writing and Resistance of Tillie Olsen and Meridel Le Sueur* (Oxford: Oxford University Press, 1995); Mara Faulkner, *Protest and Possibility in the Writing of Tillie Olsen* (Charlottesville: University of Virginia Press, 1993). Thanks go to Jeff Bowersox for drawing my attention to and translating sections from Lora Wildenthal, "Mass-Marketing Colonialism and Nationalism: The Career of Else Frobenius in the 'Weimarer Republik' and Nazi Germany," in *Nation, Politik, und Geschlecht: Frauenbewegungen und Nationalismus in der Moderne*, ed. Ute Planert (Frankfurt, Germany: Campus Verlag, 2000), 328–45.

female labor activist but also to journals such as the *American Federationist* as archives of labor writing worthy of greater attention. Unlike the articles written by committed AFL members, Holmes's fiction opens the door to a range of questions concerning radical individuals' relationships with this organization. By considering Holmes in this context and situating her work in the *American Federationist* as a part of a longer trajectory of labor activism, I seek to understand the appeal of the AFL publication to a radical writer.

Holmes was one of many who came of age within the Knights of Labor, a labor federation with a much broader and more flexible agenda than the AFL.[7] The Knights attempted to organize a wide range of workers regardless of skill, race, or gender. Moreover, conservatives, moderates, and radicals coexisted within the Knights, united by republican ideals.[8] In contrast, the remit of the AFL at the turn of the twentieth century was narrow and politically conservative, privileging white, American-born, skilled, male workers and rejecting calls for an outright end to the wage system. Nevertheless, by the end of the nineteenth century, the AFL had usurped the Knights' position as the premier labor organization in the United States, and its status no doubt attracted radical activists. Although they may not have been sympathetic to AFL president Samuel Gompers's "pure and simple" unionism, radicals and former radicals such as Holmes came into the AFL from a background in which diversity of opinion was the norm.[9]

Despite her active role in the labor movement over a number of decades, Holmes has not received enough attention from labor scholars. By taking her seriously as a writer, rather than as a minor figure in a larger political narrative, I also suggest the value of approaching labor texts with an awareness that labor writers could cover a broad range of political positions. In this respect, Holmes's representations of gender dynamics within the labor movement are particularly interesting. Although she had herself worked to organize Chicago's working women, none of her characters were female working-class labor activists; the working-class heroes of the labor movement are all male. Yet, when placed within her larger oeuvre, this disparity

---

7 On the Knights of Labor, see, for example, Susan B. Levine, *Labor's True Woman: Carpet Weavers, Industrialization, and Labor Reform in the Gilded Age* (Philadelphia: Temple University Press, 1984); Leon Fink, *Workingmen's Democracy: The Knights of Labor and American Politics* (Urbana: University of Illinois Press, 1983); Kim Voss, *The Making of American Exceptionalism: The Knights of Labor and Class Formation in the Nineteenth Century* (Ithaca, NY: Cornell University Press, 1993); Weir, *Beyond Labor's Veil*; Robert E. Weir, *Knights Unhorsed: Internal Conflict in a Gilded Age Social Movement* (Detroit: Wayne State University Press, 2000).

8 Voss, *The Making of American Exceptionalism*, 80.

9 On "pure and simple" unionism, see Julia Greene, *Pure and Simple Politics: The American Federation of Labor and Political Activism, 1881–1917* (Cambridge: Cambridge University Press: 1998).

seems less surprising. Holmes's activism and contribution to publications that spanned the political spectrum indicate that she moved between and through a number of different organizations, some of which appear in opposition with one another.

Thus, as the starting point for discussion, I discuss the questions raised at the outset about the curious fact of a radical female activist writing fictional stories for the publication of an organization whose president was virulently antiradical. From there, I consider the messages Holmes communicated via these stories and suggest the benefit of detaching individual activists from static categories and considering how individuals move among categories over their lifetimes.

The Stories

In one way or another, the eight stories that Holmes wrote for the *American Federationist* all depict workers' struggles in early-twentieth-century America. Five of them have main characters who suffered at the hands of industrial capitalism: one character dies and four others escape in various ways. In "Only an Industrial Outcast," Phillip Morland loses his job and cannot find other industrial employment because the subdivision of the work process has left him trained to do just one specific job. He resorts to tramping around the countryside before finding salvation in agricultural labor. In "Two Types of Wasted Lives," Frank Kirby enters the workforce as a boy and ends up losing his life to a machine. Holmes introduces her first female protagonist, Ellen Worth, in "Economy That Proved Disastrous." Ellen leaves her hometown after the local factory owner's campaign for thriftiness destroys all pleasurable pursuits. In "Not by Bread Alone," Holmes presents Alice Casey, a young woman physically and emotionally weakened by sewing at home. A socialite provides her escape by enlisting her as a companion. "The Path One Treads" juxtaposes two working girls as they grow into adulthood. While Myrtle Desmond finds escape in marriage, Jennie Dean continues to work and becomes tired, lonely, and dreary as a result. In each of these stories, Holmes depicts an industrial system that weakens both men and women.

The remaining three tales feature labor activists, two men and one woman, as main characters. Holmes's first and only female activist, a middle-class woman named Helen Estes who is committed to the labor movement, is the protagonist of "Her Life for Labor." Through this character, Holmes exposes the dangers of greed and the virtue of those who work for the labor movement. "Judge Newcomb's Retribution" has the first male union activist, Seth Cooper, a strong and charismatic unionist whose characteristics Holmes reproduces with John Lawrence in "Her Birthday Gift"; in both stories, the heroes' arguments win over upper-class women. These last three stories all champion the labor movement via attractive young organizers.

The Life of a Radical Woman

Lizzie Mary Hunt was born in Iowa on December 21, 1850. She spent most of her childhood in Ohio, moving there with her family by the time she was four.[10] Having received a relatively advanced education, she began to teach in a one-room schoolhouse at the age of fifteen. She continued to earn a living as a teacher even after she married Hiram J. Swank in 1867 and gave birth to a son the following year and a daughter five years after that.[11] Holmes later claimed that her husband died five years after they were married, but census records do not confirm that.[12] Life as a rural wife, mother, and schoolteacher did not necessarily lend itself to labor activism. Instead, it was the dramatic and widely reported events of the 1877 railroad strike that served as her transition.

The strike introduced her to the "labor question," and Swank (as she was called until November 26, 1885, when she married William Holmes[13]) soon "longed to know more of the people set off as belonging to a caste"—the working classes.[14] Two years later, she and her sister departed from their rural upbringings and ventured to Chicago where they found work in a cloak factory.[15] In addition to a "desire to know these people [the working classes] intimately," her inability to find work as a music teacher "in a city full of musical professors" motivated this employment decision and set her on a path to radical politics.

Over the next two years, Swank "passed through every phase of a struggling sewing woman's existence."[16] She worked in factories and sweatshops; sewed children's dresses, buttonholes, and linen coats; and earned as little as $3 a week. In her own words, during these years she learned "all the struggles, the efforts of genteel poverty, the pitiful pride with which working girls hide their destitution and drudgery from the world."[17] Two decades later, she drew upon these experiences to write her stories for the *American Federationist*. It is not surprising that the trade she

---

10   FamilySearch, "FamilySearch Record," www.familysearch.org/Eng/Search/AF/family_group_record.asp?familyid=5812647 (accessed March 19, 2005); Lizzie Swank Holmes quoted in "Work of the Sex," *Chicago Times*, September 2, 1894. I am indebted to Bettina Bradbury for pursuing Holmes through genealogical records for me.

11   "Work of the Sex."

12   FamilySearch, "Family Search Record," www.familysearch.org/Eng/Search/AF/family_group_record.asp?familyid=6522173 (accessed March 19, 2005); "Work of the Sex."

13   Lizzie Mae Holmes, "Transcript of Witness Testimony: Lizzie Mae Holmes, Former Assistant Editor of the *Alarm*, Witness for the Defense," *People for the State of Illinois vs. August Spies et al.* (August 6, 1886), vol. M, 280–307, 28 p., Chicago History Museum, www.chicagohistory.org/hadc/transcript/volumem/251–300/M280–307.htm (accessed February 20, 2007).

14   "Work of the Sex."

15   Ibid.; FamilySearch, "Family Search Record," www.familysearch.org/Eng/Search/AF/family_group_record.asp?familyid=6522173 (accessed March 19, 2005).

16   "Work of the Sex."

17   Ibid.

described in the greatest detail in these tales was the garment trade.

In an interview with the *Chicago Times* in 1894, Holmes told the reporter that after just five years of marriage her husband had died, meaning that she went to Chicago a widow, but census records do not confirm this. In addition, Holmes failed to mention that her mother, two brothers, and her seven-year-old daughter, but not her twelve-year-old son, either accompanied her and her sister to Chicago or followed soon after. The 1880 census reports that Swank lived in a house in which her mother, then aged fifty-four, was the head of the household. The household consisted of Swank and her sister, who both worked in the garment industry, her two brothers, two lodgers who worked for the telephone company, and Swank's daughter, who was at school. Contrary to what she told the *Chicago Times* reporter, the census listed Swank as still married, although her husband was not living in the same house.[18] It also listed her mother as widowed, although it appears from other records that Swank's father died in Ohio in 1900. It appears that she either separated from or lived a life independent of her husband in which her mother acted as matriarch and that she later constructed a public persona that did not concur with the historical record. Perhaps her mother's influence

also led her to journalism, as both her mother and sister wrote for *Lucifer: The Light Bearer*, Moses Harman's radical paper.[19]

Her work in the garment industry led Swank into the labor movement. In the early 1880s, after a year in Chicago, Swank joined the Working Women's Union (WWU), which was recently established by the Socialist Labor Party. The WWU struggled to organize wage-earning women, many of whom felt that other trade unions were not places for "nice girls," and campaigned for the eight-hour day.[20] Holmes was an active member; she was even fired for trying to organize her coworkers, a common occurrence among the city's trade union activists. Undeterred, she spoke regularly at WWU meetings and within a year became its secretary.[21] The WWU became Labor Local Assembly No. 1789 of the Knights of Labor in 1881, and the Knights thus framed Holmes's activism in the years that followed.[22]

Women played a prominent role among the Chicago Knights. Susan Levine and Robert Weir have pointed out that although many retained the image of domestic womanhood as the ideal, their commitment to unskilled

18 Census information found on www.familysearch.org: FamilySearch, "Census Records," www.familysearch.org/Eng/Search/frameset_search.asp?PAGE=census/search_census.asp (accessed July 21, 2005).

19 Carolyn Ashbaugh, "Women in the Haymarket Event," www.lucyparsonsproject.org/aboutlucy/ashbaugh_wmn_in_haymarket.html (accessed July 21, 2005).

20 Lizzie M. Swank Holmes, "Women Workers of Chicago," *American Federationist*, August 1905, 508; Tax, *The Rising of the Women*, 46.

21 "Work of the Sex."

22 Tax, *The Rising of Women*, 46, 51.

workers and their support for equal pay for equal work and for women's suffrage made the Knights particularly attractive to women.[23] By 1886, women activists in Chicago had organized three Knights of Labor assemblies to represent the garment industry.[24] In addition, Elizabeth Rogers, one of the founders of the WWU, became the first female master workman of a district assembly in 1887 and was well respected by both male and female Knights.[25] Via the WWU, Swank thus joined the company of a number of dedicated female labor activists, many of whom were also active in political organizations. This involvement in a range of different organizations—moderate and radical, labor and political—introduced Swank to a style of activism in which an individual's fluidity and flexibility were respected.

Along with Elizabeth Rogers, Swank met Lucy Parsons and Alzina Stevens among the WWU members. These women combined their activism in the Knights with political activism, and they introduced Holmes to socialism.[26] Swank found the socialist critique of the capitalist system, which guided the

WWU activists, to be appealing, and she too became involved in other groups, the most important of which was the American group of the International Working People's Association (IWPA).[27] Like the Knights of Labor but unlike many contemporary radical political organizations, it had a relatively inclusive approach to women, although the leaders were men.[28]

Swank was one of only 15 to 20 female members of the 175-member American group (comprising 8 to 11 percent of the membership), but these women played a far more important role than their numbers suggest.[29] Lucy Parson's biographer Carolyn Ashbaugh argues that Parsons, Swank, and other women who were active in the IWPA played a central role in the protests it organized, and they regularly published articles advocating their politics.[30] Playing on contemporary gendered language and assumptions, historian Bruce

---

23 Susan Levine, "Labor's True Woman: Domesticity and Equal Rights in the Knights of Labor," *Journal of American History* 70, no. 2 (1983): 325; Levine, *Labor's True Woman*; Weir, *Knights Unhorsed*.

24 Carolyn David McCreesh, *Women in the Campaign to Organize Garment Workers 1880–1917* (New York: Garland Publishing, 1985), 29–30.

25 "Our Women," *Journal of United Labor* (January 8, 1887): 2247.

26 Nelson, *Beyond the Martyrs*, 59.

27 The IWPA had its roots in the Workingmen's Party of the United States, founded in July 1876, which became the Socialist Labor Party in December 1877. Lucy Parson's husband, Albert Parsons, August Spies, and other midwestern trade union militants split from the Workingmen's Party in 1881 in response to its temporary merger with the Greenbacks and founded the Revolutionary Socialist Party, which was renamed as the IWPA a year later. On Chicago's anarchist movement, see Ashbaugh, *Lucy Parsons*; Paul Avrich, *The Haymarket Tragedy* (Princeton, NJ: Princeton University Press, 1984); Nelson, *Beyond the Martyrs*; Tax, *The Rising of the Women*, 42.

28 See Nelson, *Beyond the Martyrs*, 93.

29 Ibid., 103–4.

30 Ashbaugh, *Lucy Parsons*.

Nelson similarly argues that despite the restrictions of contemporary gender roles, the " 'she-communists' did more than sew revolutionary banners and serve beer."[31] Indeed, by participating in protests, writing articles, publicizing the IWPA's position, and organizing within the Knights of Labor, Parsons, Stevens, Rogers, Swank, and others articulated an active and inclusive role for women in the labor movement and set a precedent for organizations such as the Women's Trade Union League in the twentieth century.[32]

The WWU not only introduced Swank to this political world but also stimulated her career as a journalist. No doubt at times she read the Knights' *Journal of United Labor*, which had published allegorical fiction from 1881, but it was not for the Knights that Swank began writing. Her first pieces were exposés of the poor conditions in the garment trade, and she went on to author more general pieces, many of which drew upon her political activism in their critiques of capitalism. A range of radical papers published her work, including Chicago's *Anti-Monopolist* and *Labor Enquirer*, the *Nonconformist*, and

Lucifer: The Light Bearer.[33] In October 1885, Swank more explicitly connected her politics and writing when she became assistant editor of the *Alarm*, the IWPA's paper. She left this position in late 1886 but continued to contribute regular articles over the next three years. She mostly wrote news pieces reporting on anarchist activism across the country, although a few of her fictional stories occasionally appeared as well. These stories shared much with those she later wrote for the *American Federationist* and, for that matter, with contemporary dime fiction. For example, one told the tale of a young lad much like Frank Kirby who has great potential but ends up a tramp, freezing to death in a gutter.[34] Another juxtaposed chattel slavery in 1850 with wage slavery in 1886, the power resting with the foreman, who destroys the family of one of his workers through intimidation and force.[35]

Holmes, her name after her marriage to William Holmes, continued to balance her involvement in the labor movement with her radical journalism. She remained active in Labor Local Assembly No. 1789 and participated in the 1886 eight-hour-day campaign. Like much of the Knights of Labor's work, this campaign brought together radicals and trade unionists, revealing

31   Marsh, *Anarchist Women*, 110; Ashbaugh, *Lucy Parsons*; Nelson, *Beyond the Martyrs*, 94.

32   On the connections between these women and the Women's Trade Union League, see Ruth Percy, "Women or Workers? The Construction of Labour Feminism in London and Chicago, 1880s-1920s" (PhD diss., University of Toronto, 2006), ch. 1.

33   "Work of the Sex." These other works are beyond the remit of this article.

34   Lizzie M. Swank, "A Short Story for Moral Teachers," *Alarm*, January 23, 1886, 4.

35   Lizzie M. Swank, "Two Stories in One," *Alarm*, April 3, 1886, 4.

the connections, albeit tenuous, among a variety of different political groups.[36] With the Parsons, Holmes attended the May 4, 1886, meeting at Haymarket Square, which was organized to protest violence against strikers the previous day. As the police moved to disperse the crowd, a bomb was thrown amid them, and police opened fire. A total of eleven people died as a result, with many more injured.[37] Holmes later testified for the defence that Albert Parsons, one of the eight people put on trial in the aftermath, was in a café with her at the time the bomb was thrown. The court transcripts reveal a confident, strong, and defiant woman. In the cross-examination for the prosecution, she confirmed that she was both an anarchist and a socialist, explaining when pressed that by anarchy she meant "self-government." Importantly, in the context, she also asserted that the "theory of anarchy is opposed to all idea of force."[38]

The arrest, trial, and death of the Haymarket martyrs and the subsequent repression of left-wing groups took its toll on the anarchist movement, and by 1892 the Chicago anarchists had fractured and been driven underground.[39] Holmes was not alone in focusing her attention on the trade union movement, because many remained active in other organizations. Yet, the hostility to left-wing ideas that followed Haymarket led many to publicly disavow their radical politics. Nevertheless, it seems unlikely that Holmes rejected socialism outright, as she claimed in an interview in the mainstream *Chicago Times* in 1894.[40] It is more likely that Holmes renounced socialism just for the nonradical newspaper that interviewed her. Indeed, as late as 1891, she took on the bulk of the editing work alongside Lucy Parsons for *Freedom: A Revolutionary Anarchist-Communist Monthly*.[41] Regardless of her political position, though, she was among those who persisted in attempts to organize working women and, under a charter from the newly renamed AFL (Federation of Organized Trades and Labor Unions from 1881 to 1886), formed the Ladies' Federal Labor Union Local No. 2703 in 1888.[42]

As Nelson points out, many former anarchists joined more conservative trade unions and labor assemblies after 1890. However, although their skills and experience were welcomed, their politics were not. Nelson considers Holmes one of these ex-anarchists, contrasting her to Lucy Parsons, who, despite or perhaps because of her fame, became "expendable" because she was a political

---

36   Nelson, *Beyond the Martyrs*, especially 27 and 44.

37   On Haymarket, see Ashbaugh, *Lucy Parsons*; Avrich, *The Haymarket Tragedy*; Nelson, *Beyond the Martyrs*.

38   Holmes, "Transcript of Witness Testimony," *People for the State of Illinois vs. August Spies et al.*

39   Eric L. Hirsch, *Urban Revolt: Ethnic Politics in the Nineteenth-Century Chicago Labor*

Movement (Berkeley: University of California Press, 1990), 78–80.

40   "Work of the Sex."

41   Ashbaugh, *Lucy Parsons*, 196, 183.

42   Tax, *The Rising of the Women*, 54.

liability.[43] Holmes was among many in Chicago who moved between a range of different groups in the pre- and post-Haymarket years, including the citywide labor federations, local trade unions, and socialist and anarchist groups. Holmes's experiences were not unique in this regard. Despite desires for a loyal and steadfast membership, the newness of many of these groups and the complex multiethnic character of Chicago's population facilitated movement among them.

Chicago offered much in the way of political activism, but Holmes and her husband were attracted by westward opportunities. They left for Colorado in 1889 and moved to New Mexico in the mid-1890s, although Holmes appears to have returned to Chicago fairly often. She continued to write during this time, publishing factual and fictional pieces mostly in anarchist papers. Beginning in 1901, the *American Federationist* published her eight stories.[44] Although the leadership of the AFL was far more politically conservative than that of the organizations Holmes had been active in, by the turn of the twentieth century it was also a considerable force among the working classes. In addition to needing the work, Holmes likely conceded, unlike some other radicals, that the *American Federationist* was an important vehicle for continuing her political journalism and especially for attacking the capitalist system.

Writing for the *American Federationist*

The publication of Holmes's work in the *American Federationist* points to both the difficulties labor journalists faced as they tried to earn a living at the turn of the twentieth century and the connections individuals made between supposedly antagonistic branches of the left-wing movement. When fellow anarchist Emma Goldman visited Holmes and her husband in Denver in 1898, she noted that they lived "in poor quarters and barely earn[ed] enough to sustain life." [45] Money was presumably an important consideration, and we can assume the *American Federationist* paid.[46] Yet earning a living was probably not Holmes's only motivation in writing for the AFL journal. The *American Federationist* was the official organ of the largest labor organization in the country and thus gave Holmes an extremely wide readership, far wider than the more radical journals to which she also contributed. As Goldman commented, although poor, Holmes and her husband "were still as devoted to the Cause as in the days when their faith was young and

---

43   Nelson, *Beyond the Martyrs*, 236–37.
44   McKinley, "Free Love and Domesticity," 55; Holmes, "Women Workers of Chicago," 507–10.

45   Emma Goldman, *Living My Life* (1931; repr. New York: Dover Publications, 1970), 1:222.
46   Eva Valesh, needing to fund a trip to Europe to help her husband regain his health, received payment for a series of articles on European labor she wrote in 1896. Faue, *Writing the Wrongs*, 119.

their hopes high." [47] Although the AFL leadership had little time for Goldman's anarchist "Cause," through the *American Federationist* Holmes could spread her critique of capitalism to a much broader audience, many of whom would have had radical backgrounds or leanings.

Holmes's writings in mainstream labor, anarchist, and free-love papers suggest she adopted a rather flexible relationship to radical and trade union organizations that many contemporary activists neither acknowledged nor encouraged. On the radical left, Goldman disparagingly thought of this fluidity as a display of the "indefinite, uncertain mind of the American radical." [48] To the right of Goldman, AFL president Samuel Gompers, despite his own socialist background, worked toward defeating radical rivals of the AFL in favor of his "pure and simple" unionism. However, many more activists occupied the middle ground between these two extremes. There they continued a tradition established within the Knights of Labor that saw value in flexibility.

In the dual interest of securing an income and reaching new audiences, radicals such as Holmes negotiated all opportunities available to them. [49] Thus, just three years before publishing her first story in the *American Federationist*, Holmes published a far more radical piece in the *Arena*. In it, she challenged the idea of wage labor as exclusively masculine and argued not only that women had a right to freedom equal to men but also that such freedom would not impinge upon their femininity. [50] The absence of such a radical position in her stories for the AFL does not necessarily suggest contradiction, inconsistency, or insincerity. To the contrary, it points to the flexibility she brought to her writing, enabling her to write for many different audiences.

The *American Federationist*, the largest labor newspaper in the country, was "devoted to the interests and voicing the demands of the trade union movement." [51] Unlike the other vehicles through which Holmes communicated her messages, the mainstream AFL journal enabled her to reach a wide audience. The *American Federationist* in turn appears to have published her stories as part of its attempt to broaden its readership and keep up with the growing membership, just as the Knights' *Journal*

---

47 Goldman, *Living My Life*, 1:222.

48 Emma Goldman, quoted in Arthur Redding, "The Dream Life of Political Violence: Georges Sorel, Emma Goldman, and the Modern Imagination," *Modernism/Modernity* 2, no. 2 (1995): 10. Redding points out that Progressive Era fiction writers' lack of clarity when writing about the Left was "an inevitable product of the inherent tensions in radicalism and the labor movement."

49 There are two articles attributed to William Holmes in the *American Federationist* that appeared a few years before these stories, and it is possible that the author was Holmes's husband.

50 Lizzie M. Holmes, "Woman's Future Position in the World," *Arena*, 20, no. 3, September 1898, 333–43.

51 The byline appeared under the title of many of the early issues. See, for example, the first issue, *American Federationist*, March 1894, 1.

of United Labor did eleven years earlier; the AFL had 278,000 members in 1898 and 1.5 million members just five years later.[52] The publication of Holmes's fiction coincided with other changes to the journal. New editorial input in 1901 varied the type of content, expanded the number of pages, and increased the advertising revenue.

Eva Valesh, who had a long-standing relationship with Gompers and had worked as a journalist for a number of mainstream dailies, joined the AFL head-quarters as Gompers's assistant in 1901. As Elizabeth Faue points out in her study of Valesh, her job description was rather ambiguous but to all intents and purposes it included being the managing editor of the *American Federationist*.[53] The journal, Valesh later recalled, aimed to counter the "prejudice against the unions in the newspapers." "If they had a central magazine," she continued, "where they could express their own ideas, explain their own ideals, and have an interchange of thought, it would be education."[54] Perhaps it was Valesh who encouraged the publication of fiction, for, as Faue points out, she favored a "popular touch."[55]

The editor (presumably Gompers, but perhaps Valesh) introduced Holmes's series of "industrial stories" by commending Holmes as a long-time

"careful student of practical economics" who "possesses the happy faculty of weaving incidents of everyday life into stories in which the sombre realism of the workers' lives is lightened by the touch of romance which may glorify the humblest lot."[56] The escapist nature of the stories contrasted to rather dry articles, such as Valesh's "Conditions of Labor in Europe" series, which ran from April to October 1896 and gave readers an insight into working conditions in a number of European countries. Holmes also stood out as one of the few female writers and the only one with a radical political background. In the first seven years of publication, there were only seventeen articles by women, all of whom tended to come from maternalist reform backgrounds. Only five articles were actually about women.[57] This contrasted to the Knights of Labor journal, which

---

52 Faue, *Writing the Wrongs*, 144–45.

53 Ibid.

54 Eva Valesh, quoted in Faue, *Writing the Wrongs*, 147.

55 Faue, *Writing the Wrongs*, 145–46.

56 Samuel Gompers, editorial, *American Federationist*, August 1901, 307.

57 For example, other contributors included reformers Grace H. Dodge, who was involved in working girls' societies in New York, and Josephine Shaw Lowell, founder of the New York Consumers' League. On maternalism, see Molly Ladd-Taylor, *Mother-Work: Women, Child Welfare, and the State, 1890–1930* (Urbana: University of Illinois Press, 1994), 1–14; Seth Koven and Sonya Michel, eds., *Mothers of a New World: Maternalist Politics and the Origins of Welfare States* (New York: Routledge, 1993); Elizabeth Anne Payne, *Reform, Labor, and Feminism: Margaret Dreier Robins and the Women's Trade Union League* (Urbana: University of Illinois Press, 1988), 117–54; Lori D. Ginzberg, *Women and the Work of Benevolence: Morality, Politics, and Class in the Nineteenth-Century United States* (New Haven, CT: Yale University Press, 1990).

fairly regularly included articles on women's issues.

For content, Holmes drew upon her experiences as a wage earner and labor organizer; for style, she drew upon contemporary popular fiction. Her stories in the *American Federationist* explored the impact of industrial labor upon both male and female workers and as such linked back to some of the fiction that appeared in the *Journal of United Labor* in the late 1880s. However, unlike much of the Knights' fiction, which Weir notes had "an acceptance of the mutuality of capital/labor interests, an undercurrent of genteel pretensions, and a nod to Victorian morality," Holmes's stories were often more bitter.[58] Her working-class characters are invariably self-improving, respectful, respectable, and kind people. All of the workers she describes are young—and thus full of the potential of youth—white, American-born, intelligent, and, with one notable exception, physically strong people. Through these characters, Holmes spoke to the general industrial experience and did not comment on any differences within the working class. Although this seems to belie Holmes's experiences in Chicago's ethnically diverse workforce, this was also characteristic of the factual reports and opinion pieces in the *American Federationist*. Throughout its pages, writers homogenized the American working class into a white, English-speaking, native-born body.[59]

However, Holmes offered something more. She attached a range of problems to a number of different likeable characters and thereby provided readers with personalized stories to which they could easily relate. Instead of talking abstractly or theoretically, the fictional form no doubt facilitated readers' identification with the problems the characters faced and thus helped to communicate her message. In doing so, the stories offered something to both the editors and Holmes. The editors surely hoped the fictional form would appeal to more readers at the same time that it gave Holmes access to a wider readership. It is worth considering here, albeit briefly, the nature of the relationship between editor and author. Although we have little material to shed light on this relationship, clearly the editors felt that Holmes's fiction could contribute to the overall tone of the *American Federationist*. It is certainly possible that they suggested, or even dictated, the central message of each story. Holmes's willingness to write under such circumstances suggests both the necessity for flexibility among labor writers and the importance of the financial incentive to Holmes (remember Goldman's comments on her and her husband's poverty).

---

58 Weir, *Beyond Labor's Veil*, 215.

59 Articles expressing concern about the influx of immigrants were regularly featured in the labor press, but union rhetoric remained homogenizing.

Critiquing Industrial Capitalism: Worker as Victim

Holmes began her critique of industrial capitalism by focusing on the lack of control workers exercised in the contemporary workplace. Her first story, "Only an Industrial Outcast" (published in August 1901), addressed a concern regularly voiced in the press: machines and unskilled laborers were replacing skilled workers. The story tells the tale of a man unable to secure industrial labor because "labor-saving machinery, trusts and consolidations, are throwing men out of employment all the time."[60] The central character, Phillip Morland, is unable to find work in the city and resorts to tramping around the countryside in search of casual agricultural labor.

In this story, Holmes establishes a stark contrast between rural and urban environments. The city could be the land of opportunity, but it was also where the industrial system most oppressed workers. In contrast, although equally hard work was required in the countryside, it was a purer and more honest work that implied masculine independence and self-control.[61] Such a dichotomy not only accorded respect to rural laborers but also suggested a particularly virile

rural masculinity and thus accentuated Holmes's critique of industrial capitalism. Indeed, of all the stories here we see perhaps the clearest evidence of the impact of the Knights of Labor upon Holmes's labor politics. Although the AFL rarely concerned itself with agricultural labor, the Knights had tried to unite farm workers with industrial laborers, and thus the rural masculinity she depicted would have been familiar to many readers.

The story opens as Phillip approaches a farmhouse and asks for work. The farmer, Nathaniel Richards, is disparaging and dismisses Phillip. However, the farmer's daughter Tavia pities the transient worker, follows him, and secretly gives him some food and drink. During this encounter, they engage in a discussion about industrial conditions in the cities. Phillip explains to Tavia the nature of his work in a shoe factory in Massachusetts: "I know how to make a fraction of a shoe and I don't know how to do another useful thing on earth. My muscles are all trained to one set of motions and are not strong at anything else." [62] Repeating a point made several times in each edition of the *American Federationist*, Holmes uses this conversation to critique the division of labor in the contemporary industrial system and to construct a particular image of the working man who maintained his masculinity despite his inability to find industrial employment.

---

60   Lizzie M. Holmes, "Only an Industrial Outcast," *American Federationist*, August 1901, 296.

61   Renewed contact with nature was a central aspect of the progressives' idea of the "simple life." See David E. Shi, *The Simple Life: Plain Living and High Thinking in American Culture* (Oxford: Oxford University Press, 1985), 175–214.

---

62   Holmes, "Only an Industrial Outcast," 296.

The medium of fiction, in contrast to the factual articles, allowed Holmes to write her own ending to the problems of industrial capitalism. Although Phillip at first struggles to keep up with the hard labor on the farm, he persists and gains Nathaniel's respect after saving Tavia from her runaway horse. In the end, Phillip secures a permanent job on the farm and thus escapes industrial labor by returning to the land. This was a common literary trope of the period but an uncommon occurrence for America's industrial workers.[63] However, Holmes's choice of this answer to Phillip's problem suggests a lingering pastoral ideal within the labor movement.

In the second story, published two months later, Holmes makes an even more explicit critique of industrial labor through a much less fortunate character. In "Two Types of Wasted Lives," Frank Kirby is forced to leave school at age fourteen to venture to the nearest town to earn a living. There he finds a group of "working boys and girls who had formed a club for mental improvement and sociability and was invited to join." [64] He finds happiness in this club, but his factory closes, and he must leave his newfound friends as he once again moves on in search of work. He goes to a larger city and, having no friends or family around him, becomes "a mere nobody in the great human hive," the embodiment of the urban experience.[65] "This sort of neglect, with poverty and hard work," Holmes preaches, "killed the beauty of character and real ability that at first existed in his nature."

Frank's love of books and "talent for letters" had no place in the industrial world; his dreams of becoming a writer die as he turns into "a mere clod" at the industrial machine. With no one to care for him in the big city, where "every one seemed full of his own occupations and sorrows," Frank had "no joy, no beauty, no incentive in his life." [66] Indeed, Holmes explains that he "became a mere machine to create what went to make up the magnificent wealth of the country." Frank's juxtaposition with a rich, indulgent, and bored young man, George Meredith, who can find no way to amuse himself, further accentuates the harshness of the industrial system; even those

---

63 By the mid-nineteenth century, "a cult of rural domesticity" was firmly established in literature; established and polarized gender relations were not challenged in the country. James L. Machor, *Pastoral Cities: Urban Ideals and the Symbolic Landscape of America* (Madison: University of Wisconsin Press, 1987), 154. On the persistence of the country as the ideal place to live as a trope in literature, see Loren C. Owings, *Quest for Walden: A Study of the "Country Book" in American Popular Literature, with an Annotated Bibliography, 1863–1995* (Jefferson, NC: McFarland and Co., 1997), especially 9–15. Valesh also depicted the rural as ideal in the novel she wrote under the pen name Eva Gay: *Tale of the Twin Cities: Lights and Shadows of the Street Car Strike in Minneapolis and St. Paul* (Minneapolis: Thomas Clark, 1889). See Faue, *Writing the Wrongs*, 67–68.

---

64 Lizzie M. Holmes, "Two Types of Wasted Lives," *American Federationist*, October 1901, 408.

65 Ibid.

66 Ibid.

with potential have no hope, whereas those who have opportunities squander them. Perhaps trying to shock her readers, Holmes provides no glimmer of hope for the working man—Frank "met his death very recently at a machine."[67]

In her first two stories for the *American Federationist*, Holmes's construction of working-class manhood affirmed the connection between masculinity and wage labor. Within the American labor movement from the Knights of Labor to the AFL, working men's identities were intricately tied to the ideals of the male breadwinner, the skilled craftsman, and the protector of women. Working men's independence and respectability depended on their ability to prove themselves in the workplace. For Holmes, the contemporary industrial system, characterized by mindless specialized tasks that alienated workers from their labor, does not allow for a viable masculinity; Phillip finds salvation in agricultural labor and Frank loses his life. Holmes capitalized on this discourse, adding a melodramatic edge to attract readers.

Holmes continued to discuss the destructive powers of industrial capitalism in the third, fifth, and seventh stories, all of which have female heroines. She moved beyond the exclusive association of wage labor with masculinity and articulated the possibility of a wage-earning womanhood, which was unusual in the *American Federationist* but would have

been familiar to readers of popular fiction. Like Phillip and Frank, these female characters suffer in various ways at the hand of industrial labor. In this respect, these stories share contemporary literary devices that suggested the ambiguous status of women in the workplace and labor movement at the turn of the twentieth century—were they workers equal to men or did they truly belong in the home?[68] In contrast to many of her fiction-writing contemporaries, Holmes does not simply represent wage labor as the first step on the downward spiral to prostitution.[69]

At first reading, these female characters seem to belie Holmes's radical past and her own experiences organizing working women in Chicago. None of the working-class women she creates are active unionists; only two even come into contact with trade unions. Nonetheless, these characters contribute to her overall critique. Indeed, the fact that she depicts unskilled women workers as having the same industrial experiences as men suggests that they

---

67   Ibid.

68   See Amal Amireh, *The Factory Girl and the Seamstress: Imagining Gender and Class in Nineteenth-Century American Fiction* (New York: Garland, 2000); Laura Hapke, *Tales of the Working Girl: Wage-Earning Women in American Literature, 1890–1925* (New York: Twayne, 1992).

69   See, for example, Stephen Crane, *Maggie: A Girl of the Streets* (1896; repr. Peterborough, ON: Broadview Press, 2006); Edgar Fawcett, *The Evil That Men Do: A Novel* (New York: Belford Co., 1889). Laura Hapke discusses the prevalence in fiction of this descent into prostitution in *Tales of the Working Girl*, especially 15–17 and 35–37.

too should have the recognition and support of the AFL. Moreover, Holmes offers this suggestion to her readers via familiar tropes of escape. Dime novels, story-papers, and popular theater were filled with tales of morally strong yet financially destitute women who end up discovering they are in fact wealthy and/or who marry wealthy men and thus escape the factory or the street.[70] However, Holmes complicates this escape in her collection of stories by also including one woman who is unable to escape, Jennie Dean, and another who does not seem to need or want to, Mary Casey. Holmes's message is thus that escape is fine for those who find it but does not solve the problems caused by industrial capitalism.

With the descriptions of Alice Casey and Jennie Dean in the fifth and seventh stories, Holmes continues her explicit critique of "wage slavery" using women as victims. In these two tales, she draws upon her own experiences as a garment worker and union organizer, as well as upon contemporary debates surrounding women's wage earning. Many AFL members opposed women's wage earning, and their role in the organization was marginal well into the twentieth century.[71] (It

was not until 1980 that a woman sat on the executive of the AFL-CIO, as it was then known.[72]) Holmes plays with these ideas in her critique of industrial capitalism, subtly suggesting the possibility of a working womanhood to her readers.

As was the case with male characters, close descriptions of working women's physical and psychological experiences of wage labor are a central aspect of Holmes's message in these two tales. Just as she did with Frank's character, Holmes capitalized on the powerful imagery of a body or mind destroyed by labor.[73] The feminine dynamic further accentuates this established destructive-industry paradigm.

The worker-destroyed-by-industry construction is most evident in "Not by Bread Alone," published in January 1902. Holmes opens with a description of a "young woman, pale and faded," who sews by a window in a room that "was simply sordid, ugly, dreary."[74] This woman, Alice Casey, is a home worker in the garment trade whose work and living conditions have left her with a "hungry

---

70 Denning, *Mechanic Accents*; Hapke, *Tales of the Working Girl*; Amireh, *The Factory Girl*; Weir, *Beyond Labor's Veil*.

71 See, for example, two articles published around the same time: John Stafford, "The Good That Trade Unions Do, Part 1," *American Federationist*, July 1902, 353; Samuel Gompers, "Should the Wife Help to Support the Family?" *American Federationist*, January 1906, 36.

72 Joyce D. Miller, president of the Coalition of Labor Union Women, was elected as executive of the AFL-CIO in 1980. Dorothy Sue Cobble, *The Other Women's Movement: Workplace Justice and Social Rights in Modern America* (Princeton, NJ: Princeton University Press, 2004), 205.

73 This imagery was fairly common. See, for example, Harold Frederic, *The Lawton Girl* (New York: Scribner's Sons, 1890); Fawcett, *The Evil That Men Do*; Crane, *Maggie*; Jack London, *The People of the Abyss* (1903; repr. London: Pluto, 2001). See also Hapke, *Tales of the Working Girl*.

74 Lizzie M. Holmes, " 'Not by Bread Alone,' " *American Federationist*, January 1902, 11.

look in her eyes [that] was not due alone to lack of nourishing food"; having inherited "fine tastes" from her father, Alice "would willingly have sacrificed some of her best meals for the sake of a beautiful picture of any work of real art."[75] Like Frank Kirby's, this artistic temperament had little potential for development within the industrial workforce. In both these stories, Holmes makes reference to the American standard of living, including leisure and cultural activities, that labor activists had been demanding since the late nineteenth century.[76]

Alice is the most dramatic described of any of Holmes's female characters, and she stood out in the pages of the *American Federationist*. The description of Alice's weakened body lends itself to certain assumptions about the inappropriateness of women's wage labor, particularly as such descriptions recalled the language used by antisweatshop campaigners and would have been familiar to many readers.[77] As the story continues, Holmes complicates this message: Alice lives with her sister Mary, who is stronger, still goes to work in the factory, and brings work home for Alice. In contrast to Alice, Mary "had been endowed with her mother's practical good

sense and energy" and could thus handle factory labor.[78]

Holmes's descriptions of the sisters contrast starkly: Mary "was older, plainer, but more cheerful and matter-of-fact. She did not seem so much out of place in the surroundings, and it was evident they did not worry her as they did her sister."[79] Thus, a wage-earning womanhood was possible. Through Mary, Holmes made some connections to her more radical nonfiction writings, such as the aforementioned article in the *Arena*. These radical works critiqued the dominant masculinity of the workforce and labor movement and offered an alternative in which women could retain their femininity and share the freedom of men. With Alice and Mary's story, Holmes introduced some of that critique, albeit in a softened and even ambiguous way.

Nevertheless, aware of the official politics of the AFL, Holmes did not push the idea of gender equality in the labor movement. She does not tell readers what happened to Mary more than to say that she continued to work in the factory, apparently less troubled than Alice by the struggle to earn a living. Instead, the story focuses on Alice's escape from a life of drudgery. Even though her tale appeared in a labor journal, Alice's salvation does not come from a union *per se*. Although local union organizer Mortimer Graham shows an interest

---

75 Ibid.
76 See page 84 for a fuller discussion of the American standard of living.
77 For a discussion of the language of the antisweatshop campaigns, see Daniel E. Bender, *Sweated Work, Weak Bodies: Anti-sweatshop Campaigns and the Languages of Labor* (New Brunswick, NJ: Rutgers University Press, 2004), especially 105–31.

---

78 Holmes, "Not by Bread Alone," 11.
79 Ibid.

in Alice's well-being, she escapes destruction via a sympathetic upper-class woman. Mrs. Thornton takes Alice in as a companion, enabling her to recuperate and then enjoy the pleasures of the leisured class's artistic and cultural world.

Mrs. Thornton's rescue does not make for only a happy ending. Just as she did with Frank Kirby's story, Holmes uses the juxtaposition of rich and poor characters to represent the lack of justice and fairness in the industrial world. It is only once Alice is "saved" that she regains her health, her beauty, and her spirit.[80] We assume that without Mrs. Thornton, she would have met a fate similar to Frank—death at the machine. Holmes makes a plea for reform in the industrial world: although there are many women suffering under "the destructive power of wage slavery," there are not enough Mrs. Thorntons to come to everyone's rescue.

In "The Path One Treads," published in May 1902, Holmes points out the difficulties women, like men, have finding fulfillment through industrial employment by juxtaposing Jennie Dean, who remains a worker, and Myrtle Desmond, who escapes industrial labor. In this, the penultimate story, Holmes follows the parallel paths of two working girls. At the beginning, they are eighteen and "full of the joy of life."[81] They are physically strong and walk, well dressed, to the factory every day: "It was a delight to watch these young girls as they

started away in the morning with a brisk, springy step; their eyes beaming; their bright faces glowing; jokes, light chatter, and smiles springing to their lips as naturally as songs pour forth from the throats of the birds."[82] In these descriptions, Holmes offers up to readers a respectable working womanhood (or perhaps girlhood). Their gender enables Holmes to accentuate both their youth and their beauty, as she does with Alice, and this makes Jennie's downfall all the more dramatic.

Nonetheless, Jennie and Myrtle do not find fulfillment solely in the workplace. Like Frank Kirby and Alice Casey, these two girls enjoy a range of cultural activities. In addition to their work in the factory, the two girls attend a literary club, a singing society, and socials every week, and at these they meet Evan Hamilton, whom they both admire. Through Evan, Holmes falls back on the general perception that wage labor was only a way station on the track to full womanhood; marriage was the terminus. The girls' paths diverge when Myrtle leaves the factory town after her father inherits some money. Unbeknown to Jennie, Myrtle finds fulfillment through marrying Evan and lives a leisured life with enough money to employ two maids. Jennie has no such luck and continues to work in the factory. Several years pass, and industrial labor has beaten her down. She is no longer pretty or full of life but "thin

80 Ibid., 14.
81 Lizzie M. Holmes, "The Path One Treads," *American Federationist*, May 1902, 224.

82 Ibid.

and wistful" with a "little worn figure," reminiscent of Alice Casey.[83]

Jennie is left alone after her parents die and her brothers move or get married. When we return to her, she is thirty-eight and occasionally attends church in her search for fulfillment that she cannot find in the workplace. After hearing a sermon that preached about the contentment achieved by hard work, economy, and persistence, she assesses her own position.[84] Jennie has worked hard since she was twelve, has taken good care of her possessions, has mended her clothes to make them last longer, and has been polite and patient. Yet she is far more removed from the happiness and prosperity of which the preacher spoke than she had been at age twelve. Holmes criticizes the preacher's message by pointing out that in contemporary industrial society the qualities he listed were no longer enough to ensure happiness and prosperity. Like Phillip Morland and Frank Kirby, Jennie had followed the rules of the industrial system. Like the men, her failure to succeed was not a personal failure but the result of a broken and corrupt system.

Published in November 1901, "Economy That Proved Disastrous" tells a more subtle tale of industrial woe than those of Frank Kirby, Alice Casey, or Jennie Dean.[85] At the beginning of the story, the town is full of happy, industrious people who find pleasure in small things such as social clubs, a pretty ribbon, or an ice cream. The image is one of an idealized early industrial town where the whole community benefits from the local factory. As the story continues, however, Holmes makes it clear that such a relationship is impossible.

The protagonist, Ellen Worth, works in Mr. Blatchford's factory. She is engaged to Frank Towne, who works in a different department of the same factory. The seemingly idyllic industrial setting is gradually destroyed by Mr. Blatchford's obsession with doctrines of "economy." As he preaches the values of economy to his workers and to the town in general, they slowly stop engaging in unessential leisure activities. Luxury businesses such as saloons and ice cream parlors go out of business, and ultimately Mr. Blatchford's doctrine destroys the whole town. In a message similar to that in both Frank Kirby's and Phillip Morland's tales, the power of capital, this time in the manifestation of the penny-pinching Mr. Blatchford, is corrupt and destructive. Like Phillip but unlike Frank, Ellen escapes the industrial system. She leaves the town and her fiancé "for regions a little less economical and thrifty."[86]

Although Frank Towne and Mr. Blatchford only look for fulfillment in the world of work and profit-making, Holmes uses Ellen to suggest a more rewarding balance between work and

---

83 Ibid., 225.
84 Ibid.
85 Lizzie M. Holmes, "Economy That Proved Disastrous," *American Federationist*, November 1901, 471–72.

86 Ibid., 472.

leisure; Ellen works hard in the factory but also enjoys culture, social activities, and little luxuries. Via Ellen, Holmes critiques a world centered solely on wage earning and suggests that it needs to be combined with leisure activities. This message would have been familiar to many readers as the call for the American standard of living. Since the late nineteenth century, the labor movement, in accepting the permanence of wage labor, had demanded a living wage and a standard of living that allowed for cultural activities and engagement in consumer society. However, as Lawrence Glickman points out, the American standard "reestablished male/female and American/alien dichotomies.... If it allowed white, male workers to escape 'slave' status, it also gave them a way to call others 'slaves' and to exclude working-class immigrants, African Americans, and *women* from participation in the American standard."[87] By including Ellen and Alice alongside Frank as workers who enjoy and need leisure, Holmes thus suggests that women should be just as entitled as men to the American standard of living.

In these stories about working-class victims, Holmes both conforms to and complicates contemporary arguments about the harsh nature of industrial labor. Her overall critique is similar to that of other pieces in the *American*

Federationist; she constructed male characters presumably familiar to her male readers and capitalized upon the feminine image of victimized workers. The fact that she was writing fiction also enabled Holmes to quietly suggest the possibility of a working womanhood and that women also deserved the American standard of living. In addition, her medium makes for entertaining reading for the historian and undoubtedly did for her contemporaries too.

Critiquing Industrial Capitalism: Organizer as Hero

Holmes encouraged readers to pity these victims of the industrial system, but she also used labor leaders as heroes. These characters offered an alternative to the worker-as-victim construction to inspire sympathy for the trade union movement. In contrast to Phillip, Frank, and the women workers, Holmes personified the idealized working man in two male characters, both labor leaders. Mirroring the physical representation of oppression, the strong will and sense of fairness in these two men are evident in their physical features. In her sixth story, Seth Cooper's "manly beauty, love of justice, intellect, powerful character and physical strength, all combined to make him a leader among men,"[88] and in the final tale Holmes introduces John Lawrence to readers: "a tall, athletic looking young

87 Emphasis added. Lawrence B. Glickman, *A Living Wage: American Workers and the Making of Consumer Society* (Ithaca, NY: Cornell University Press, 1997), 78. See also Currarino, "The Politics of 'More,' " 17–36.

88 Lizzie M. Holmes, "Judge Newcomb's Retribution," *American Federationist*, February 1902, 65.

man, with a fine head, well set on broad shoulders and a clean-cut, firm and thoughtful face, full of character and decision."[89] With these two admirable men, Holmes champions the potential of the working man and the labor movement.

In addition to being admired by their fellow workers, Seth and John both convert women from the leisured classes to the workers' cause. With this plotline, Holmes flatters her unionist readers as she presents the unionists' message that "the wealth should belong to those who labor" as commonsensical and suggests that it can convert even the most unlikely candidates.[90] In the sixth story, "Judge Newcomb's Retribution," published in February 1902, Holmes describes Seth as "a strong, active, enthusiastic young unionist" who plays an active role in a railroad strike.[91] Recognizing his influence, the police arrest him on false charges. Holmes gives the story a twist—orphaned Seth turns out to be the illegitimate son of the judge who sentences him to twenty years of hard labor. The more interesting tale is the vague relationship between Seth and Berenice Brown, the daughter of a large shareholder in the railroad company. Berenice is sympathetic to the strikers and finds Seth an "eloquent" speaker. Much to her friends' dismay, his speeches make her realize that the strikers "are the useful ones of earth," whereas she and her friends are "pampered" and "idle."[92] The two meet only briefly when Seth protects Berenice from some soldiers who are harassing her because she supports the strike; the police arrest him as a result. Nevertheless, Seth's impact on Berenice is considerable. Not only had Berenice "ever since taken a deep interest in everything pertaining to labor," but Berenice also compares all potential suitors to Seth.[93]

In the final story, printed in March 1903, Holmes returns to this theme of male labor leaders winning over upper-class women. "Her Birthday Gift" tells the tale of Edith Langford, the only daughter of a rich banker, who falls in love with labor man John Lawrence although she is due to marry her self-absorbed second cousin Ernest Wilberforce. Despite Ernest's protestations, Edith decides to attend a labor meeting to see "what rights can the diggers of a sewer want."[94] There she meets John, whom she questions after his talk. He teaches her about the labor cause, and Edith finds the conversation enlightening and stimulating. Over the next few months, she attends more talks and continues to quiz John about workers' concerns. His arguments are reasonable and his manner respectable; he is the ideal labor leader capable of winning over others through his intellectual,

---

89   Lizzie M. Holmes, "Her Birthday Gift," *American Federationist*, March 1903, 166.

90   Ibid.

91   Holmes, "Judge Newcomb's Retribution," 65.

92   Ibid., 66.

93   Ibid., 67.

94   Holmes, "Her Birthday Gift," 165.

moral, and physical strength. Holmes complements her physical glorification of working-class masculinity by having John save Edith from drowning on a lake during a storm. In a perfect example of what the editor referred to as "a touch of romance," Holmes completes her construction of the respectable labor organizer by ending the story with Edith and John's marriage.

In the fourth story, "Her Life for Labor," printed in December 1901, Holmes raises many of the same issues surrounding labor organizing, but significantly the protagonist is female. Just as she constructs a wage-earning womanhood through Mary in "Not by Bread Alone" and the young Jennie and Myrtle in "The Path One Treads," Holmes constructs an active union womanhood through Helen Estes. Like the other women, Helen is an unusual figure in the *American Federationist*. However, she would not have been unusual to many working people, particularly those who had lived or worked in Chicago and had come into contact with Jane Addams and the other women who worked out of Hull House.[95]

Although the majority of women writers who contributed to the journal were women like Helen or Addams, financially secure individuals who were able to spend their time working to improve society, these women's lives never actually appear in the pages of the journal. Even after such women formed the Women's Trade Union League (WTUL) in 1903, it was not until late 1905 that the *American Federationist* made reference to this organization. This omission belied the WTUL's importance to the organization of women workers and suggests its ambiguous relationship with the AFL. It is thus especially striking that Helen appears in this story as a champion of the working man, like Seth and John. Holmes could draw upon her own experiences in late-nineteenth-century Chicago to emphasize middle-class women's importance to the organization of working women.[96] Nevertheless, unlike Seth and

---

95 On Hull House, see, for example, Jane Addams, *Twenty Years at Hull-House: With Autobiographical Notes* (New York: Macmillan, 1910), and *The Second Twenty Years at Hull-House, September 1909 to September 1929: With a Record of a Growing World Consciousness* (New York: Macmillan, 1930); Barbara Garland Polikoff, *With One Bold Act: The Story of Jane Addams* (Chicago: Boswell Books, 1999); Eleanor J. Stebner, *The Women of Hull House: A Study in Spirituality, Vocation, and Friendship* (Albany: State University of New York Press,

1997); Hilda Satt Polacheck, *I Came a Stranger: The Story of a Hull-House Girl* (Urbana: University of Illinois Press, 1991); Rivka Shpak Lissak, *Pluralism and Progressives: Hull House and the New Immigrants, 1890–1919* (Chicago: University of Chicago Press, 1989); Allen F. Davis and Mary Lynn McCree, eds., *Eighty Years at Hull-House* (Chicago: Quadrangle, 1969).

96 Holmes, "Women Workers of Chicago," 508–10; "Work of the Sex." Men dominated the trade union movement and marginalized women, whom they did not recognize as "authentic" workers. Continued male resistance and reluctance to organizing women resulted in the formation of a number of women's labor organizations in the late nineteenth and early twentieth centuries, including the ones in Chicago in which Holmes was involved.

John, Helen is not a working woman but rather an independent, middle-class woman whose activities are subsumed within the framework of charity.

"Her Life for Labor" begins with middle-class labor organizer Helen discussing the values of working for the labor movement with her suitor Willis Dryden. Willis wants Helen to marry him and then settle down at home while he engages in some business venture. He suggests that when they are financially secure they can both return to labor organizing. Helen rejects this proposal, presumably able to do so because of her class, which allows her to remain financially independent. Although Willis admires Helen's "spirit of devotion," he believes that she is "casting pearls before swine." Voicing concerns about appropriate behavior for a middle-class woman, he explains: "People look askance at young ladies who spend their time among the workers and the poor and entertain strong opinions. There is no honor in it, only hard work and ignominy, and you will not even have the enjoyment of seeing yourself victorious in bringing about the reforms for which you are working."[97]

Helen's rebuttal demonstrates a noble, selfless person but also one entirely in keeping with the contemporary construction of middle- and upper-class women's charitable and maternalist role in society. She did not do her work for honor or glory but to help less fortunate people: "If I should succeed in persuading a few people to think earnestly, should inspire the workers, especially women, with better and higher desires; or help the world along a very little toward the era of co-operation, fraternity, equal duties and equal privileges, I shall feel fully repaid."[98] As the story develops, Holmes continues her critique of capitalism. Helen doubts that it is possible for a rich man to be sympathetic to the labor movement, on the grounds that money corrupts. Her concerns are proved correct when the two meet years after going their separate ways. Willis is a rich man who refuses to negotiate with his unionized employees, while Helen is still committed to the labor movement. The story ends tragically when Helen is shot trying to protect Willis from an angry mob that has hijacked the picket lines. (Holmes is careful not to incriminate the strikers.)

Although the model labor woman was very different to the idealized male organizer represented by John or Seth, the woman union activist that Holmes constructed in Helen similarly reflected contemporary concerns within the labor movement. Holmes's construction of Helen and her broader association of female trade union activity with middle- and upper-class women can be best understood within the context of the gendering and classing of the labor movement at the turn of the century. As Holmes found in the late 1870s when she

---

97   Lizzie M. Holmes, "Her Life for Labor," *American Federationist*, December 1901, 521.

98   Ibid.

was organizing Chicago women for the WWU, the commonly held belief that "no nice girl would belong" to a union complicated the task of organizing working-class women into trade unions.[99] The lack of working-class women's participation, particularly among native-born, English-speaking women workers—the subjects of her stories—was a common complaint at the turn of the twentieth century. However, after the demise of the Knights of Labor, male unionists rarely tried to organize working women, and well into the twentieth century the most important unionization campaigns were organized by middle-class women. By depicting a romantic, feminine, and at times quite glamorous middle- or upper-class woman organizer, Holmes constructed a respectable labor woman to which working-class female readers could perhaps aspire—even Helen's tragic death reaffirmed her "woman's compassion."[100] At the same time, she presented a positive model that male readers of the *American Federationist* could respect.

---

99 Holmes, "Women Workers of Chicago," 508.

100 Laura Hapke and Nan Enstad both discuss working-class women's modification of middle- and upper-class behavior; Hapke does so in specific relation to fiction. See Laura Hapke, *Labor's Text: The Worker in American Fiction* (New Brunswick, NJ: Rutgers University Press, 2001), 14–55, especially 145; Nan Enstad, *Ladies of Labor, Girls of Adventure: Working Women, Popular Culture, and Labor Politics at the Turn of the Twentieth Century* (New York: Columbia University Press, 1999).

Conclusion

The eight stories Holmes published in the *American Federationist* offered a critique of industrial capitalism. Through her fiction, Holmes communicated her position to a much broader audience than she could access in more radical journals. The tales suggest the value of a closer examination of the *American Federationist* as a working-class journal, the potential and limits of fiction as a political medium, and the flexible approach to labor journalism many writers took at the turn of the twentieth century.

The *American Federationist* was read by thousands, if not hundreds of thousands, of American workers across the country. Drawing upon her own wage-earning and organizing experiences and a life that had taken her from the Midwest to the West, from the Knights of Labor to socialism and anarchism to "pure and simple" unionism, Holmes created environments, circumstances, and characters familiar to these readers and used that familiarity to communicate her critique of capitalism. That critique of capitalism was rooted in the American labor tradition through which Holmes had moved. Indeed, the diversity of Holmes's activism no doubt enabled her to write for such a wide-ranging audience. Holmes's descriptions of the bodies of her working-class characters reveal much about her understanding of the modern industrial system. Both men and women suffer as a result of industrial labor. Their bodies are bent, thin, dirty, worn down, and made ugly, and their minds are wasted; both are ultimately destroyed. This critique was the central message of the stories, but they also touched upon gender and class dynamics in the labor movement.

Although the leadership of the AFL was not sympathetic to her radical background nor her ideas of gender equality, Holmes was able to provide a strong critique of the capitalist system and to suggest that women deserved the same rights as men—access to the American standard of living and, without rejecting women's domestic role, the right to wage labor if they so wanted. Holmes's fiction benefited both parties, albeit in different ways. Although Holmes's radical past makes her an unlikely bedfellow of the AFL, the editors of the *American Federationist* presumably felt that melodramatic fiction would appeal to its current readers and even attract more. Financial compensation and the broader audience likely motivated Holmes to see the *American Federationist* as a valuable vehicle to spread her critique of capitalism, despite the need to modify her radical politics. The fact that this was a marriage of convenience does not make these stories any less valuable as a source for the labor historian. To the contrary, the differences between Holmes's more radical life and her publications in the *American Federationist* offer historians a way to consider the flexibility of left-wing politics in turn of the century America.

DISCUSSION QUESTIONS

1. What is the author's thesis? In other words, what is she saying about Lizzy Holmes?

2. What does the author tell us about the relationship between the Knights of Labor and the American Federation of Labor?

3. Describe the fictional stories Holmes wrote for the *American Federationist*.

4. What event began Holmes's lifelong interest in the labor struggle?

5. What was Holmes's role in the Haymarket Riot?

6. Although earning money was one reason Holmes published in the *American Federationist,* there was another reason. What was it?

7. How do Holmes's stories contrast rural labor with urban labor?

8. Although it was courageous of Holmes to use women as heroines in her stories, she stops short of advocating gender equality by doing what?

9. In the story "Her Life for Labor," how is Holmes's heroine different from ones in her earlier stories?

CHAPTER SIX

Environmentalism Redefined

FROM *Forcing the Spring*
BY ROBERT GOTTLIEB

INTRODUCTION

The history of environmentalism in the United States is one of ideological battles fought over what environmentalism should be. In 1913 Congress passed the Raker Act, ending a long battle between Teddy Roosevelt's conservationist approach and John Muir's deeply spiritual environmentalism. Teddy won. The twin valleys of Yosemite and Hetch Hetchy would have separate fates. Yosemite would be preserved and Hetch Hetchy would be flooded in order to construct a hydroelectric dam to service the growing state of California. Practical conservation defeated nature-as-holy-shrine.[1] But that was just one particular battle. The war continued, as various parts of the "environmental movement" fought over its meaning and significance. The children of Teddy Roosevelt became mainstream environmentalists. They were bureaucrats who got things done through the system. The children of John Muir became the idealists, the "tree-huggers," the activists, operating outside the system. Both groups have played important roles in the history of environmentalism. But can they be brought

FIGURE 6.1.
"Rachel Carson," https://commons.wiki-media.org/wiki/File:Rachel_Carson_w.jpg. Copyright in the Public Domain.

---

1   Robert Righter, *The Battle over Hetch Hetchy: America's Most Controversial Dam and the Birth of Modern Environmentalism* (New York: Oxford University Press, 2005).

together? That is the question Robert Gottlieb asks in his book, *Forcing the Spring*.

Rachel Carson, the famous biologist and nature writer, was dying of cancer when her book *Silent Spring* was published in 1962. Up to that time she had been famous as a nature writer, having written two bestselling books on nature in the 1950s. Now at the end of her life, she was publishing a book that would earn her numerous enemies and expose her to vitriolic criticism, especially from those connected to the chemicals industries. This new book was an expose on how pesticides, especially the much-used DDT, were poisoning the environment. The birds were all being killed off. No birds, no bird songs, thus a Silent Spring. Furthermore, these dangerous chemicals caused cancer in humans. The threat was not only to the environment, but to people as well. The hatred heaped on Rachel Carson was more than anyone should have to endure. She died of cancer in 1964. But the war that chemical companies had waged on her backfired. Even before she died, people started becoming aware that her warnings deserved to be heeded. A new strength came to environmentalism thanks to Rachel Carson's work. Her writing and research had transcended the normal divides within the larger environmental community, and created a somewhat unified movement.[2] Gottlieb believes we could use another Rachel Carson today.

Another towering figure in environmental history is Alice Hamilton, who in 1919 became the first woman to be appointed to the Harvard faculty. Her work in toxicology led to important changes in industrial workplaces all over the country. Her research explored how certain chemicals in the workplace were harmful to humans. She died at the age of 101 in 1970. Posthumously, her work has been seen as an important part of environmental efforts. Like Carson, she bridged the gap between the professional, bureaucratic side of environmentalism and the grassroots activist side of environmentalism. This was especially true because of Hamilton's long association with Jane Addams' Hull House.[3]

Will the future of environmentalism see more inspiring figures like Rachel Carson and Alice Hamilton? What will the environmental movement of the future look like? How can it unite its many factions? These are the questions Gottlieb sought to answer back in the 1990s. We are still asking those questions today.

* * *

2   Linda Lear, *Rachel Carson: Witness for Nature* (New York: H. Holt, 1997).
3   Alice Hamilton, *Exploring the Dangerous Trades: The Autobiography of Alice Hamilton* (Boston: Little Brown and Co., 1943).

Opportunities for Change

When Vice-president-elect Albert Gore convened the session addressing environmental and technology issues on the afternoon of the last day of the December 1992 Economic Summit in Little Rock, Arkansas, there was already speculation among the press and policy makers that there would emerge, as the *Los Angeles Times* put it the day after the summit, a "green tilt" to the new administration. Even more than the election of Jimmy Carter sixteen years earlier, there was enormous anticipation that change—a Clinton buzzword during the campaign—was in the air.

Speakers at the session had proposed a number of environmental policy approaches, some of which were likely to be contradictory: pollution taxes; a non-adversarial relationship among industry, environmentalists, and government; pollution prevention strategies; rationalizing regulatory and permit processes. There was even talk of a "new paradigm of environmental governance," as Gus Speth (NRDC cofounder and Jimmy Carter's chair of the Council on Environmental Quality) put it. Such talk inevitably reflected raised expectations, a feeling that so much more was possible than at any previous period during environmentalism's short but complex history as both movement and policy system manager and watchdog.

One month later in his inauguration speech, Clinton spoke of "forcing the spring" by his election. This evocation of change, which had been so prominent at both the economic summit and in pre-inaugural events, was beginning to have a life of its own. For one, it was suggesting in environmental terms that the historic divisions between jobs and environment or economic development and environmental governance, as the Clinton campaign rhetoric had insisted, would now, at last, be overcome.

The mood of change, however, does not necessarily reflect the realities of change. The divisions over policy, between movements and policy makers, and among movements themselves, are potentially as sharp and contentious as ever. What becomes different is the level of expectation, the promise of change to come. And such a promise has arrived at a moment in time when the possibilities of environmental change have become increasingly linked to the redefinition of the environmental movement and its capacity to transform American society itself.

We live today in a period of great upheaval, when environmental issues increasingly reflect crucial social and economic choices, and when new opportunities for change are emerging both within the movement and throughout society. Such opportunities for change have turned out to be unexpected, broad in scope, potentially far-reaching, and radical in their implications. They involve questions of technology and production, decision making and empowerment, social organization and cultural values. They reflect changes at the global level—most significantly, the end of the Cold War. They also reflect local struggles and victims, as demonstrated by new constituencies and new social claims that may influence the direction of environmentalism. Of all these changes, it is the passing of the Cold War that has the greatest consequences.

More than thirty years ago, the Students for a Democratic Society argued forcefully in *The Port Huron Statement* that the Cold War had become the defining event of the post–World War II order. Cold War realities, the SDS manifesto declared, affected the "whole living conditions of each American citizen," with "defense mechanisms" in the nuclear age altering the very "character of the system that creates them for protection."[4]

The Cold War, pervasive at the time this statement was written, dominated public life for more than four decades. Government budgets became heavily weighted toward military expenditures. The new technologies of such Cold War–related industries as aerospace, electronics, and petrochemicals have all left huge legacies of pollution. And for much of the post–World War II period, the rhetoric of national mission became intertwined with Cold War–linked themes concerning national security, access to resources, and strategic competition.

The Cold War was a pivotal factor in influencing the state of the environment. It stimulated the nuclear industry, whose severe environmental impacts have included the contamination of local communities where nuclear facilities (from mines to generators) have been located. It shaped energy and industrial policies that both exhausted resources and intensified the development of an economy significantly based on the use of toxic or hazardous materials and processes.

The Cold War also influenced the state of environmental politics. During the early years of the Cold War, key conservationist figures, such as Fairfield Osborn of the Conservation Foundation and Joseph Fisher of Resources for the Future, incorporated Cold War themes such as national security into the conservationist argument. If materials shortages threatened to "impair the long-run economic growth and security of the United States and other free nations," as the 1952 report of the President's Materials Policy Commission explicitly warned, then, according to Joseph Fisher, the "availability of a wide variety of resource materials [was] essential to our defense and security." A strong conservationist approach was therefore connected to Cold War agendas and presented as integral to sustaining what Fairfield Osborn called the values that make "American life what it is."[5]

---

4 See Students for a Democratic Society, *The Port Huron Statement* (New York: Students for a Democratic Society, August 1962), pp. 23, 24.

5 The national security dimension of resource policy is discussed in President's Materials Policy Commission, *Resources for Freedom*, A Report to

Response to the Cold War also differentiated between the types of environmental groups that emerged in the post–World War II era. The opposition to nuclear testing that developed in the late 1950s and early 1960s began a direct line of dissent through the New Left to the antinuclear and antitoxics movements of the 1970s and 1980s. These contrasted with the national security–oriented approaches of the cold-warrior conservationists and with later arguments by mainstream environmentalists that nuclear issues especially were not appropriate subjects for an environmental movement.

Yet the Cold War remained, for environmental groups, a reality from which it was never quite possible to escape. Through the 1970s to middle 1980s, while mainstream environmentalism grew and matured, Cold War politics still influenced the direction of policy. The imperatives of the Cold War, reinforced by the massive military buildup

that was begun in the last years of the Carter administration and was escalated dramatically during the Reagan years, remained dominant in setting the priorities for government expenditures and in structuring economic and industrial policies. For mainstream environmentalists, a continuous Cold War created uncomfortable choices: either deny Cold War realities or accommodate to the culture of the Cold War in policy debates.

In the area of nuclear weapons policy, for example, most mainstream groups (with the significant exceptions of the NRDC, Friends of the Earth, and Environmental Action) avoided involvement with the issue. Distancing themselves from the tactics and perspectives of the anti–nuclear power protesters, mainstream groups remained uneasy about the efforts of organizations such as Mobilization for Survival to link explicitly energy and Cold War–based military and arms race issues. Even the NRDC, which promoted policies for managing an arms race that had spun dangerously out of control, tried to avoid association with the direct-action wing of the movement.

In contrast, among the alternative groups, the escalating arms race of the 1970s and 1980s generated new and important organizing efforts. Community-based groups emerged to contest particular facilities, such as the weapons production center at Hanford, Washington, and the Rocky Flats facility near Denver, Colorado. Other groups focused on the impacts of proposed new

---

the President (Washington, D.C.: Government Printing Office, 1952), vol. 1, p. 2. The same theme is discussed by Samuel Hays in his essay "The Myth of Conservation" in *Perspectives on Conservation*, edited by Henry Jarrett (Baltimore: Johns Hopkins Press, 1958), pp. 40–45. The "availability of a wide variety of resources" quote is from Joseph L. Fisher, "Long-Range Research in Times Like These," in Resources for the Future, *Annual Report* (for the year ending September 30, 1961) (Washington, D.C.: Resources for the Future, December 1961), p. 4. Fairfield Osborn's remarks are cited in Peter Collier and David Horowitz, *The Rockefellers: An American Dynasty* (New York: Holt, Rinehart and Winston, 1976), p. 305.

weapons systems or high-level radioactive waste dumps or opposed specific programs such as the mobile, land-based MX missile in southern Utah. The emergence of many of these grassroots groups, which became integral to the rise of the antitoxics movements of the 1980s, helped transform the question of the Cold War from an issue of ideological conflict to one concerning the environmental hazards of military production. By the late 1980s, what had begun as a series of local protests against the pollution generated by hazardous facilities had evolved into a full-blown movement exposing the country's most extraordinary toxics scandal. Military facilities—weapons production centers, military bases, and other units of the military's production complex—had become the largest and most unregulated source of pollution and toxic hazards and a major polluter overseas. Documented problems included the nearly 15,000 toxic waste sites, with about 100 of those areas listed on Superfund's National Priorities List of most contaminated sites; extensive contamination at nearly all of the military's major foreign installations; contract arrangements based on a system of military specifications that encouraged the use of hazardous materials; and the almost blanket exemption of military facilities from environmental laws and regulations. The Cold War had left a toxic legacy, as the military created "a chemical plague over the land through its misuse and disposal of dangerous chemicals."[6]

The strategic limits of existing environmental policy in addressing this toxic legacy became more visible and intolerable with the sudden passing of the Cold War in the late 1980s and early 1990s. How to clean up polluting industries— many spawned and nurtured by a Cold War system—no longer seemed a question of how best to manage such pollution, but, more appropriately, how to restructure the country's toxics-centered, military-based economy. The longstanding, presumedly utopian desire of antinuclear movements for economic conversion—turning swords into plowshares, or toxic military facilities into socially useful, clean-technology operations—had suddenly become, in the wake of the Cold War's demise, an issue of some urgency and practicality. Questions about the future role—or restructuring—of Cold War–related military production have been transformed in the new post–Cold War era into a broader set of issues linked to the concepts of pollution prevention and toxics use reduction raised by the alternative environmental groups. The end of the Cold War exposed a production system toxic at its core and an environmental politics that continually limited the possibilities for change. The conversion of production to *what*? Controlled by

6 The "chemical plague" quote is from Lenny Siegal and Gary Cohen, "America's Worst Environmental Nightmare: The U.S. Military's Toxic Legacy," *New Solutions*, Winter 1991, p. 37.

whom? These have become the central questions for post–Cold War environmentalism. How to advocate and organize concerning such issues and the related question of what kind of post-Cold War environmental politics might emerge have therefore become defining points for the movement.

As the end of the Cold War has created enormous opportunities for restructuring the urban industrial order, it has also provided an opportunity for new visions about environmental change and social transformation. Not since the period of social rebellion during the 1960s, with its search for a new quality of life, have circumstances appeared to create the basis for such new visions. During the 1960s, many of the generational challenges that arose were associated with a desperate search for community in the midst of Cold War realities. Participants in the youth movements, including but not limited to students, were essentially children of the Cold War. Today, the end of the Cold War presents opportunities for a post–Cold War generation to establish a new framework for change.

Contemporary environmental groups, especially the mainstream organizations, have largely ignored young people, including students. During the rise of mainstream environmentalism in the 1970s and 1980s, young people and students served primarily as ground troops for the particular activities of an evolving environmental movement, such as electoral initiative campaigns and mega-events such as Earth Day. Even organizations such as the PIRGs or the National Wildlife Federation's "Cool It" program (which focused on issues such as recycling and global warming) were organized directly as youth and student-based efforts, and relied on older professional staff or the larger mainstream organizations to set their agendas or establish their directions.

The relative lack of environmental activity among young people began to change in the late 1980s, linked to the upsurge in environmental activism in general. Several new student environmental groups especially took root, in some cases inspired by the rise of the alternative community-based and direct-action groups and the growing interest in class, ethnicity, race, and gender-related questions in environmentalism. In 1988, one of those groups, based at the University of North Carolina at Chapel Hill, began to explore the possibility of establishing a network with other student environmental groups. Taking the name Student Environmental Action Coalition (SEAC), the students placed a notice to this effect in *Greenpeace* magazine. To their astonishment, they received responses from some 200 campus-based environmental groups, many less than a year old themselves. An informal association of student groups, based on phone, fax, mail, and computer networks, was then established. A conference, hosted by the University of North Carolina group, was organized for October 1989. Entitled "Threshold," the meeting represented the first national student environmental conference ever held.[7]

With more than 1700 students in attendance and spirited talk of new organ-izing and action, Threshold far surpassed everyone's expectations. It appeared to transform SEAC overnight into a major new player within the environmental movement. Conference speakers, including Barry Commoner, David Brower, and John O'Connor of the National Toxics Campaign, found a receptive audience hungry for information and strategic direction.

After Threshold, SEAC became a loose amalgam of campaigns, network functions, campus organizing activities, and occasional lobbying work. One of the network's most successful undertakings was the campus environmental audit, a program modeled after a study by UCLA graduate students of the environmental problems and issues associated with that university. More than 200 student activist groups undertook audits of their own campuses as part of Earth Day 1990 activities, with SEAC integrating the audit concept into a newly established university accountability campaign, paralleling SEAC's own corporate accountability theme. With its network mushrooming, foundation interest in the new organization blossoming, and active courtship by both mainstream and alternative

environmental groups increasing, SEAC prepared to emerge as a viable national organization. SEAC leaders hoped that process would culminate at "Catalyst," the group's second annual student environmental conference, to be held in October 1990 at the University of Illinois campus in Champaign-Urbana.[8]

The Catalyst gathering turned out to be an even headier experience for the students than the previous year's Threshold event. This time, 7600 students from all fifty states registered, with additional representatives from eleven foreign countries. The presence of so many potential student activists was inspiring. The numbers alone seemed to suggest that this new student environmental force might change the shape of environmental politics in the years

---

7 See "Join SEAC!" *Greenpeace*, November-December 1988, vol. 13, no. 6, p. 12.

8 The author was the faculty supervisor for the UCLA study, by Tamra Brink et al., *In Our Backyard: Environmental Issues at UCLA, Proposals for Change, and the Institution's Potential as a Model* (Los Angeles: UCLA Urban Planning Program Comprehensive Project, June 1989). See also April A. Smith and Robert Gottlieb, "Campus Environmental Audits: The UCLA Experience," in *The Campus and Environmental Responsibility*, edited by David J. Eagan and David W. Orr (San Francisco: Jossey-Bass, New Directions for Higher Education Series, no. 77, Spring 1992), and UCLA Environmental Research Group, *Campus Environmental Audit* (Palo Alto, Ca.: Earth Day, 1990, February 1990). April Smith, one of the coauthors of *In Our Backyard* and the *Campus Environmental Audit*, became the liaison with SEAC and its university accountability campaign. See also April E. Smith and the Student Environmental Action Coalition, *Campus Ecology: A Guide to Assessing Environmental Quality and Creating Strategies for Change* (Los Angeles: Living Planet Press, 1993).

to come. The mass media also began to take note, with several publications commenting warily on the unabashed radicalism of SEAC and its affinity with the New Left. *Forbes* magazine, for example, labeled the group's constituents as "the children of the children of the 1960s" and warned readers that the anticorporate, activist-oriented SEAC had "a clear line of descent from SDS."[9]

Within the year, however, SEAC unexpectedly found itself at an impasse. Overwhelmed by the attention, distracted by its instant celebrity status, unprepared to consolidate and extend initial student interest into a coherent campus organizing strategy, and uncertain about its own status as a national player as it continued to function as a loose collection of campus contacts and activities, the organization appeared unable to contend with its enormous growing pains.

These growth pains were compounded by the continuing division among environmental groups. Although mainstream groups welcomed student participation, they worried about the potential radicalism of student activists and the tendency of the activists to accuse the Group of Ten of having sold out concerning issues and tactics. And the alternative groups, while identifying with the activism of students, remained wary that these were students likely to be trained as future professionals who in turn would likely be ignorant of community or workplace experiences. Unlike SDS, whose formative role within the New Left helped define a larger social movement, the new student activism thus finds itself emerging at a point in time when the environmental movement has already become divided and an institutionalization process has narrowed certain definitions of the movement's role. Student groups such as SEAC and youth groups in general therefore tend to see themselves as limited in their capacity to set new directions or establish a new spirit or framework for movement activity.

Despite these constraints, a student and youth-based environmentalism has the capacity to play an important role in creating new opportunities for environmentalism. One crucial arena for action is the university itself, as student environmental groups seek to transform this powerful institution, which is a major environmental player through its infrastructure activities (waste generation and disposal, resource use, land use policies) and, most importantly, through the influence of its research on environmental policy. A student-based environmentalism also has the potential to help revive campus activism in general. By the early 1990s, SEAC and other campus environmental groups were becoming "the biggest and often the only source of campus activism attempting to stimulate

---

9 The *Forbes* article, by Martin Kihn, is entitled "SDS Jr." (June 10, 1991, pp. 51–52). For background on the SEAC, see Barbara Ruben, "Catalyzing Student Action," *Environmental Action*, January-February 1991, p. 7, and Jim McNeill, "Jonathan Goldman: Student SEACer," *In These Times*, September 18–24, 1991, pp. 4–5.

a new movement," as Swarthmore College activist Heather Abel put it.[10] The 1992 presidential election, with its large youth vote (some of it environmentally related) for Clinton and Gore, also suggested an opening toward activism, which had been suspended during the 1980s but seemed ready to emerge once again.

Beyond the possibilities for activism, young people have come to represent the first generation to be aware of the dimensions of environmental crisis and its relationship to everyday experience. Young people are not simply becoming early eco-activists (children taking up environmental values as moral absolutes has become increasingly common and noted), but they are also increasingly aware that the economic and social choices they face about their future work and lives have become more and more limited. At a moment when the end of the Cold War creates new possibilities for economic and environmental restructuring, young people seem destined to become the first generation likely to experience downward mobility combined with more degraded environments. The environmental crisis becomes the metaphor for the larger social crisis, while a generational politics, including a student and youth-based environmentalism, becomes one crucial route for linking issues and movements that must be linked if that crisis is to be addressed. A youth politics, like the

post–Cold War future to which it is now intricately tied, thus offers another kind of opening for change, part of a renewed activism capable of undertaking its own "long march through the institutions" in its quest for environmental redefinition and transformation.[11]

Inerest Group or Social Movement?

What is an environmental group? Who is an environmentalist? How might different kinds of environmental groups influence the state of the environment— and the state of society? These charged questions lie at the heart of the problem of how to define environmentalism and its future direction. Does environmentalism represent new kinds of social movements, democratic and populist insurgencies seeking a fundamental restructuring of the urban and industrial order? Or is it a set of interest groups influencing policy to better manage or protect the environment and help rationalize that same urban and industrial order? Is it a left-wing movement in disguise, as George Will and other conservative commentators have complained? Or is environmentalism

---

10   Author's 1992 interview with Heather Abel.

11   The phrase "long march through the institutions" was first used in 1967 by German New Left activist (and German Green cofounder) Rudi Dutschke in describing the New Left's link to what would subsequently be defined by European and U.S. analysts as "the new social movements." (Author's notes from his attendance at the annual convention of the German SDS in Munich, June 1967.)

apolitical, concerned with science rather than ideology, as Sierra Club executive director Carl Pope has argued? Is it a movement primarily about Nature or about industry, about production or about consumption, about wilderness or about pollution, about natural environments or about human environments, or do such distinctions themselves indicate differing interpretations of what environmentalism has been and ought to be?[12]

In describing the complexity, distinctive roots, and different contemporary forms of environmentalism, this book provides an analysis of environmentalism as both interest group and social movement. The origins of environmentalism derive in part from the development of a set of social claims about Nature and urban and industrial life. During the Progressive Era, one set of groups came to be associated with the rise of resource agencies and environmental bureaucracies, adopting a perspective related to the uses of science and expertise for a more efficient and rational management of the natural environment and the urban and industrial order. Similarly, concerns about wilderness and protection of the environment came to be linked to the

activities of specific constituencies who saw themselves as "consumption users of wildlife" (as Thomas Kimball of the National Wildlife Federation described NWF members) or consumers of other environmental amenities. At the same time, there were groups that saw themselves fighting for the public interest by challenging powerful special interests, such as the timber companies and mining interests, in their attempt to exploit the environment for private gain.[13]

These Progressive Era conservationist and protectionist groups were similar to and contrasted with urban and industrial groups of the same period that focused on the environmental conditions of daily life. Such groups as settlement house workers, regional planning advocates, and occupational health activists shared a faith in scientific analysis and the power of rational judgment pervasive in that era. But these groups also sought to empower powerless constituencies and organize for the minimal conditions of well-being and community identity in a harsh urban and industrial age.

With the significant social and technological changes of World War II and the postwar era, environmentalism became increasingly identified with changes in the patterns of consumption associated with an expanding urban and industrial order. Scenic resources came to be valued as recreational resources, although the mobilizations

---

12 See George Will, "The Green Thrill Has Replaced the Red Scare," *Los Angeles Times*, April 19, 1990. See also Charles Krauthammer, "An Insidious Rejuvenation of the Old Left," *Los Angeles Times*, December 24, 1990, and, along the same lines, Martin W. Lewis, *Green Delusions: An Environmentalist Critique of Radical Environmentalism* (Durham, N.C.: Duke University Press, 1992).

13 Author's 1991 interview with Thomas Kimball.

in defense of wilderness at Dinosaur National Monument and the Grand Canyon tentatively (and inadequately in terms of outcome) sought to define a public interest value in protecting Nature for its own sake. The changes in consumption also helped to shape the rebellious politics of the New Left and the counterculture, with their concerns about quality of life and the hazards of technology. Consumption thus became at once an economic activity, with a defined set of interests associated with it, and a social condition giving rise to the new social movements of the post–World War II period.

By Earth Day 1970, some confusion about the new environmentalism and what it represented had set in. This reflected its eclectic origins, which included 1960s New Left and counter-culture activism, recreational/leisure time–oriented protectionist politics of the post–World War II period, and the resource management emphasis of several of the old-line conservationist groups. Even the trend toward profes-sionalization that so quickly prevailed among environmental groups during the 1970s nevertheless incorporated both adversarial and system management perspectives on how to achieve envi-ronmental change. Environmentalists were activists *and* lobbyists, system opponents *and* system managers. But by the late 1970s, most of the professional groups had become thoroughly linked to the environmental policy system, a system designed to manage and control rather than reduce or restructure the sources of pollution and other environ-mental ills. Though at times contesting how policies were implemented, the ties that developed between professional or mainstream groups (mainstream in part because of those very ties) and the environmental policy system itself made mainstream environmentalism espe-cially vulnerable to the charge of interest group politics.

Through the 1980s and into the 1990s, mainstream groups have been continually subject to criticism about their interest group status. Mainstream environmentalists are defined as elitists in class terms, upper-middle-class whites who have a lack of concern for job loss. At the same time, the national focus of the mainstream groups, their emphasis on professionalization, and their unwillingness to organize specific con-stituencies or in specific communities have provided an opening for blatantly transparent pro-industry campaigns, such as the Sagebrush Rebellion of the late 1970s and the more recent "wise use" movement to erode public support for certain environmentalist goals. The contemporary "wise use" movement is particularly instructive in its effort to appropriate long-standing conservation-ist language about efficient "use" of resources and then seeking to charge the mainstream groups with hostility to the "use" concept itself.

Today, the interest group identity for mainstream environmentalism seems more entrenched than ever. With their chief executive officers, targeted mailings, and continuing emphasis on lobbying, litigation, and the use of expertise, mainstream groups have replicated certain key aspects of interest group organization. Even the shift in focus of groups such as the EDF away from environmental "command and control" regulatory policies to market incentives has only reinforced the interest group connection. Through market arrangements such as pollution credits, the environment becomes a commodity to be traded and sold, with environmental groups seen as defining their objectives increasingly in terms of their economic value.

As they have grown in size and reach, mainstream groups have successfully secured for themselves a seat at the negotiating table and are now powerful organizations contending with other powerful interest groups. For example, since 1990, a "three-way" negotiating process concerning water policy in California has taken place. The three parties to the negotiations include urban interests (signifying large urban water agencies), agriculture interests (associated with the large landowners and irrigation districts), and environmental interests (consisting largely of mainstream environmental groups interested in protecting the Sacramento Bay Delta environment in northern California). These three-way negotiators have sought to reach a consensus position about water policy for the state. For the environmental interests, the key objective in

this regard has been the creation of an Environmental Water Authority with the power to purchase water to help protect the Delta environment. The key to the three-way process has thus evolved into the effort to establish a political process for the purchase and sale of water among contending interest groups. In the process, environmental negotiators, defined as a quasi–economic interest group, begin to lose their public interest status as a social force fighting on behalf of groups not represented at the table.[14]

This interest group association most directly separates the mainstream groups from alternative environmental groups, grassroots networks, and community-based groups, as well as direct-action and more ideologically oriented "green" organizations. The use of the term *alternative* for environmental groups suggests different scenarios for these organizations. On the one hand, it implies that they are outside the mainstream, different from the way that environmentalism has come to be defined, especially in terms of its interest group status. It is in this context that many activists within alternative groups, such as antitoxics organizers, don't like to call themselves environmentalists. "Calling our movement an environmental movement," Lois Gibbs declares, "would inhibit our organizing and undercut our claim that we are about protecting people,

---

14 On the "three-way" process, see Judith Redmond and Robert Gottlieb, "The Select Few Who Still Control State's Water Policy Discussions," *Sacramento Bee*, June 1, 1992.

not birds and bees."[15] Similarly, Richard Moore of the Southwest Organizing Project and Tony Mazzochi of the Oil, Atomic, and Chemical Workers Union, among others, have argued that people of color and workers are turned off by the environmentalist label, suggesting the term conjures up associations with middle- and upper-class Anglo yuppie types seen as consumers of Nature or policy technicians.

At the same time, alternative approaches are noteworthy for their critical view of the existing urban and industrial order, similar to ways that the new social movements of the 1960s defined their activities. Such a view is critical in the sense that environmental problems are seen as rooted in the structures of production and consumption in society. Such a viewpoint also extends to the critique of mainstream interest-group forms of environmental organization and activity. In this context, the term *alternative* suggests a social change movement, as well as efforts to construct a prefigurative movement seeking new forms of community and technology. As opposed to mainstream environmentalism's interest group identity, alternative groups can be seen as inheriting the mantle of the new social movements, or at least the tradition of social claims about equity, empowerment, and daily life concerns.

As part of this critical tradition, antinuclear groups challenged the nuclear industry during the 1970s, questioning the technologies employed and advocating replacing such environmentally harmful technologies with a clean production system. The direct-action antinuclear groups became especially wedded to a vision of a decentralist, democratic, solar energy–based society, connecting their vision to earlier New Left and counterculture ideas about transforming a post-scarcity society. Similarly, antitoxics groups, which first mobilized against local landfills and incinerators, expanded their claims to talk about empowerment and environmental democracy as well as the new sense of community that their struggles had helped define. Concepts such as toxics use reduction and environmental justice, which became central to the antitoxics campaigns, also spoke to the need for restructuring industry decision making to account for industrial impacts on daily life.

Unlike the mainstream groups, the social claims of these alternative groups directly address questions of gender, ethnicity, race, and class. Many, though not all, of the alternative groups have established a feminist perspective that is both more interactive and democratic. By pursuing a message of environmental justice and equity, some alternative groups, especially those in the antitoxics area, have necessarily become focused on issues of discrimination and racism embedded in the toxics economy. And with the tentative efforts to link workplace and community environmental

---

15   Author's 1992 interview with Lois Gibbs.

concerns, some alternative groups have begun to shift the definition of environmentalism away from an exclusive focus on consumption to the sphere of work and production. By elevating issues of work and production, the dynamics of ethnicity race, and gender, and questions of community and empowerment, a reconstituted environmentalism has the capacity to establish a common ground between and among constituencies and issues, bridging a new politics of social and environmental change.

Who, then, will speak for environmentalism in the 1990s and beyond? Will it be the mainstream groups with their big budgets, large staff, and interest group identity? Can alternative groups, many of whom reject the label "environmentalist," lay claim to a tradition that has yet to be considered environmental? Will the opportunities for transformation, heightened by a mood of change associated with the end of the Reagan and Bush era and the raised expectations of the 1992 elections, translate into more vigorous and broader-based social movements that can influence and frame "a new paradigm of environmental governance"? Can mainstream and alternative groups find a common language, a shared history, a common conceptual and organizational home?

The figures of Alice Hamilton and Rachel Carson provide a clue. These compassionate, methodical, bitterly criticized women, accused of being sentimentalists, biased researchers, and pseudoscientists, opened up new ways of understanding what it meant to be concerned about human and natural environments. They were figures who transcended the narrow, limiting discourse of their eras, forcing their contemporaries to realize that much more was at stake than one industrial poison or one dying bird. Their language was transformative, their environmentalism expressed in both daily life and ecological dimensions.

To understand these women as connected rather than disparate parts of a tradition helps answer the question posed by Dana Alston at the People of Color Environmental Leadership Summit discussed in the introduction to this book. How should environmentalism be defined? Alston asked. Should we keep to the narrow definitions that have provided environmental legitimacy for some groups and ideas to the exclusion of others? To learn the lessons of Rachel Carson and Alice Hamilton and how they are linked in their concern for the world we live in helps begin that process of redefining and reconstituting environmentalism in the broader terms that Alston urged. It involves a redefinition that leads toward an environmentalism that is democratic and inclusive, an environmentalism of equity and social justice, an environmentalism of linked natural and human environments, an environmentalism of transformation. The complex and continuing history of this movement points the way toward these new possibilities for change.

DISCUSSION QUESTIONS

1. What do you think the author means by "forcing the Spring"?
2. According to the author, what event in the 1990s sparked a new approach to environmentalism?
3. According to the author, how is the Student Environmental Action Coalition (SEAC) an example of a new style of environmental action?
4. What problems did the SEAC have after its initial success?
5. According to the author, is environmentalism an interest group or a social movement?
6. What does it mean when environmental groups use the term "alternative" to define themselves?

CHAPTER SEVEN

Worrisome Changes in US Labor Force and Employment Since 2007

BY ROBERT RIGGS

INTRODUCTION

In the 1990s *The Wall Street Journal* reported some interesting statistics. Comparing corporate profits in 1980 with those in 1994, they found that in 1980, seventy percent of corporate profits came from manufacturing, while thirty percent came from investment banking. By 1994 that had been reversed, so that seventy percent of profits came from investment banking and thirty percent from manufacturing. They also reported that corporate profits were up fifty percent in 1994, while production was down twenty percent and the labor force was down twelve percent.[1] How should we interpret these statistics? The answer is, it depends on who you are. If you are *The Wall Street Journal* or the corporate leaders who read it every day, this is all good news. What could be better news than making more money with less effort and less investment in a labor force? On the other hand, if you are a member of the labor force, these statistics should be troubling. Have we created a system that will eventually not need us? What exactly would that look like? We are talking about a world where people (or at least most people) are irrelevant to the functioning of the system, the government, the workings of the entire economy. It seems absurd that we should have a world where we don't matter, but the trends are headed in that direction. A book that comes to mind on this is Aldous Huxley's novel *Brave New World*, in which he imagines this future society where people have been relieved of all their responsibilities to produce goods, to have families, and even to reproduce. His characters often seem bored to death with this utopia of ease and

---

1   *The Wall Street Journal*, November 7, 1994.

privilege.[2] But that would be the best-case scenario. What we may be facing instead is a world where we no longer have a function, but that world will not be able or willing to support our most basic needs. It is starting to get a little scary when *Brave New World* is your best-case scenario.

The better questions are, who is blame for this and what do we do about it? Some blame capitalism itself. Marx warned us that it carried the seeds of its own destruction. But a quick look at twentieth-century history tells us that attempts to do away with capitalism have mostly led to great suffering and bloodshed. So if capitalism is what we are stuck with, how do we make it better? One answer to that question is that we greatly restrain the corporation, which has come to dominate our world. Corporations are not evil. They are simply doing what they were designed to do: snuff out competition, promote investment, and dominate markets. They are like sharks in that they chew people up and swallow them from time to time. But we don't call sharks evil, because they are just a part of nature that can be dangerous. We do our best to keep them off our beaches. Perhaps the same attitude toward corporations is in order. Don't condemn them, but control them. Maybe that is the best way for humans to save their relevance in the system they created for themselves.

In the following article by Robert Riggs, he offers a different set of statistics that he finds worrisome. He shows how, despite recent improvement in the unemployment rate, the number of workers in the labor market is diminishing. Perhaps realizing that *Brave New World* is unlikely to happen any time soon, he finds this to be a dangerous trend.

* * *

------

2   Aldous Huxley, *Brave New World* (New York: RosettaBooks, 2002).

Recent Labor-Force Anomalies

The United States has a long history of population growth and concomitant labor-force growth. As figure 7.1 shows, the number of men in the civilian labor force (that is, men either working in paid employment or actively seeking work) increased fairly steadily over the past half-century, at least until the onset of the current recession.

For the past six years, however, the number of men in the labor force has fluctuated around a fairly level trend line at approximately 82–83 million. This cessation of growth came on the heels of a 6-million-man increase during the previous seven years.

In the post–World War II era, the number of women in the labor force grew even more quickly than the number of men and also tended to grow fairly steadily. When the current

Civilian Labor-Force Level: Men
Original Source U.S. Department of Labor: Bureau of Labor Statistics

Shaded areas indicate U.S. recessions.
2013 research.stlouisfed.org
Source: Federal Reserve Bank of St. Louis

FIGURE 7.1.

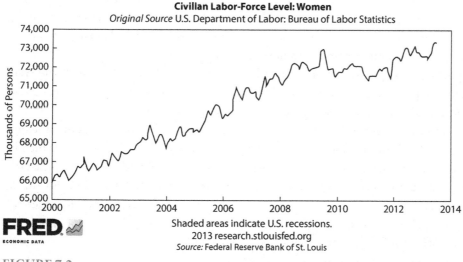

Civilian Labor-Force Level: Women
Original Source U.S. Department of Labor: Bureau of Labor Statistics

Shaded areas indicate U.S. recessions.
2013 research.stlouisfed.org
Source: Federal Reserve Bank of St. Louis

FIGURE 7.2.

recession began, the female labor force continued to grow, increasing by about a million women between the officially designated beginning and end of the economic contraction (December 2007 to June 2009) (see figure 7.2). In the second half of 2009, however, this growth stopped, and a slight reversal occurred, putting the total on a lower, fairly level trend line throughout 2010 and 2011, albeit still at a slightly higher level than the female labor force had reached before the recession began. Early in 2012, the female labor rose quickly by about a million women, but it then settled at that higher level for the next year or more, with no sustained tendency to rise further, as of the latest report available (for July 2013).

Labor economists and others have been puzzling over what has happened. Although labor-force growth tended to slow or even to halt momentarily during past recessions of the postwar era, the current cessation of growth has no precedent in that era; hence, analysts have found an explanation of it to be a challenge.

Whatever the answer(s), one thing is clear: unless the labor force resumes something like its historically normal growth, we cannot expect a resumption of historically normal economic growth. Labor inputs are major contributors to the production of goods and services. Increases in labor productivity are only a partial substitute unless the rate of productivity growth can be made much greater than observed historically over long periods.

One also wonders: How are the millions of people who normally would have been in the labor force now occupying themselves? Who is supporting them? What are their expectations and plans? Their extended stay outside the labor force joins a number of other puzzling features of the present recession, during which many patterns of economic change and policy responses have differed significantly from those observed during previous macroeconomic busts. We are living, as the cliché has it, in interesting times. Unfortunately, many of the developments that make these times interesting also make them worrisome.

Labor Markets Are Still in Bad Shape

The recent report that the standard (U-3) rate of unemployment in the United States fell to 7.4 percent in July 2013 seems to have stirred considerable joy in Mudville. But before we spend a lot of time shouting hurrah, we might well bear in mind a few other data and, of course, recall that not so long ago an unemployment rate of 7.4 percent would have been a cause for lament rather than celebration.

Because the data on which the various official rates of unemployment rest are so problematic (see Higgs 2009), we often do better to examine not unemployment, but employment, which is subject to fewer difficulties of measurement and interpretation. On this front, the news—especially when it is viewed in historical perspective—does not look so good.

As figure 7.3 shows, total civilian employment, though it has tended to increase during the past four years, still stands about 2 million jobs below its level at the end of 2007. So after six years the job total still has a long way to go merely to get back to where it was before the bust began.

FIGURE 7.3.

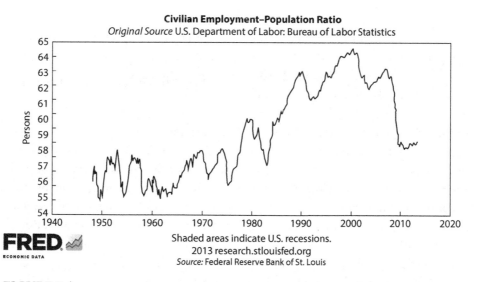

FIGURE 7.4.

Meanwhile, however, the population has continued to grow, and therefore the ratio of civilian employment to civilian noninstitutional population age sixteen and older is in much worse shape than total employment (see figure 7.4).

This ratio plummeted during the economic contraction, and although the overall economy hit bottom in mid-2009 and began to rebound, albeit slowly, the ratio of employment to population has scarcely budged, remaining stuck

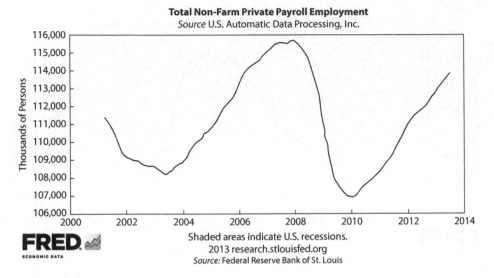

Total Non-Farm Private Payroll Employment
Source U.S. Automatic Data Processing, Inc.

Shaded areas indicate U.S. recessions.
2013 research.stlouisfed.org
Source: Federal Reserve Bank of St. Louis

FIGURE 7.5.

at 58–59 percent. To find a time with a comparable ratio, we must go back thirty years to the recession of the early 1980s.

Clearly, the labor markets remain in a funk. Although they have improved during the past four years in some regards, they have failed to improve in other regards. However we measure their condition, it is clear that the situation remains poor by historical standards and, in some ways, even by the standards of only a few years ago. The collapse of the employment/population ratio in particular indicates that something must have occurred since 2008 or 2009—perhaps the many additional or increased government subsidies of unemployment and of absence from the labor market—to keep the job market stuck in a distinctly subpar position.

Private Employment has Recouped Only about Three-Fourths of Its Recent Loss

As the most widely reported rate of unemployment (U-3) has fallen in recent months, people with a political agenda served by painting a rosy picture of the recovery have made considerable noise about this decrease. Their political opponents have responded that one reason for the decline is that the labor force has shrunk as more people have given up looking for work, some of them going into retirement sooner than they would have if the labor market had been more robust and others using the disability-insurance program as a de facto unemployment-insurance program.[3]

The best way to avoid the parsing and cherry-picking that plague such debates is to look not at unemployment, but at employment. After all, it is employment that contributes to the production of goods and services and generates earnings for the job holders. Employment is less subject to interpretive ambiguity than unemployment is.

As I write, the most recently reported data on private nonfarm employment (for July 2013; see figure 7.5) show that employment has indeed continued its recovery. Since reaching its current-recession trough at the end of 2009, it has increased by almost 7 million persons. Before starting a celebration, however, we should recognize that private nonfarm employment is still about 2 million persons less than it was at its pre-recession peak at the end of 2007.

Moreover, such private employment is currently only about 2.4 million persons greater than it was in December 2000, more than twelve years ago, on the eve of the dot-com bust. So at this point we have suffered the proverbial "lost decade" in the private labor market—the market in which employees are hired to produce goods and services that consumers and investors have demonstrated they actually value (or for which producers are convinced that such demand will be forthcoming in the future).

To be sure, labor productivity has increased during this period, yet the likelihood is slight that sustained economic growth can take place in the future without long-term growth in private employment. A large recession-related loss of private employment still remains to be recouped, however, before we can even begin to think about the long-term growth of employment. The situation has improved somewhat since the end of 2009, no doubt, yet the labor market has a long way to go—it has almost 25 percent of its recent loss to make up—merely to get back to its pre-recession peak.

It seems clear that uncertainties related to the future costs of Obamacare, the Dodd-Frank financial reform act, and other looming regulations and taxes are a significant factor in deterring hiring.[4] Note, too, that because many businesses sell to other businesses, when firms are not hiring because (as often reported) they do not foresee sufficient demand to justify expanding their payroll, this reason may also reflect indirectly the effect of regime uncertainty, which may have depressed demands by the firms' potential customers.

---

3   For evidence about and discussion of the disability program's effects, see de Rugv 2013 and Rosiak 2013.

4   See, for example, Cochran 2012; Ohanian, Taylor, and Wright 2012; Leduc and Liu 2013. A great deal of evidence and discussion (by me and others) of regime uncertainty during recent years appears at the Independent Institute's group blog *The Beacon*; these sources are available at http://blog.independent.org/?s=%22regime+uncertainty%22&submit=go.

References

Cochran, John P. 2012. Malinvestment and Regime Uncertainty. *Miscs Daily*, October 29. Available at: http://mises.org/daily/6245/.

De Rugy, Veronique. 2013. Unfit for Work: The Startling Rise of Disability in America. *The Corner: National Review Online,* August 1. Available at: http://www.nationalreview.com/corner/354988/unfit-work-startling-rise-disability-america-veronique-de-rugy.

Federal Reserve Bank of St. Louis, n.d. Federal Reserve Economic Data (FRED). Available at http://research.stlouisfed.org/fred2/categories/10. Accessed August 3, 2013.

Higgs, Robert. 2009. Will the Real Rate of Unemployment Please Stand Up. *The Beacon,* November 24. Available at: http://blog.independent.org/2009/ll/24/will-the-real-rate-of-unemployment-please-stand-up/.

Leduc, Sylvain, and Zheng Liu. 2013. Uncertainty and the Slow Labor Market Recovery. *Federal Reserve Bank of San Francisco Economic Letter,* July 22. Available at: http://www.frbsf.org/economic-research/publications/economic-letter/2013/july/us-labor-market- uncertainty-slow-recovery/.

Ohanian, Lee E., John B. Taylor, and Ian J. Wright, eds. 2012. *Government Policies and the Delayed Economic Recovery.* Stanford, Calif.: Hoover Institution Press.

Rosiak, Luke. 2013. EXography: Many Disability Recipients Admit They Could Work. *Washington Examiner,* July 30. Available at: http://washingtonexaminer.com/exography-many-disability-recipients-admit-they-could-work/article/2533626.

DISCUSSION QUESTIONS

1. What trend does the author discuss in the first few paragraphs?
2. Why should we measure employment rather than unemployment?
3. What does the author mean by the "Lost Decade"?
4. Labor productivity has grown over the last fifteen years. According to the author, does this help make up for the shrinking labor force?
5. In your opinion, is the author critical of programs like Obamacare and Dodd–Frank?

CHAPTER EIGHT

If Corporations Are Not People, What Are They?

FROM *Corporations Are Not People: Reclaiming Democracy*
BY JEFFREY CLEMENTS

INTRODUCTION

During the 2012 presidential race, Republican candidate Mitt Romney was asked by a reporter, "Are corporations people?" Romney's answer was that of course they are. People working together make up a corporation. Whether Romney was evading the question or not, he was certainly not taking it head on. The question is not, do people make up the workforce of a corporation? Of course they do. The question is, can corporations be treated by law as if they are persons? And it is not just a partisan debate. Chief Justice John Roberts, a conservative judge appointed by George W. Bush, believes that corporate personhood is a fallacy. Jeffrey Clements's book, *Corporations Are Not People: Reclaiming Democracy*, deals with this important topic in lieu of the 2010 decision Citizens United vs. FEC. In Chapter 3 he asks the question, if corporations are not people, what are they?

In this chapter he writes about a Supreme Court case back in 1886, Southern Pacific Railroad vs. Santa Clara County. He explains how this case became a rallying point around which corporations would claim protection under the Fourteenth Amendment. What is particularly interesting about that case is that the judges seem to have assumed corporate personhood despite the fact that the idea had never been debated by the courts. Why would Supreme Court judges just assume such a thing while ruling in favor of the railroad? The answer lies in what is called the Conkling controversy. Roscoe Conkling was a Republican senator back in 1868. He was on the committee that wrote the Fourteenth Amendment, which declared equal protection under the law for all persons, no matter their race or ethnicity. It was an attempt to establish legal equality for freed slaves. Years later, Conkling testified on behalf of Southern Pacific Railroad. He claimed

FIGURE 8.1.
Source: https://spencercraig.files.wordpress.com/2013/03/corporate-logos1.jpg

that the wording of the Fourteenth Amendment was meant to include corporations as "persons." It is widely believed that he perjured himself in order to help his friends in the railroad business. This, it seems, caused the judges in the Southern Pacific case to assume the railroad was protected under the Fourteenth Amendment. Over the next twenty-four years the Fourteenth Amendment would be invoked in 288 Supreme Court cases. Of those, 269 were by corporations, while only 19 were by African Americans. Corporations had hijacked a constitutional amendment.[1]

Clements also points out the radical change wrought by the 2010 Citizens United case. This bears looking at. Citizens United was a nonprofit organization that championed conservative causes. During the 2007–2008 presidential primary, with Barack Obama and Hillary Clinton fighting for the Democratic Party candidacy, Citizens United sought to air their documentary, *Hillary: The Movie*, which some have described as an elongated version of a thirty-second negative campaign ad. By advertising it as a documentary, they left the impression with the public that it was fair and balanced. The Federal Election Commission sued Citizens United on the grounds that it had violated the McCain–Feingold Act. In 2010 the case made it to the Supreme Court, which held in favor of Citizens United on the grounds that corporations have a First Amendment

---

1 Ted Nace, *Gangs of America: The Rise of Corporate Power and the Disabling of Democracy* (San Francisco: Berrett-Koehler, 2005).

right to spend money as they see fit on political campaigns. To prevent them from doing so is a violation of free speech. In other words, money equals speech. Here was Chief Justice John Roberts's dissenting opinion:

"A corporation is an artificial being, invisible, intangible, and existing only in contemplation of law. Being the mere creature of law, it possesses only those properties which the charter of its creation confers upon it."[2]

In other words, corporations are *not* people. So what are they? Read on.

* * *

---

2 Adam Liptak, "Justices, 5–4, Reject Corporate Spending Limit," *New York Times*, January 21, 2010

Metaphor ... is the peculiarity of a language, the object of which is to tell everything and conceal everything, to abound in figures. Metaphor is an enigma which offers itself as a refuge to a robber who plots a blow, to a prisoner who plans an escape.
—Victor Hugo, *Les Miserables*[3]

I am compelled to say something about corporate "personhood." ... Human beings are persons, and it is an affront to the inviolable dignity of our species that courts have created a legal fiction which forces people— human beings—to share fundamental, natural rights with soulless creations of government.
—Justice James Nelson, Montana Supreme Court, December 30, 2011[4]

---

3 Victor Hugo, *Les Miserables: A Novel,* trans. Charles Wilbour (New York: Carleton, 1862), p. 95.
4 *Western Tradition Partnership v. Bullock,* Montana Supreme Ct. No. DA-11-0081, at 79 (Nelson, J. dissenting).

What is a corporation? One might expect to find a good description of a corporation in *Citizens United* or the other corporate rights cases, but the Supreme Court is strangely silent on that point. Instead, corporate rights decisions from the Court come packaged in metaphorical clouds. It is not corporations attacking our laws; it is "speakers" and "advocates of ideas," "voices" and "persons," and variations on what Justice John Paul Stevens called in his *Citizens United* dissent, "glittering generalities."

Corporations are economic tools created by state law; corporate shares are property. Yet the majority decision in *Citizens United* did not explain even the most basic features of a corporation, an entity created and defined by state laws. The Court did not examine why, for more than a century, Congress and dozens of state legislatures thought it made sense to distinguish between corporations and human beings when making election rules. One reading the *Citizens United* decision might forget that the case concerned a corporate regulation at all; the Court described the timid corporate spending rule it struck down as a "ban on speech," government "silencing" of some "voices," some "speakers," and some "disadvantaged classes of persons."[5]

Metaphor Marches On

The use of the "speaker" and "speech" metaphor in *Citizens United* follows the playbook dating back to the corporate rights pioneer, Justice Lewis Powell. In 1978, Powell wrote the *First National Bank of Boston* decision that created the new corporate rights theory to strike down a Massachusetts law banning corporate spending in citizen referenda. He sidestepped the question of what a corporation is, saying, "If the speakers here were not corporations, no one would suggest that the State could silence their proposed speech."[6] The people of Massachusetts, however, did suggest exactly that because corporations are not "speakers." And the corporations did not propose "speech." Rather, the corporations proposed to spend corporate money to influence a citizen referendum vote. A law prohibiting this did not "silence" anyone; it defined a prohibited activity of corporate entities in elections.

In a 1980 corporate rights case, Justice Powell described the Consolidated Edison Corporation as "a single speaker." The Court struck down a New York law regulating this corporate monopoly because, according to Powell, the law "restricts the speech of a private person."[7] Later that year, Justice Powell wrote the *Central Hudson* decision creating a "right" of utility corporations to promote energy consumption in defiance of a government policy of conservation. Justice Powell identified "the critical inquiry in this case" as whether or not the First Amendment allowed the state's "complete suppression of speech."[8] (Who's for the complete suppression of speech? If that is really the question, the answer is pretty easy: the Court struck down the law.) In a 1986 decision using the corporate speech theory to strike down regulation of utility corporations, Justice Powell identified the corporation as a "speaker," with an "identity" seeking to make "speech."

Justice Powell's successors on the Court have followed this pattern of euphemism and distortion. In the 2001 *Lorillard v. Reilly* case about cigarette advertising directed to school children, Justice Clarence Thomas explained that corporations selling cigarettes and targeting children are no different from

---

5   *Citizens United*, 24.
6   *First National Bank of Boston v. Bellotti*, 435 US 765, 777 (1978).

7   *Consolidated Edison Co. of New York v. Public Service Commission of New York*, 447 US 530, 540 (1980). Justice Rehnquist joined Justice Blackmun in dissent.
8   *Central Hudson Gas & Electric Corp. v. Public Service Commission of New York*, 447 US 557, 570 (1980). Only Justice Rehnquist in dissent pointed out that a "public utility is a state-created monopoly," and that the state law was an economic regulation," not a "speech" restriction.

"advocates of harmful ideas. When the State seeks to silence them, they are all entitled to the protection of the First Amendment."⁹

Justice Thomas wrote the Court's 1995 decision in *Rubin v. Coors Brewing Company*, which ruled that Coors has a First Amendment right to ignore a federal law banning the display of alcohol levels on beer labels. Coors, now part of Molson Coors, is an international conglomerate of corporations with billions of dollars in sales around the globe. At the time of the 1995 corporate speech case, Coors Brewing Company was, among other things, a Colorado corporation; a subsidiary corporation of a larger corporation listed on the New York Stock exchange; one of a web of corporations with international operations, including alcohol products in Spain and Korea, and a joint venture among corporations for an aluminum processing operation; it had sales of nearly $2 billion and had its corporate name on the largest sports stadium in Colorado.¹⁰

Writing the 1995 decision in *Coors Brewing Company*, Justice Thomas set out to describe exactly who or what it was that came before the Court claiming a free speech right to strike down a law passed by Congress and on the books for more than fifty years. Here is

Justice Thomas's complete description: "Respondent brews beer."¹¹

It is true enough, I suppose, that Coors "brews beer," but that is hardly the only relevant fact about a corporate entity created by the law of Colorado that demands that the Court invalidate a federal law. Why is the fact that Coors is a corporation relevant? Before the justices or the rest of us reach any conclusion about that question, it would seem useful first to define *corporation*. A definition would certainly seem in order before we attribute to the entity any capacity for "speech," participation in elections, and the constitutional rights with which humans are born.

What Is a Corporation?

A corporation is a government-defined legal structure for doing business, with "legal privileges that can only be provided by government."¹² Corporations are defined by state legislatures to advance what the state deems to be in the public interest. Corporate entities are government policy tools; only government makes incorporation possible.¹³ Unlike other associations

9 *Lorillard v. Reilly*, 53 US 525 (2001) (Thomas, concurring).
10 Not long after the 1971 Powell memo, Joseph Coors, the Coors Charitable Foundation, and eighty-seven corporations helped start and fund the Heritage Foundation.
11 *Rubin v. Coors Brewing Co.*, 514 US 476, 479 (1995). "Respondent" refers to the party that won the case in the federal court below the Supreme Court and is "responding" to the other party's appeal.
12 David Ciepley 1 *Journal of Law and Courts* 221–245, Fall 2013.
13 "A corporation is a legal entity created through the laws of its state of incorporation." Cornell University Law School, Legal Information Institute, "Corporations: An

or ways of doing business, a corporation cannot exist by private arrangement.[14]

Many good reasons support state laws that permit ready incorporation of enterprises. The corporate legal entity is supremely effective at bringing together and channeling ideas, capital, and labor to make a productive, growing enterprise. The corporate form streamlines the making and enforcement of contracts; it encourages, secures, and rewards investment; it enables risk-taking as well as sustained operations, expansion, and innovation over long periods of time; and it can efficiently spread risk (and reward) over many diverse shareholders. All this and more makes incorporation a very useful tool to encourage and reward investment, innovation, job creation, and economic growth. That's why my business, the publisher of this book, and many thousands of other businesses take advantage of the privilege of incorporation.

Because the corporate entity is so useful and so prevalent, we can forget that it is a legal tool created by government to advance government policy. People can start and run businesses without government permission or a government form of organization. People can form advocacy groups, associations, unions, political parties, clubs, religious organizations, and other institutions without incorporating and without the government's permission

or involvement. People, or even "associations of people," however, cannot form or operate a corporation unless the state enacts a law authorizing the formation of a corporation and providing rules for operations as a corporation.

Most modern incorporation laws provide attributes of a corporation such as limited liability, perpetual life, and legal identification as a unitary actor. These attributes encourage simplicity and efficiency for a corporation to own property, make and enforce contracts, sue and defend lawsuits in court, and so on. State law, not the Constitution, provides these attributes. That law offers, but does not require, a useful vehicle for the individuals involved in doing business. No one is required to use the corporate form, with its relative benefits and burdens, but if people decide to do so, the privilege of incorporation is a package deal. We cannot decide to comply with some of the law to get the benefits and defy the parts of the corporate laws we find inconvenient.

Some people mistakenly call corporations mere "associations of people" or a "product of private contract."[15] This is incorrect. Corporations are not private matters, and they are not mere "associations of citizens."[16] Corporations exist

Overview," n.d., http://topics.law.cornell.edu/wex/Corporations (accessed July 23, 2011).

14 Harry G. Henn and John R. Alexander, *Law of Corporations,* 3rd ed. (Saint Paul, Minn.: West, 1991).

15 Kent Greenfield, *The Failure of Corporate Law* (Chicago: University of Chicago Press, 2006), pp. 30–33.

16 "Those who feel that the essence of the corporation rests in the contract among its members rather than in the government decree ... fail to distinguish, as the eighteenth century did, between the corporation and the voluntary

only because states enact laws defining exactly what a corporation is, what it can do, and what it cannot do. In virtually every state, it is illegal for people to do business as a corporation unless the corporation is incorporated or registered under the laws of that state.[17]

Most transnational corporations are incorporated under the law of Delaware. Three hundred of the mega-corporations listed on the Fortune 500 list are incorporated under Delaware law, as are more than half of all publicly traded companies in the United States.[18] The reason for this is a matter of some debate. Some say that giant global conglomerate corporations such as BP, Dow Chemical, and Goldman Sachs incorporate under the law of Delaware, where the corporations do little business, to ensure low corporate standards

that benefit the few at the expense of the many.[19] Others defend the dominance of Delaware, arguing that by now the state has a detailed body of corporate law.[20] Either way, as with the corporate law of every state, none of the features of the Delaware corporation law are "required." Rather, they are policy choices made by elected legislatures.

Take shareholder limited liability, for example. The concept of limited liability for corporate shareholders means that if you invest in a company, you might lose your investment if things go badly, but you will not be responsible for paying all of the debts of the corporation or for compensating victims of any misconduct or neglect by the corporation. Imagine that you owned some shares in the BP corporation in April 2010 when the Deepwater Horizon oil well exploded in the Gulf of Mexico. If the corporation cut corners on safety, resulting in the death of eleven people and a catastrophe that ruins a vast ecosystem and fishery that had sustained millions of people for eons, are you as a shareholder to blame? If BP is liable for this death and destruction but the corporation runs out of money to pay its debts, why are the shareholders who own the company and who profited in the safety-cutting years not forced to sell their personal property, their houses,

---

association." [Oscar Handlin and Mary Flug Handlin, *Commonwealth: A Study of the Role of Government in the American Economy: Massachusetts, 1774–1861* (Cambridge, Mass.: Belknap Press, 1961; originally published 1947), p. 92 and n. 18.]

17 See, for example, Virginia Statutes, §13.1-812 ("unlawful for any person to transact business in the Commonwealth as a corporation or to offer or advertise to transact business in the Commonwealth as a corporation unless the alleged corporation is either a domestic corporation or a foreign corporation authorized to transact business in the Commonwealth. Any person who violates this section shall be guilty of a Class 1 misdemeanor."

18 "More than 50% of all publicly-traded companies in the United States including 63% of the *Fortune* 500 have chosen Delaware as their legal home." http://www.corp.delaware.gov/aboutagency.shtml. See also Greenfield, *Failure of Corporate Law*, pp. 107–108.

19 Greenfield, *Failure of Corporate Law*, pp. 107–108.

20 Daniel R. Fischel, The "Race to the Bottom" Revisited: Reflections on Recent Developments in Delaware's Corporation Law, 76 *Northwestern University Law Review* 913 (1982).

their cars, and their kids' college savings accounts to pay BP's bills? After all, the shareholders own and are presumed to control the corporation that caused so much damage in the pursuit of their profit. Why are the shareholders not held to account?

The rule of limited liability, that's why. Limited liability of corporate shareholders did not come down from on high. Only because people in the state of incorporation (in BP's case, Delaware) decided to include limited liability in their corporate laws, the shareholders are not responsible for the debts of the corporation. Here's how the elected state representatives in Delaware put limited liability into the law, which they call the Delaware Corporations Code: "The stockholders of a corporation shall not be personally liable for the payment of the corporation's debts except as they may be liable by reason of their own conduct or acts."[21]

As with many other features of incorporation law, I think limited liability probably is good policy because it encourages efficient, effective capital investment in economic activity that benefits all of us. Others disagree and make strong arguments that limited liability encourages excessive risk, "externalizes" losses and damage of all kinds onto society, and directs profits only to a few individuals.[22] Whether limited liability is good policy or bad policy, though, it

is public policy that we decide on. It is not a private arrangement among people involved in the corporation.

The same is true of the other basic features of a corporation. How is it possible that the GE corporation keeps going on, decade after decade, long after every shareholder, director, executive, and other human being involved in forming and building GE has long since died? How does something called the GE corporation sign contracts, go into court, or prove to a creditor or a bank that it exists as an entity that will pay its bills, no matter how the people involved in the corporation may come and go? GE and other corporations can do that because we, the people in our states elect representatives in government who decide to make corporate "perpetual life" possible. Again, we very well could decide otherwise if we chose to do so.

Look at Delaware law again, by way of example. Corporations organized under Delaware law have "perpetual existence" because the Delaware legislature said so. Here's how the legislature of Delaware wrote the law: "A provision [may limit] the duration of the corporation's existence to a specified date; otherwise, the corporation shall have perpetual existence."[23] Notice that the Delaware law does say that "the duration of the corporation's existence" can be limited "to a specified date." This used to be the norm with corporate

---

21 Delaware Code, Annotated title 8, §102.
22 See Henry Hansmann Reinier Kraakman, "Toward Unlimited Shareholder Liability for Corporate Torts," 100 *Yale Law Journal* 1879, 1880 (1991).
23 Delaware Code, Annotated title 8, §102.

law. Years ago, traditional American distrust of concentrated power and caution about corporate dominance of government led most state laws to limit the life span of corporations. The period in which a corporation could exist was usually limited to a defined term of years, often twenty years.[24] Is it not strange that a thing that exists only by the policy of the state, a thing as to which the state can decide "the duration of the corporation's existence," can successfully take control of the people's Bill of Rights to strike down federal, state, and local laws?

Delaware Cannot Rewrite the Constitution

This brings us to the notion that some call "corporate person-hood," the idea that under the law, corporations are treated as "persons." As with perpetual existence, limited liability, and other features of corporations, the source of this concept of a "corporate person" is not particularly complicated. We came up with it, or rather, our state and federal legislatures did, because treating the corporation as a legal "person" makes sense for certain purposes. That policy choice, though, is our choice and has nothing to

do with the Constitution or corporate "rights."[25]

There are lots of good reasons why states and the federal government enact laws that say, in some instances, that the word *person* includes corporations. For example, the Clean Water Act prohibits unpermitted discharge of toxics and pollutants into the waters of the United States by any person. Congress wrote the Clean Water Act to create civil and criminal penalties for "any person" who violated the law. Obviously, we want to make sure those penalties apply to corporations that violate the Clean Water Act. For that reason, here's what Congress said in section 502 of the Clean Water Act: "The term 'person' means an individual, corporation, partnership, association, State, municipality, commission, or political subdivision of a State, or any interstate body."

Congress and the states take the same approach to include corporations when we say "no person shall violate another person's trademark" or "no person shall sell drugs that have not been approved

---

24 See e.g., Handlin and Handlin, *Commonwealth;* Horowitz, Morton. *The Transformation of American Law,* Vol. 1. (Cambridge: Harvard University Press, 1979).

25 In attributing the "corporate person" to legislatures, I recognize the role of common law courts in developing the metaphor. Ultimately, however, the common law is subject to legislative choice. Legislatures may keep, modify or, as often is the case, abolish common law. Where and when the "person" metaphor is appropriate for corporations, then, depends on legislative choice, not Constitutional mandate. See, e.g. *FCC v. AT & T Inc.,* 131 S. Ct. 1177, 1185 (2011). (interpreting Congressional intent in statutory meaning in FOIA of "person" and "personal privacy," concluding that corporations were not capable of asserting "personal privacy" under statute).

by the FDA." Similarly, it makes sense as a matter of policy to treat a corporation like a "person" when a corporation makes a contract or is sued or brings a lawsuit or engages in any one of many activities that state law may authorize a corporation to do. We do this because we have decided as a matter of state law that the "person" metaphor can help make the corporation better as a tool of public policy. Yes, corporations create private wealth, and shareholders own shares as private property, but the corporation as an artificial entity, and the rules that define it are public choices.

The Constitution is different from state laws and federal statutes. Our Bill of Rights is not a "policy choice" that government can decide. Rather, the Bill of Rights defines the relationship between we human beings and our government. The First Amendment and our other rights in the Constitution are the natural human rights that we insist on ensuring to ourselves when we consent to the Constitution's plan of government.

When we decide, as we might, that under our state or federal laws, corporations are "persons" that can be prosecuted (or that can contract or be sued), that decision cannot transform corporations into "persons" under the Constitution's protections of rights. We can change state laws of incorporation anytime we can muster a majority in the legislature for a particular change. We do not change the meaning of the Constitution anytime a legislature,

let alone the legislature of Delaware alone, decides it might be efficient to do so. The rights in our Constitution, including the rights of "life," "liberty," "property," and "equal protection" for all "persons" are human rights.

The Constitution cannot be changed by state or federal laws; it can be changed only by the process of amendment as set forth in Article 5 of the Constitution. The people have never added corporations to the definition of *persons* in the Constitution by using the amendment process. As the Supreme Court declared in the 1800s when rebuffing early corporate efforts to create corporate rights, "State laws, by combining large masses of men under a corporate name, cannot repeal the Constitution."[26]

To appreciate the distinction between *person* under state or federal law and *person* under the Constitution, consider Delaware law again. Recall that Delaware law declares that corporations can exist for a defined period of years or may have "perpetual existence." If a majority of the Delaware legislature wanted to delete that last part of the law and simply declare that corporations may exist for a period of twenty years, they could do so. In contrast, neither Delaware nor any other state or federal legislature in America can decide that people shall have a limited period of existence. No matter how good the policy justification for such a law, that law obviously would

---

26 *Marshall v. Baltimore and Ohio Railroad Co.*, 57 US 314 (1853).

violate the Constitution's due process clause protecting the life of all persons.

The Right Thing in the Wrong Place

Corporations, then, are policy tools; they are not people or holders of constitutional rights. As economic tools, corporations are highly effective. Yet the same traits that make corporations such useful economic policy tools can also make them dangerous to republican government and democracy if people and lawmakers do not watch and restrain abuses. Corporations can aggregate immense power, corrupt government, drive down wages, trash public resources, concentrate markets to squeeze out competitors, and more. As Justice William Rehnquist said in one of his many dissents from the corporate rights decisions in the late 1970s and the 1980s, a "State grants to a business corporation the blessings of potentially perpetual life and limited liability to enhance its efficiency as an economic entity. It might reasonably be concluded that those properties, so beneficial in the economic sphere, pose special dangers in the political sphere."[27]

As with all tools, use of the corporate entity requires oversight and care. Gasoline is fantastic. It is also dangerous. I enjoy working with a chainsaw or taking out guns for hunting or practice,

but I know that care and rules are necessary to prevent potentially disastrous consequences of using either one. Great tools, but we would not hand them out to anyone without having some clarity about how they will be used.

The problem of corporate power is not the personal failings of the many good and decent people who work for corporations, often creating wonderful products or services that benefit us all. Rather, corporate power is now subverting our democracy because we have forgotten that corporations are just tools, and we have forgotten our duty to keep an eye on them. Until the corporate rights offensive of recent years, the idea of restraining corporate power was a mainstream, basic American proposition, not a fringe viewpoint.

The Southern Pacific Case

Occasionally, the 1886 Supreme Court case of *Santa Clara County v. Southern Pacific Railroad Company* is cited to claim that corporations are constitutional "persons" with rights. In that case, the Southern Pacific Railroad Company tried to avoid state and county taxes by claiming that it was a "person" under the recently adopted Fourteenth Amendment to the Constitution. The Fourteenth Amendment had been enacted after the Civil War to ensure that freed slaves and all people in America had equal rights to due process, liberty, property, and equal protection of the law. The Southern Pacific Railroad

---

27 *First National Bank of Boston v. Bellotti*, 435 US 765 (1978) (Rehnquist, dissenting).

corporation sued Santa Clara County, California, arguing that a tax assessment violated its rights as a "person" under the Fourteenth Amendment because the tax was not "equal" with taxes applied to other "persons."

The Court decided the case in favor of the railroad, but not for the reasons for which the case became known. In fact, in the *Santa Clara* decision, the Court did not discuss Southern Pacific's Fourteenth Amendment argument at all. Instead, the outcome of the case rested on California law rather than a constitutional question.[28] Nevertheless, the Gilded Age courts, almost as corporate-oriented as today's Court, repeatedly used *Santa Clara* as authority to fabricate corporate rights and strike down workers compensation, child labor, conservation, and other laws.[29]

Following *Santa Clara* in 1886, the Supreme Court faced a wave of cases in which large corporations and the infamous corporate monopoly "trusts" demanded constitutional rights to shield them from the growing movement for laws to protect employees (including child labor), the environment, fair taxes, and other public interests. On several occasions in the 1890s and early 1900s, the Supreme Court agreed with the corporations. The cases stated, without any explanation whatsoever, that "a corporation is a person under the Fourteenth Amendment," as if saying that with a straight face would make it true.[30] Could it be true?

Not a chance. Absolutely no evidence suggests that corporations were intended to be included in the Fourteenth Amendment or in the Constitution generally. Indeed, the evidence is exactly to the contrary. Since the beginning of our country, virtually every generation of Americans has acted to prevent corporate power from being leveraged into political power at the expense of the people. During the colonial era, only "a handful of native business corporations carried on business ... four water companies, two wharf companies, two trading societies, and one mutual fire insurance society," and only twenty business corporations were formed by

---

28 *Santa Clara County v. Southern Pacific Railroad Co.*, 118 US 394 (1886) ("As the judgment can be sustained upon this [state law] ground it is not necessary to consider any other questions raised by the pleadings and the facts found by the court"; 416.)

29 Thom Hartmann, *Unequal Protection: How Corporations Became "People" and How You Can Fight Back*, 2nd ed. (San Francisco: Berrett-Koehler, 2010); Ted Nace, *Gangs of America: The Rise of Corporate Power and the Disabling of Democracy* (San Francisco: Berrett-Koehler, 2003).

30 *Pembina Consolidated Silver Mining and Milling Co. v. Commonwealth of Pennsylvania*, 125 US 81, 188–189 (1888); *Missouri Pacific Railway Co. v. Mackey*, 127 US 205 (1888); *Minneapolis & Saint Louis Railway Co. v. Herrick*, 127 US 210 (1888); *Minneapolis & Saint Louis Railway Co. v. Beckwith*, 129 US 26 (1889); *Charlotte, Columbia and Augusta Railroad Co. v. Gibbes*, 142 US 386 (1892); *Covington and Lexington Turnpike Road Co. v. Sandford*, 164 US 578 (1896); *Gulf, Colorado and Santa Fe Railway Co. v. Ellis*, 165 US 150 (1897); and *Kentucky Finance Corp. v. Paramount Auto Exchange Corp.*, 262 US 544 (1923).

1787, when the American people convened the Constitutional Convention in Philadelphia.[31] Legislatures, however, increasingly permitted the creation of corporations in the new republic to facilitate and expedite all kinds of public purposes, such as the building of roads, dams, and bridges.[32] Yet it remained clear that corporations were legal instruments of the state, defined and controlled by the state, with limitations on their purposes and their duration.[33]

It would be bizarre if the generation that defiantly declared to the world that "all men are created equal" and that "they are endowed by their Creator with certain unalienable Rights" and who wrote a constitution opening with "We, the People" would have tolerated corporate constitutional rights. Founders such as Thomas Jefferson and James Madison could not have been more clear about the danger of unregulated corporations and the need for, as Madison put it, "proper restraints and guards." Another founder, James Wilson, a Pennsylvania man who signed the Declaration of Independence, served in the Continental Congress, helped draft the Constitution, and was nominated by George Washington to be one of the first six justices on the Supreme Court, agreed. He well expressed the prevailing view of the time that corporations can be useful tools of the state but must always be controlled by the people:

> *A corporation is described to be a person in a political capacity created by the law, to endure in perpetual succession.... It must be admitted, however, that, in too many instances, those bodies politick have, in their progress, counteracted the design of their original formation.... This is not mentioned with a view to insinuate, that such establishments ought to be prevented or destroyed: I mean only to intimate, that they should be erected with caution, and inspected with care.*[34]

The Supreme Court at the time knew that any "rights" of corporations come from the state charter, not from

---

31 Henn and Alexander, *Law of Corporations*, p. 24 and n. 2, citing Edwin Merrick Dodd, *American Business Corporations Until 1860* (1954); Joseph Stancliffe Davis, *Essays in the Earlier History of American Corporations* (1917); Simeon E. Baldwin, "American Business Corporations Before 1789," in *Annual Report of the American Historical Association*, pp. 253–274 (1902). See also Handlin and Handlin, *Commonwealth*, pp. 99, 162.

32 Handlin and Handlin, *Commonwealth*, pp. 106–133; *Louis K. Liggett Co. v. Lee*, 288 US 517, 548–560 (1933) (Brandeis, dissenting).

33 Restrictions on corporate purposes were the norm. See ibid. See also *Head and Amory v. Providence Insurance Co.*, 6 US (2 Cranch) 127, 166–167 (1804) ("a corporation can only act in the manner prescribed by law").

---

34 James Wilson, "Of Corporations," in ed. Kermit L. Hall and Mark David Hall, *Collected Works of James Wilson*, (Indianapolis, Ind.: Liberty Fund, 2007), vol. 2, ch. 10, http://oll.libertyfund.org/title/2074/166648/2957866 (accessed July 22, 2009).

the Constitution (let alone from our Creator). The corporate legal form today is not fundamentally different than when Chief Justice Marshall explained in 1819 that a corporation, as a "mere creature of law . . . possesses only those properties which the charter confers upon it, either expressly or as incidental to its very existence."[35] A corporation today is chartered from the state just as in 1809 when a unanimous Supreme Court held that "a body corporate as such cannot be a citizen within the meaning of the Constitution."[36]

For nearly two hundred years, the Supreme Court rejected the argument that corporations were entitled to the rights of citizens under the Constitution's "privileges and immunities" clause. In 1839, the Court said, "The only rights [a corporation] can claim are the rights which are given to it in that character, and not the rights which belong to its members as citizens of a state."[37] Fifty years later, the Court said that the term *citizens* in the Constitution "applies only to natural persons, members of the body politic owing allegiance to the state, not to artificial persons created by the legislature, and possessing only such attributes as the legislature has prescribed."[38]

At least until recently, the vigilance of American leadership about corporate power did not waver as corporations became more dominant in our economy. "Corporations, which should be the carefully restrained creatures of the law and the servants of the people, are fast becoming the people's masters," warned President Grover Cleveland.[39] Theodore Roosevelt sought to end "a riot of individualistic materialism" and successfully called for a ban on corporate political contributions: "Let individuals contribute as they desire; but let us prohibit in effective fashion all corporations from making contributions for any political purpose, directly or indirectly."[40] President Roosevelt said he "recognized that corporations and combinations had become indispensable in the business world, that it is folly to try to prohibit them, but that it was also folly to leave them without thoroughgoing control."[41]

---

35 *Trustees of Dartmouth College v. Woodward,* 17 US 518, 636 (1819).

36 *Hope Insurance Co. v. Boardman,* 9 US (5 Cranch) 57, 58 (1809).

37 *Bank of Augusta v. Earle,* 38 US 519, 587 (1839).

38 *Pembina Consolidated Silver Mining and Milling Co. v. Commonwealth of Pennsylvania,* 125 US 181, 188–189 (1888).

39 Grover Cleveland, "Fourth Annual Message to Congress (December 3, 1888)," Miller Center, http://millercenter.org/scripps/archive/speeches/detail/3758 -(accessed July 24, 2011).

40 Theodore Roosevelt, *Theodore Roosevelt: An Autobiography* (New York: Scribner, 1929) (originally published 1913), p. 423; Theodore Roosevelt, "Sixth Annual Message to Congress (December 3, 1906)," Miller Center, http://millercenter.org/scripps/archive/speeches/detail/3778 (accessed July 24, 2011).

41 Roosevelt, *Roosevelt,* p. 425. And he went further, writing supportively of the Progressive reformers: "They realized that the Government must now interfere to protect labor, to subordinate the big corporation to the public welfare, and to shackle cunning and fraud exactly as centuries before it had interfered to shackle the physical force which does wrong by violence" (p. 425).

This vigilance did not mean that powerful corporations simply accepted or cooperated with the public's "thoroughgoing control." As those who came before us understood, the opportunity for using the advantages of corporate privileges to concentrate power and aggregate wealth have always led corporations to seek to evade control or oversight by claiming "rights." In a democracy, an assertive, vigilant citizenry and leadership always is needed to push back.

Until the success of the Powell–Chamber of Commerce plan, Americans knew this. That is why the *Santa Clara* line of "corporate person" cases was rendered largely meaningless by the people's rejection of corporate rights throughout the twentieth century. Under Theodore Roosevelt, a Republican, Americans restrained corporate power with effective antitrust enforcement, labor laws, environmental laws, and laws banning corporate political spending. In Roosevelt's words, "There can be no effective control of corporations while their political activity remains."[42] Under Woodrow Wilson and Franklin Roosevelt, both Democrats, Americans likewise regulated corporate power to ensure the strength of the people and the country as a whole. Republicans, Democrats, and Independents came together to amend the Constitution twice in 1913 to weaken the hold on government by

corporations and the extreme wealth of the few: first, by overturning a Supreme Court case striking down the federal income tax, and second, by requiring senators to be elected by the people rather than appointed by state legislatures.[43]

Finally, in a 1938 dissenting opinion, Justice Hugo Black, a former Alabama senator, demolished the idea that corporations were "persons" with rights under the Constitution's Fourteenth Amendment. Although he wrote in dissent, the clarity of his expression about corporations and persons sounded a warning to any justice who might try to slip corporate rights into the Constitution with "glittering generalities" and glib citation of *Santa Clara*. His lengthy dissenting opinion examined the words, history, meaning, and purpose of the Fourteenth Amendment:

> *I do not believe that the word "person" in the Fourteenth Amendment includes corporations.... A constitutional interpretation that is wrong should not stand. I believe this Court should now overrule previous decisions which interpreted the Fourteenth Amendment to include corporations.*
>
> *Neither the history nor the language of the Fourteenth Amendment justifies the belief*

---

42 Theodore Roosevelt, speech delivered August 31, 1910, cited in Hartmann, *Unequal Protection,* p. 161.

43 US Constitution, Amend. XVI and Amend. XVII.

that corporations are included within its protections.

Certainly, when the Fourteenth Amendment was submitted for approval, the people were not told that the states of the South were to be denied their normal relationship with the Federal Government unless they ratified an amendment granting new and revolutionary rights to corporations.... The records of the time can be searched in vain for evidence that this amendment was adopted for the benefit of corporations.[44]

With Justice Black's warning shot that there would be no more free rides for corporate rights on the Supreme Court, *Santa Clara* "corporate personhood" was a dead issue for decades. Indeed, the Court said little more about corporations' "rights" until Justice Lewis Powell and his Chamber of Commerce plan came to the Supreme Court following the death of Justice Black in September 1971. Through most of the twentieth century, the Court returned to the basic American understanding that corporations were economic, not political, entities.

For example, in rejecting the claim of corporations for privacy rights in 1950, the Supreme Court said:

Corporations can claim no equality with individuals in the enjoyment of a right to privacy. They are endowed with public attributes. They have a collective impact upon society, from which they derive the privilege of acting as artificial entities.... Law-enforcing agencies have a legitimate right to satisfy themselves that corporate behavior is consistent with the law and the public interest.[45]

For more than a century until *Citizens United*, most states and the federal government banned corporate political contributions and spending. Some states, such as Kentucky, even made the control of corporate political activity part of their state constitutions.[46] This basic understanding of the place of corporations in American democracy guided the Supreme Court, even as Justice Powell's "corporate speech" cases worked away at creating the new corporate rights doctrine.

The one time before *Citizens United* when the Supreme Court went off the rails with respect to corporate political spending occurred with Justice Powell's maiden corporate rights decision in *First National Bank of Boston*, striking down a state law banning corporate spending in referendum elections. That exception

---

44 *Connecticut General Life Insurance Co. v. Johnson,* 303 US 77, 85–87 (1938).

45 *United States v. Morton Salt Co.,* 338 US 632, 651–652 (1950).
46 Kentucky Constitution, §150 (1891).

should have proved the rule, in large part because of the force of Justice Rehnquist's dissent. Rehnquist concluded that the "Fourteenth Amendment does not require a State to endow a business corporation with the power of political speech."[47] Instead, Rehnquist forcefully pressed the truth that corporations are not people with rights but are entities defined by the states, with restrictions that the legislatures find appropriate. Congress, he wrote, and numerous

> *States of this Republic have considered the matter, and have concluded that restrictions upon the political activity of business corporations are both politically desirable and constitutionally permissible. The judgment of such a broad consensus of governmental bodies expressed over a period of many decades is entitled to considerable deference from this Court.*[48]

Again, the different opinions of these two Richard Nixon appointees—William Rehnquist and Lewis Powell—showed the stark gap between the corporatist and the conservative understanding of our American republic. For a time, the conservative Rehnquist was able to form a majority on the Court. In 1990, the Chamber of Commerce in

Michigan attacked a law restricting corporate political spending and lost. The Court upheld the right of the people to keep corporations out of politics. In that case, *Austin v. Michigan Chamber of Commerce*, Justice Rehnquist's dissenting views in the corporate speech cases became the majority view.[49]

Rehnquist joined Thurgood Marshall, who wrote for the Court in affirming Michigan's regulation of corporate spending in elections. Marshall's words for the Court were drawn from the earlier Rehnquist dissents:

> *State law grants corporations special advantages.... These state-created advantages not only allow corporations to play a dominant role in the Nation's economy, but also permit them to use "resources amassed in the economic marketplace" to obtain "an unfair advantage in the political marketplace."*[50]

Even as late as 2003, before Chief Justice John Roberts and Justice Samuel Alito replaced Chief Justice Rehnquist and Justice Sandra Day O'Connor, the Court agreed that the same corporate election spending law that the Court would later strike down in *Citizens United* was perfectly fine

---

47   *First National Bank of Boston v. Bellotti*, 435 US 765, 826 and n.6 (Rehnquist, dissenting).
48   Ibid., 822–823.

49   *Austin v. Michigan Chamber of Commerce*, 494 US 652 (1990).
50   Ibid., 658–659 (1990), quoting *Federal Election Commission v. Massachusetts Citizens for Life*, 479 US 238, 257 (1986).

under our Constitution. In that 2003 case, *McConnell v. Federal Election Commission*, the Court affirmed that the people's representatives in Congress were entitled to "the legislative judgment that the special characteristics of the corporate structure require particularly careful regulation."[51]

Citizens United: Corporations Back on the Track, People to the Back

We then come to *Citizens United* a mere seven years later, posing again this fundamental question of American democracy: Can Congress and state legislatures make laws to ensure that government of the people does not become government of the corporations? What had changed since 2003, 1990, the New Deal, Theodore Roosevelt's presidency, the 1800s, or the days of Madison, Jefferson, and President Washington's Supreme Court justice and national founding father James Wilson?

Is *Citizens United* different because that case involved a nonprofit corporation? Although that point may have been worthy of examination, it made no difference to the Court. The Court in *Citizens United* made very clear that its decision applied to all corporations (or, as Justice Kennedy's decision called them, all "voices" and "speakers"). That is

why Chevron, Koch Industries, Target, News Corporation, and other global, for-profit corporations have funneled hundreds of millions of dollars into elections since *Citizens United*.

Although the claims of a nonprofit corporation seeking to express the views of its members are more sympathetic, all corporations, whether for-profit or not-for-profit, are creatures of the state. Take *Citizens United*, for example. *Citizens United* is a corporation organized under Virginia law. It exists as a nonprofit corporation because the people of Virginia passed an incorporation law. Under this law, people may create a nonprofit corporation only if they file with the state a set of articles of incorporation containing elements that the state requires, pay a filing fee of $75, designate a registered agent to deal with the state's annual assessment packet, and comply with recordkeeping and other requirements set out in the Virginia law.[52]

Without all of these steps, *Citizens United* (or any other nonprofit corporation) does not exist. In fact, the state provides the equivalent of the corporate death penalty for noncompliance with these laws. No one forced people to incorporate their activity as *Citizens United*, the nonprofit corporation, but once they chose to do that, is it too much to ask that the corporation comply with the laws on the books?

---

51 *McConnell v. Federal Election Commission*, 540 US93, 205 (2002).

52 The Commonwealth of Virginia provides an on-line guide to the steps to forming a nonprofit corporation at http://vdba.virginia.gov/non_profit.shtml.

That does not mean that the people who support *Citizens United*, who work there, or who believe in its mission lose any rights whatsoever. They have all the same rights they had before they decided to incorporate and the same inalienable rights of all Americans. The corporation, however, does not, and we are not required to pretend that the corporation is the same as the people.

Once we recall that the rules for corporations come from us, for the betterment of our nation, the idea of "corporate rights" will be exposed as ridiculous. If we return to recognition that corporations are policy tools, rather than people with constitutional rights, we can then begin to realize many possibilities to improve the tool so that it better serves the purposes for which we Americans permitted the corporate entity in our laws in the first place. We can begin to rethink and reinvigorate our incorporation laws.

We might decide that the 315 million Americans who do not live in Delaware ought to have as much say about corporate law as the 900,000 people who live in Delaware now have.

We might decide to create new and better corporate entities under the law, such as for-benefit "B Corporations," and options for sustainable "low-profit" hybrids between for-profits and nonprofits. We can change the rules to make real shareholder democracy and to make corporations justify their corporate charters and show how they have served the public and complied with the law. We can use the corporate chartering and charter revocation process and other features of corporate law to prevent and punish corporate crime and misconduct. We can insist on accounting for externalities—the dumping onto society of costs from pollution, destruction of our global ecosystem, and financial bailouts.[53]

That's not all. When people—voters, legislators, businesspeople, everyone—take responsibility for the public tool of incorporation, we are not only saving our republic; we may also be saving our economy. With new corporate rules, we can make corporations more effective at business, protect innovation and competition, create more jobs, and free human creativity.

---

53 Charlie Cray, "Using Charters to Redesign Corporations in the Public Interest," in William H. Wist, ed., *The Bottom Line or Public Health* (Oxford: Oxford University Press, 2010), http://www.corporatepolicy.org/pdf/CrayCharters2010.pdf (accessed June 13, 2011).

DISCUSSION QUESTIONS

1. How do the courts use metaphors when speaking of corporations? Why do they do this?

2. The author says a corporation is a "government defined legal structure." What does that mean?

3. Why are most transnational corporations incorporated under Delaware law?

4. What does it mean that corporations have "perpetual life"?

5. What is the difference between "persons" under state or federal law and "persons" under the Constitution?

6. How did President Theodore Roosevelt handle corporate power?

7. How is the Citizens United case a departure from the Court's rulings throughout most of the twentieth century?

8. What suggestions for change does the author make?

CPSIA information can be obtained
at www.ICGtesting.com
Printed in the USA
LVOW05s0221010217
522764LV00013B/115/P